Microsoft®
Training &
Certification

AF697840

2830A: Designing Security for Microsoft® Networks

Microsoft®

Course Number: 2830A
Part Number: X10-29855
Released: 12/2002

END-USER LICENSE AGREEMENT FOR MICROSOFT OFFICIAL CURRICULUM COURSEWARE -STUDENT EDITION

PLEASE READ THIS END-USER LICENSE AGREEMENT ("EULA") CAREFULLY. BY USING THE MATERIALS AND/OR USING OR INSTALLING THE SOFTWARE THAT ACCOMPANIES THIS EULA (COLLECTIVELY, THE "LICENSED CONTENT"), YOU AGREE TO THE TERMS OF THIS EULA. IF YOU DO NOT AGREE, DO NOT USE THE LICENSED CONTENT.

---

1. GENERAL. This EULA is a legal agreement between you (either an individual or a single entity) and Microsoft Corporation ("Microsoft"). This EULA governs the Licensed Content, which includes computer software (including online and electronic documentation), training materials, and any other associated media and printed materials. This EULA applies to updates, supplements, add-on components, and Internet-based services components of the Licensed Content that Microsoft may provide or make available to you unless Microsoft provides other terms with the update, supplement, add-on component, or Internet-based services component. Microsoft reserves the right to discontinue any Internet-based services provided to you or made available to you through the use of the Licensed Content. This EULA also governs any product support services relating to the Licensed Content except as may be included in another agreement between you and Microsoft. An amendment or addendum to this EULA may accompany the Licensed Content.

2. **GENERAL GRANT OF LICENSE.** Microsoft grants you the following rights, conditioned on your compliance with all the terms and conditions of this EULA. Microsoft grants you a limited, non-exclusive, royalty-free license to install and use the Licensed Content solely in conjunction with your participation as a student in an Authorized Training Session (as defined below). You may install and use one copy of the software on a single computer, device, workstation, terminal, or other digital electronic or analog device ("Device"). You may make a second copy of the software and install it on a portable Device for the exclusive use of the person who is the primary user of the first copy of the software. A license for the software may not be shared for use by multiple end users. An "Authorized Training Session" means a training session conducted at a Microsoft Certified Technical Education Center, an IT Academy, via a Microsoft Certified Partner, or such other entity as Microsoft may designate from time to time in writing, by a Microsoft Certified Trainer (for more information on these entities, please visit www.microsoft.com). WITHOUT LIMITING THE FOREGOING, COPYING OR REPRODUCTION OF THE LICENSED CONTENT TO ANY SERVER OR LOCATION FOR FURTHER REPRODUCTION OR REDISTRIBUTION IS EXPRESSLY PROHIBITED.

3. DESCRIPTION OF OTHER RIGHTS AND LICENSE LIMITATIONS

3.1 *Use of Documentation and Printed Training Materials.*

3.1.1 The documents and related graphics included in the Licensed Content may include technical inaccuracies or typographical errors. Changes are periodically made to the content. Microsoft may make improvements and/or changes in any of the components of the Licensed Content at any time without notice. The names of companies, products, people, characters and/or data mentioned in the Licensed Content may be fictitious and are in no way intended to represent any real individual, company, product or event, unless otherwise noted.

3.1.2 Microsoft grants you the right to reproduce portions of documents (such as student workbooks, white papers, press releases, datasheets and FAQs) (the "Documents") provided with the Licensed Content. You may not print any book (either electronic or print version) in its entirety. If you choose to reproduce Documents, you agree that: (a) use of such printed Documents will be solely in conjunction with your personal training use; (b) the Documents will not republished or posted on any network computer or broadcast in any media; (c) any reproduction will include either the Document's original copyright notice or a copyright notice to Microsoft's benefit substantially in the format provided below; and (d) to comply with all terms and conditions of this EULA. In addition, no modifications may made to any Document.

Form of Notice:

© 2002. Reprinted with permission by Microsoft Corporation. All rights reserved.

Microsoft and Windows are either registered trademarks or trademarks of Microsoft Corporation in the US and/or other countries. Other product and company names mentioned herein may be the trademarks of their respective owners.

3.2 *Use of Media Elements.* The Licensed Content may include certain photographs, clip art, animations, sounds, music, and video clips (together "Media Elements"). You may not modify these Media Elements.

3.3 *Use of Sample Code.* In the event that the Licensed Content includes sample code in source or object format ("Sample Code"), Microsoft grants you a limited, non-exclusive, royalty-free license to use, copy and modify the Sample Code; if you elect to exercise the foregoing rights, you agree to comply with all other terms and conditions of this EULA, including without limitation Sections 3.4, 3.5, and 6.

3.4 *Permitted Modifications.* In the event that you exercise any rights provided under this EULA to create modifications of the Licensed Content, you agree that any such modifications: (a) will not be used for providing training where a fee is charged in public or private classes; (b) indemnify, hold harmless, and defend Microsoft from and against any claims or lawsuits, including attorneys' fees, which arise from or result from your use of any modified version of the Licensed Content; and (c) not to transfer or assign any rights to any modified version of the Licensed Content to any third party without the express written permission of Microsoft.

3.5 *Reproduction/Redistribution Licensed Content.* Except as expressly provided in this EULA, you may not reproduce or distribute the Licensed Content or any portion thereof (including any permitted modifications) to any third parties without the express written permission of Microsoft.

4. **RESERVATION OF RIGHTS AND OWNERSHIP.** Microsoft reserves all rights not expressly granted to you in this EULA. The Licensed Content is protected by copyright and other intellectual property laws and treaties. Microsoft or its suppliers own the title, copyright, and other intellectual property rights in the Licensed Content. You may not remove or obscure any copyright, trademark or patent notices that appear on the Licensed Content, or any components thereof, as delivered to you. **The Licensed Content is licensed, not sold.**

5. **LIMITATIONS ON REVERSE ENGINEERING, DECOMPILATION, AND DISASSEMBLY.** You may not reverse engineer, decompile, or disassemble the Software or Media Elements, except and only to the extent that such activity is expressly permitted by applicable law notwithstanding this limitation.

6. **LIMITATIONS ON SALE, RENTAL, ETC. AND CERTAIN ASSIGNMENTS.** You may not provide commercial hosting services with, sell, rent, lease, lend, sublicense, or assign copies of the Licensed Content, or any portion thereof (including any permitted modifications thereof) on a stand-alone basis or as part of any collection, product or service.

7. **CONSENT TO USE OF DATA.** You agree that Microsoft and its affiliates may collect and use technical information gathered as part of the product support services provided to you, if any, related to the Licensed Content. Microsoft may use this information solely to improve our products or to provide customized services or technologies to you and will not disclose this information in a form that personally identifies you.

8. **LINKS TO THIRD PARTY SITES.** You may link to third party sites through the use of the Licensed Content. The third party sites are not under the control of Microsoft, and Microsoft is not responsible for the contents of any third party sites, any links contained in third party sites, or any changes or updates to third party sites. Microsoft is not responsible for webcasting or any other form of transmission received from any third party sites. Microsoft is providing these links to third party sites to you only as a convenience, and the inclusion of any link does not imply an endorsement by Microsoft of the third party site.

9. **ADDITIONAL LICENSED CONTENT/SERVICES.** This EULA applies to updates, supplements, add-on components, or Internet-based services components, of the Licensed Content that Microsoft may provide to you or make available to you after the date you obtain your initial copy of the Licensed Content, unless we provide other terms along with the update, supplement, add-on component, or Internet-based services component. Microsoft reserves the right to discontinue any Internet-based services provided to you or made available to you through the use of the Licensed Content.

10. **U.S. GOVERNMENT LICENSE RIGHTS**. All software provided to the U.S. Government pursuant to solicitations issued on or after December 1, 1995 is provided with the commercial license rights and restrictions described elsewhere herein. All software provided to the U.S. Government pursuant to solicitations issued prior to December 1, 1995 is provided with "Restricted Rights" as provided for in FAR, 48 CFR 52.227-14 (JUNE 1987) or DFAR, 48 CFR 252.227-7013 (OCT 1988), as applicable.

11. **EXPORT RESTRICTIONS**. You acknowledge that the Licensed Content is subject to U.S. export jurisdiction. You agree to comply with all applicable international and national laws that apply to the Licensed Content, including the U.S. Export Administration Regulations, as well as end-user, end-use, and destination restrictions issued by U.S. and other governments. For additional information see <http://www.microsoft.com/exporting/>.

12. **TRANSFER.** The initial user of the Licensed Content may make a one-time permanent transfer of this EULA and Licensed Content to another end user, provided the initial user retains no copies of the Licensed Content. The transfer may not be an indirect transfer, such as a consignment. Prior to the transfer, the end user receiving the Licensed Content must agree to all the EULA terms.

13. **"NOT FOR RESALE" LICENSED CONTENT.** Licensed Content identified as "Not For Resale" or "NFR," may not be sold or otherwise transferred for value, or used for any purpose other than demonstration, test or evaluation.

14. **TERMINATION.** Without prejudice to any other rights, Microsoft may terminate this EULA if you fail to comply with the terms and conditions of this EULA. In such event, you must destroy all copies of the Licensed Content and all of its component parts.

15. **DISCLAIMER OF WARRANTIES. TO THE MAXIMUM EXTENT PERMITTED BY APPLICABLE LAW, MICROSOFT AND ITS SUPPLIERS PROVIDE THE LICENSED CONTENT AND SUPPORT SERVICES (IF ANY) *AS IS AND WITH ALL FAULTS*, AND MICROSOFT AND ITS SUPPLIERS HEREBY DISCLAIM ALL OTHER WARRANTIES AND CONDITIONS, WHETHER EXPRESS, IMPLIED OR STATUTORY, INCLUDING, BUT NOT LIMITED TO, ANY (IF ANY) IMPLIED WARRANTIES, DUTIES OR CONDITIONS OF MERCHANTABILITY, OF FITNESS FOR A PARTICULAR PURPOSE, OF RELIABILITY OR AVAILABILITY, OF ACCURACY OR COMPLETENESS OF RESPONSES, OF RESULTS, OF WORKMANLIKE EFFORT, OF LACK OF VIRUSES, AND OF LACK OF NEGLIGENCE, ALL WITH REGARD TO THE LICENSED CONTENT, AND THE PROVISION OF OR FAILURE TO PROVIDE SUPPORT OR OTHER SERVICES, INFORMATION, SOFTWARE, AND RELATED CONTENT THROUGH THE LICENSED CONTENT, OR OTHERWISE ARISING OUT OF THE USE OF THE LICENSED CONTENT. ALSO, THERE IS NO WARRANTY OR CONDITION OF TITLE, QUIET ENJOYMENT, QUIET POSSESSION, CORRESPONDENCE TO DESCRIPTION OR NON-INFRINGEMENT WITH REGARD TO THE LICENSED CONTENT. THE ENTIRE RISK AS TO THE QUALITY, OR ARISING OUT OF THE USE OR PERFORMANCE OF THE LICENSED CONTENT, AND ANY SUPPORT SERVICES, REMAINS WITH YOU.**

16. **EXCLUSION OF INCIDENTAL, CONSEQUENTIAL AND CERTAIN OTHER DAMAGES. TO THE MAXIMUM EXTENT PERMITTED BY APPLICABLE LAW, IN NO EVENT SHALL MICROSOFT OR ITS SUPPLIERS BE LIABLE FOR ANY SPECIAL, INCIDENTAL, PUNITIVE, INDIRECT, OR CONSEQUENTIAL DAMAGES WHATSOEVER (INCLUDING, BUT NOT**

LIMITED TO, DAMAGES FOR LOSS OF PROFITS OR CONFIDENTIAL OR OTHER INFORMATION, FOR BUSINESS INTERRUPTION, FOR PERSONAL INJURY, FOR LOSS OF PRIVACY, FOR FAILURE TO MEET ANY DUTY INCLUDING OF GOOD FAITH OR OF REASONABLE CARE, FOR NEGLIGENCE, AND FOR ANY OTHER PECUNIARY OR OTHER LOSS WHATSOEVER) ARISING OUT OF OR IN ANY WAY RELATED TO THE USE OF OR INABILITY TO USE THE LICENSED CONTENT, THE PROVISION OF OR FAILURE TO PROVIDE SUPPORT OR OTHER SERVICES, INFORMATION, SOFTWARE, AND RELATED CONTENT THROUGH THE LICENSED CONTENT, OR OTHERWISE ARISING OUT OF THE USE OF THE LICENSED CONTENT, OR OTHERWISE UNDER OR IN CONNECTION WITH ANY PROVISION OF THIS EULA, EVEN IN THE EVENT OF THE FAULT, TORT (INCLUDING NEGLIGENCE), MISREPRESENTATION, STRICT LIABILITY, BREACH OF CONTRACT OR BREACH OF WARRANTY OF MICROSOFT OR ANY SUPPLIER, AND EVEN IF MICROSOFT OR ANY SUPPLIER HAS BEEN ADVISED OF THE POSSIBILITY OF SUCH DAMAGES. BECAUSE SOME STATES/JURISDICTIONS DO NOT ALLOW THE EXCLUSION OR LIMITATION OF LIABILITY FOR CONSEQUENTIAL OR INCIDENTAL DAMAGES, THE ABOVE LIMITATION MAY NOT APPLY TO YOU.**

17. <u>**LIMITATION OF LIABILITY AND REMEDIES**</u>. **NOTWITHSTANDING ANY DAMAGES THAT YOU MIGHT INCUR FOR ANY REASON WHATSOEVER (INCLUDING, WITHOUT LIMITATION, ALL DAMAGES REFERENCED HEREIN AND ALL DIRECT OR GENERAL DAMAGES IN CONTRACT OR ANYTHING ELSE), THE ENTIRE LIABILITY OF MICROSOFT AND ANY OF ITS SUPPLIERS UNDER ANY PROVISION OF THIS EULA AND YOUR EXCLUSIVE REMEDY HEREUNDER SHALL BE LIMITED TO THE GREATER OF THE ACTUAL DAMAGES YOU INCUR IN REASONABLE RELIANCE ON THE LICENSED CONTENT UP TO THE AMOUNT ACTUALLY PAID BY YOU FOR THE LICENSED CONTENT OR US$5.00. THE FOREGOING LIMITATIONS, EXCLUSIONS AND DISCLAIMERS SHALL APPLY TO THE MAXIMUM EXTENT PERMITTED BY APPLICABLE LAW, EVEN IF ANY REMEDY FAILS ITS ESSENTIAL PURPOSE.**

18. **APPLICABLE LAW.** If you acquired this Licensed Content in the United States, this EULA is governed by the laws of the State of Washington. If you acquired this Licensed Content in Canada, unless expressly prohibited by local law, this EULA is governed by the laws in force in the Province of Ontario, Canada; and, in respect of any dispute which may arise hereunder, you consent to the jurisdiction of the federal and provincial courts sitting in Toronto, Ontario. If you acquired this Licensed Content in the European Union, Iceland, Norway, or Switzerland, then local law applies. If you acquired this Licensed Content in any other country, then local law may apply.

19. **ENTIRE AGREEMENT; SEVERABILITY.** This EULA (including any addendum or amendment to this EULA which is included with the Licensed Content) are the entire agreement between you and Microsoft relating to the Licensed Content and the support services (if any) and they supersede all prior or contemporaneous oral or written communications, proposals and representations with respect to the Licensed Content or any other subject matter covered by this EULA. To the extent the terms of any Microsoft policies or programs for support services conflict with the terms of this EULA, the terms of this EULA shall control. If any provision of this EULA is held to be void, invalid, unenforceable or illegal, the other provisions shall continue in full force and effect.

Should you have any questions concerning this EULA, or if you desire to contact Microsoft for any reason, please use the address information enclosed in this Licensed Content to contact the Microsoft subsidiary serving your country or visit Microsoft on the World Wide Web at <u>http://www.microsoft.com</u>.

Si vous avez acquis votre Contenu Sous Licence Microsoft au CANADA :

DÉNI DE GARANTIES. Dans la mesure maximale permise par les lois applicables, le Contenu Sous Licence et les services de soutien technique (le cas échéant) sont fournis *TELS QUELS ET AVEC TOUS LES DÉFAUTS* par Microsoft et ses fournisseurs, lesquels par les présentes dénient toutes autres garanties et conditions expresses, implicites ou en vertu de la loi, notamment, mais sans limitation, (le cas échéant) les garanties, devoirs ou conditions implicites de qualité marchande, d'adaptation à une fin usage particulière, de fiabilité ou de disponibilité, d'exactitude ou d'exhaustivité des réponses, des résultats, des efforts déployés selon les règles de l'art, d'absence de virus et d'absence de négligence, le tout à l'égard du Contenu Sous Licence et de la prestation des services de soutien technique ou de l'omission de la 'une telle prestation des services de soutien technique ou à l'égard de la fourniture ou de l'omission de la fourniture de tous autres services, renseignements, Contenus Sous Licence, et contenu qui s'y rapporte grâce au Contenu Sous Licence ou provenant autrement de l'utilisation du Contenu Sous Licence. PAR AILLEURS, IL N'Y A AUCUNE GARANTIE OU CONDITION QUANT AU TITRE DE PROPRIÉTÉ, À LA JOUISSANCE OU LA POSSESSION PAISIBLE, À LA CONCORDANCE À UNE DESCRIPTION NI QUANT À UNE ABSENCE DE CONTREFAÇON CONCERNANT LE CONTENU SOUS LICENCE.

<u>**EXCLUSION DES DOMMAGES ACCESSOIRES, INDIRECTS ET DE CERTAINS AUTRES DOMMAGES**</u>. **DANS LA MESURE MAXIMALE PERMISE PAR LES LOIS APPLICABLES, EN AUCUN CAS MICROSOFT OU SES FOURNISSEURS NE SERONT RESPONSABLES DES DOMMAGES SPÉCIAUX, CONSÉCUTIFS, ACCESSOIRES OU INDIRECTS DE QUELQUE NATURE QUE CE SOIT (NOTAMMENT, LES DOMMAGES À L'ÉGARD DU MANQUE À GAGNER OU DE LA DIVULGATION DE RENSEIGNEMENTS CONFIDENTIELS OU AUTRES, DE LA PERTE D'EXPLOITATION, DE BLESSURES CORPORELLES, DE LA VIOLATION DE LA VIE PRIVÉE, DE L'OMISSION DE REMPLIR TOUT DEVOIR, Y COMPRIS D'AGIR DE BONNE FOI OU D'EXERCER UN SOIN RAISONNABLE, DE LA NÉGLIGENCE ET DE TOUTE AUTRE PERTE PÉCUNIAIRE OU AUTRE PERTE**

DE QUELQUE NATURE QUE CE SOIT) SE RAPPORTANT DE QUELQUE MANIÈRE QUE CE SOIT À L'UTILISATION DU CONTENU SOUS LICENCE OU À L'INCAPACITÉ DE S'EN SERVIR, À LA PRESTATION OU À L'OMISSION DE LA 'UNE TELLE PRESTATION DE SERVICES DE SOUTIEN TECHNIQUE OU À LA FOURNITURE OU À L'OMISSION DE LA FOURNITURE DE TOUS AUTRES SERVICES, RENSEIGNEMENTS, CONTENUS SOUS LICENCE, ET CONTENU QUI S'Y RAPPORTE GRÂCE AU CONTENU SOUS LICENCE OU PROVENANT AUTREMENT DE L'UTILISATION DU CONTENU SOUS LICENCE OU AUTREMENT AUX TERMES DE TOUTE DISPOSITION DE LA U PRÉSENTE CONVENTION EULA OU RELATIVEMENT À UNE TELLE DISPOSITION, MÊME EN CAS DE FAUTE, DE DÉLIT CIVIL (Y COMPRIS LA NÉGLIGENCE), DE RESPONSABILITÉ STRICTE, DE VIOLATION DE CONTRAT OU DE VIOLATION DE GARANTIE DE MICROSOFT OU DE TOUT FOURNISSEUR ET MÊME SI MICROSOFT OU TOUT FOURNISSEUR A ÉTÉ AVISÉ DE LA POSSIBILITÉ DE TELS DOMMAGES.

LIMITATION DE RESPONSABILITÉ ET RECOURS. MALGRÉ LES DOMMAGES QUE VOUS PUISSIEZ SUBIR POUR QUELQUE MOTIF QUE CE SOIT (NOTAMMENT, MAIS SANS LIMITATION, TOUS LES DOMMAGES SUSMENTIONNÉS ET TOUS LES DOMMAGES DIRECTS OU GÉNÉRAUX OU AUTRES), LA SEULE RESPONSABILITÉ 'OBLIGATION INTÉGRALE DE MICROSOFT ET DE L'UN OU L'AUTRE DE SES FOURNISSEURS AUX TERMES DE TOUTE DISPOSITION DEU LA PRÉSENTE CONVENTION EULA ET VOTRE RECOURS EXCLUSIF À L'ÉGARD DE TOUT CE QUI PRÉCÈDE SE LIMITE AU PLUS ÉLEVÉ ENTRE LES MONTANTS SUIVANTS : LE MONTANT QUE VOUS AVEZ RÉELLEMENT PAYÉ POUR LE CONTENU SOUS LICENCE OU 5,00 $US. LES LIMITES, EXCLUSIONS ET DÉNIS QUI PRÉCÈDENT (Y COMPRIS LES CLAUSES CI-DESSUS), S'APPLIQUENT DANS LA MESURE MAXIMALE PERMISE PAR LES LOIS APPLICABLES, MÊME SI TOUT RECOURS N'ATTEINT PAS SON BUT ESSENTIEL.

À moins que cela ne soit prohibé par le droit local applicable, la présente Convention est régie par les lois de la province d'Ontario, Canada. Vous consentez Chacune des parties à la présente reconnaît irrévocablement à la compétence des tribunaux fédéraux et provinciaux siégeant à Toronto, dans de la province d'Ontario et consent à instituer tout litige qui pourrait découler de la présente auprès des tribunaux situés dans le district judiciaire de York, province d'Ontario.

Au cas où vous auriez des questions concernant cette licence ou que vous désiriez vous mettre en rapport avec Microsoft pour quelque raison que ce soit, veuillez utiliser l'information contenue dans le Contenu Sous Licence pour contacter la filiale de succursale Microsoft desservant votre pays, dont l'adresse est fournie dans ce produit, ou visitez écrivez à : Microsoft sur le World Wide Web à http://www.microsoft.com

Contents

About This Course

This section provides you with a brief description of the course, audience, suggested prerequisites, and course objectives.

Description

This three-day, instructor-led course teaches the skills necessary to design a secure network infrastructure. Topics include assembling the design team, modeling threats, and analyzing security risks in order to derive business requirements for securing computers in a networked environment. The course encourages decision-making skills through an interactive tool that simulates real-life scenarios that the target audience may encounter. Students are given the task of collecting the information and sorting through the details to resolve the given security requirement.

Audience

This course is intended for IT systems engineers and security specialists who are responsible for establishing security policies and procedures for an organization. Students should have one to three years of experience designing related business solutions.

Student prerequisites

This course requires that students meet the following prerequisites:

- A strong familiarity with Microsoft® Windows® 2000 core technologies, such as those covered in Course 2152, *Implementing Microsoft Windows 2000 Professional and Server*.
- A strong familiarity with Windows 2000 networking technologies and implementation, such as those covered in Microsoft Official Curriculum (MOC) Course 2153, *Implementing a Microsoft Windows 2000 Network Infrastructure*.
- A strong familiarity with Windows 2000 directory services technologies and implementation, such as those covered in MOC Course 2154, *Implementing and Administering Microsoft Windows 2000 Directory Services*.

Course objectives

After completing this course, students will be able to:

- Plan a framework for security network.
- Identify threats to network security.
- Analyze security risks.
- Design security for physical resources.
- Design security for computers.
- Design security for accounts.
- Design security for authentication.
- Design security for data.
- Design security for data transmission.
- Design security for network perimeters.
- Design an incident response procedure.

In addition, this course contains three teachable appendices that cover designing an acceptable use policy, designing policies for managing networks, and designing an operations framework for managing security.

Student Materials Compact Disc Contents

The Student Materials compact disc contains the following files and folders:

- *Autorun.exe.* When the compact disc is inserted into the CD-ROM drive, or when you double-click the **Autorun.exe** file, this file opens the compact disc and allows you to browse the Student Materials compact disc.
- *Autorun.inf.* When the compact disc is inserted into the compact disc drive, this file opens Autorun.exe.
- *Default.htm.* This file opens the Student Materials Web page. It provides you with resources pertaining to this course, including additional reading, review and lab answers, lab files, multimedia presentations, and course-related Web sites.
- *Readme.txt.* This file explains how to install the software for viewing the Student Materials compact disc and its contents and how to open the Student Materials Web page.
- *settings.xml.* This file is used to display the course materials on this compact disc.
- *viewer.htm.* This file is used to display the course materials on this compact disc.
- *Addread.* This folder contains additional reading pertaining to this course.
- *Flash.* This folder contains the installer for the Macromedia Flash version 5.0 browser plug-in.
- *Fonts.* This folder contains fonts that may be required to view the Microsoft Word documents that are included with this course.
- *Labfiles.* This folder contains files that are used in the hands-on labs. These files may be used to prepare the student computers for the hands-on labs.
- *Media.* This folder contains files that are used in multimedia presentations for this course.
- *Mplayer.* This folder contains the setup file to install Microsoft Windows Media™ Player.
- *Viewer.* This folder contains files that are used to display the course materials on this compact disc.
- *Visio.* This folder contains the Microsoft Visio® Viewer Web Component that is used to view Visio diagrams on computers that do not have Microsoft Visio 2002 installed.
- *Webfiles.* This folder contains the files that are required to view the course Web page. To open the Web page, open Windows Explorer, and in the root directory of the compact disc, double-click **Default.htm** or **Autorun.exe**.
- *Wordview.* This folder contains the Word Viewer that is used to view any Word document (.doc) files that are included on the compact disc.

Document Conventions

The following conventions are used in course materials to distinguish elements of the text.

Convention	Use
Bold	Represents commands, command options, and syntax that must be typed exactly as shown. It also indicates commands on menus and buttons, dialog box titles and options, and icon and menu names.
Italic	In syntax statements or descriptive text, indicates argument names or placeholders for variable information. Italic is also used for introducing new terms, for book titles, and for emphasis in the text.
Title Capitals	Indicate domain names, user names, computer names, directory names, and folder and file names, except when specifically referring to case-sensitive names. Unless otherwise indicated, you can use lowercase letters when you type a directory name or file name in a dialog box or at a command prompt.
ALL CAPITALS	Indicate the names of keys, key sequences, and key combinations—for example, ALT+SPACEBAR.
`monospace`	Represents code samples or examples of screen text.
[ ]	In syntax statements, enclose optional items. For example, [*filename*] in command syntax indicates that you can choose to type a file name with the command. Type only the information within the brackets, not the brackets themselves.
{ }	In syntax statements, enclose required items. Type only the information within the braces, not the braces themselves.
|	In syntax statements, separates an either/or choice.
▶	Indicates a procedure with sequential steps.
...	In syntax statements, specifies that the preceding item may be repeated.
. . .	Represents an omitted portion of a code sample.

Microsoft®
Training &
Certification

Introduction

Contents

Microsoft®

Introduction

- Name
- Company affiliation
- Title/function
- Job responsibility
- Networking experience
- Expectations for the course

Course Materials

- **Name card**
- **Student workbook**
- **Student Materials compact disc**
- **Course evaluation**

The following materials are included with your kit:

- *Name card.* Write your name on both sides of the name card.
- *Student workbook.* The student workbook contains the material covered in class, in addition to the hands-on lab exercises.
- *Student Materials compact disc.* The Student Materials compact disc contains the Web page that provides you with links to resources pertaining to this course, including additional readings, review and lab answers, lab files, multimedia presentations, and course-related Web sites.

  Note To open the Web page, insert the Student Materials compact disc into the CD-ROM drive, and then in the root directory of the compact disc, double-click **Autorun.exe** or **Default.htm**.

- *Assessments.* There are assessments for each lesson, located on the Student Materials compact disc. You can use them as pre-assessments to identify areas of difficulty, or you can use them as post-assessments to validate learning.
- *Course evaluation.* To provide feedback on the course, training facility, and instructor, you will have the opportunity to complete an online evaluation near the end of the course.

  To provide additional comments or inquire about the Microsoft® Certified Professional (MCP) program, send e-mail to mcphelp@microsoft.com.

Prerequisites

Strong familiarity with:

- **Windows 2000 core technologies**
- **Windows 2000 networking technologies and implementation**
- **Windows 2000 directory services technologies and implementation**

This course is intended for Information Technology (IT) systems engineers and security specialists who are responsible for establishing security policies and procedures for an organization. Students should have one to three years of experience designing related business solutions.

This course requires that you meet the following prerequisites:

- A strong familiarity with Microsoft® Windows® 2000 core technologies, such as those covered in Course 2152, *Implementing Microsoft Windows 2000 Professional and Server*.
- A strong familiarity with Windows 2000 networking technologies and implementation, such as those covered in MOC Course 2153, *Implementing a Microsoft Windows 2000 Network Infrastructure*.
- A strong familiarity with Windows 2000 directory services technologies and implementation, such as those covered in MOC Course 2154, *Implementing and Administering Microsoft Windows 2000 Directory Services*.

Course Outline

- **Module 1: Introduction to Designing Security**
- **Module 2: Creating a Plan for Network Security**
- **Module 3: Identifying Threats to Network Security**
- **Module 4: Analyzing Security Risks**
- **Module 5: Creating a Security Design for Physical Resources**
- **Module 6: Creating a Security Design for Computers**
- **Module 7: Creating a Security Design for Accounts**

Module 1, "Introduction to Designing Security," describes the basic framework for designing network security and introduces key concepts used throughout the course. It also introduces an ongoing case study that is utilized in the labs.

Module 2, "Creating a Plan for Network Security," discusses the importance of security policies and procedures in a security design. It also explains how a security design team must include representation from various roles in your organization. After completing this module, you will be able use a framework for designing security and creating a security design team.

Module 3, "Identifying Threats to Network Security," explains how to identify likely threats to a network, and it explains attacker motivations. After completing this module, you will be able to explain common threats and predict threats by using a threat model.

Module 4, "Analyzing Security Risks," explains how to determine what resources in an organization require protection and how to categorize them in order to determine an appropriate level of protection. After completing this module, you will be able to apply a framework for planning risk management.

Module 5, "Creating a Security Design for Physical Resources," describes threats and risks to physical resources in an organization and how to secure facilities, computers, and hardware. After completing this module, you will be able to design security for physical resources.

Module 6, "Creating a Security Design for Computers," explains how to determine threats and analyze risks to computers on your network. After completing this module, you will be able to design security for computers.

Module 7, "Creating a Security Design for Accounts," describes the threats and risks to accounts in an organization. After completing this module, you will be able to design security for accounts.

Course Outline *(continued)*

- Module 8: Creating a Security Design for Authentication
- Module 9: Creating a Security Design for Data
- Module 10: Creating a Security Design for Data Transmission
- Module 11: Creating a Security Design for Network Perimeters
- Module 12: Designing Responses to Security Incidents
- Appendix A: Designing an Acceptable Use Policy
- Appendix B: Designing Policies for Managing Networks
- Appendix C: Designing an Operations Framework to Manage Security

Module 8, "Creating a Security Design for Authentication," describes threats and risks to authentication. After completing this module, you will be able to design security for authentication.

Module 9, "Creating a Security Design for Data," examines threats and risks to data. After completing this module, you will be able to design security for data.

Module 10, "Creating a Security Design for Data Transmission," discusses threats and risks to data transmission. After completing this module, you will be able to design security for data transmission.

Module 11, "Creating a Security Design for Network Perimeters," describes threats to the points where your network connects to other networks, such as the Internet. After completing this module, you will be able to design security for network perimeters.

Module 12, "Designing Responses to Security Incidents," provides information about auditing and creating procedures to direct how you respond to security incidents. After completing this module, you will be able to design an audit policy and incident response procedures.

Appendix A, "Designing an Acceptable Use Policy," explains how to create policies for acceptable use of network resources by users.

Appendix B, "Designing Policies for Managing Networks," offers guidelines for ensuring that network administrators manage the network in a secure manner.

Appendix C, "Designing an Operations Framework to Manage Security," explains how to create a framework to ensure security of a network as the network changes and as the security requirements of the organization change.

Initial Logon Procedure

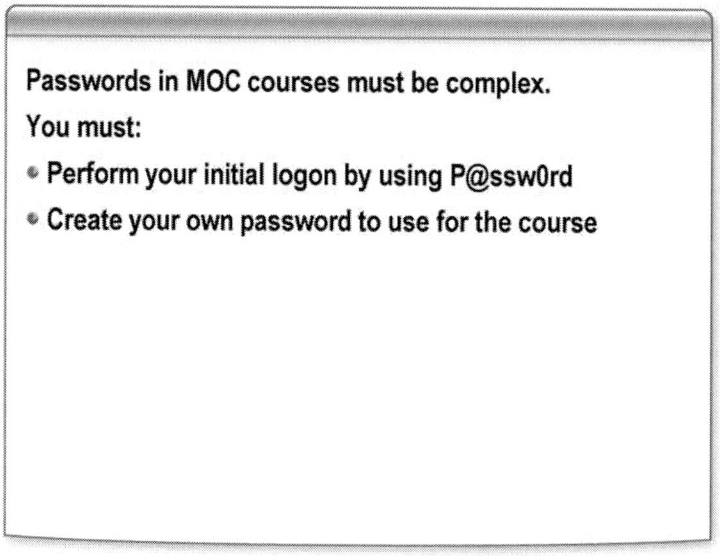

Complex passwords

To meet the complexity requirements for the password that you will use in this course, you must include characters in your password from at least three of the following four categories:

- Uppercase letters (A to Z)
- Lowercase letters (a to z)
- Numbers (0 to 9)
- Symbols (! @ # $)

To create the password that you will use in this course, you must log on either as **Student***xx*, where *xx* is your student number, or as **Student**, depending on the classroom setup.

Tasks

► **Log on to your account**

1. Press CTRL+ALT+DEL to open the **Log On to Windows** dialog box.
2. In the **User name** box, type **Student***xx* or **Student**
3. In the **Password** box, type **P@ssw0rd**
4. In the **Log on to** box, select the name of the domain that is used in the course or the name of your computer, and then click **OK**.

   The **Logon Message** dialog box appears, stating that your password must be changed at initial logon.

► **Change your password**

1. In the **Logon Message** dialog box, click **OK**.
2. In the **New Password** box, type your new password.
3. In the **Confirm New Password** box, retype your password, and then click **OK**.
4. In the **Change Password** dialog box, click **OK**.

Microsoft Official Curriculum

Introduction

Microsoft Training and Certification develops Microsoft Official Curriculum (MOC), including MSDN® Training, for computer professionals who design, develop, support, implement, or manage solutions by using Microsoft products and technologies. These courses provide comprehensive skills-based training in instructor-led and online formats.

Microsoft Training and Certification information

For more information, visit the Microsoft Training and Certification Web site at http://www.microsoft.com/traincert/.

Microsoft Certified Professional Program

Microsoft CERTIFIED Professional

http://www.microsoft.com/traincert/

Introduction

Microsoft Training and Certification offers a variety of certification credentials for developers and IT professionals. The Microsoft Certified Professional program is the leading certification program for validating your experience and skills, keeping you competitive in today's changing business environment.

MCP certifications

The Microsoft Certified Professional program includes the following certifications.

- MCSA on Microsoft Windows 2000

  The Microsoft Certified Systems Administrator (MCSA) certification is designed for professionals who implement, manage, and troubleshoot existing network and system environments based on Windows 2000 platforms, including the Windows .NET Server family. Implementation responsibilities include installing and configuring parts of the systems. Management responsibilities include administering and supporting the systems.

- MCSE on Windows 2000

  The Microsoft Certified Systems Engineer (MCSE) credential is the premier certification for professionals who analyze the business requirements and design and implement the infrastructure for business solutions based on the Windows 2000 platform and Microsoft server software, including the Windows .NET Server family. Implementation responsibilities include installing, configuring, and troubleshooting network systems.

- MCAD

  The Microsoft Certified Application Developer (MCAD) for Microsoft .NET credential is appropriate for professionals who use Microsoft technologies to develop and maintain department-level applications, components, Web or desktop clients, or back-end data services or work in teams developing enterprise applications. The credential covers job tasks ranging from developing to deploying and maintaining these solutions.

- MCSD

  The Microsoft Certified Solution Developer (MCSD) credential is the premier certification for professionals who design and develop leading-edge business solutions with Microsoft development tools, technologies, platforms, and the Microsoft Windows DNA architecture. The types of applications MCSDs can develop include desktop applications and multi-user, Web-based, N-tier, and transaction-based applications. The credential covers job tasks ranging from analyzing business requirements to maintaining solutions.

- MCDBA on Microsoft SQL Server™ 2000

  The Microsoft Certified Database Administrator (MCDBA) credential is the premier certification for professionals who implement and administer Microsoft SQL Server databases. The certification is appropriate for individuals who derive physical database designs, develop logical data models, create physical databases, create data services by using Transact-SQL, manage and maintain databases, configure and manage security, monitor and optimize databases, and install and configure SQL Server.

- MCP

  The Microsoft Certified Professional (MCP) credential is for individuals who have the skills to successfully implement a Microsoft product or technology as part of a business solution in an organization. Hands-on experience with the product is necessary to successfully achieve certification.

- MCT

  Microsoft Certified Trainers (MCTs) demonstrate the instructional and technical skills that qualify them to deliver Microsoft Official Curriculum through Microsoft Certified Technical Education Centers (Microsoft CTECs).

Certification requirements

The certification requirements differ for each certification category and are specific to the products and job functions addressed by the certification. To become an MCP, you must pass rigorous certification exams that provide a valid and reliable measure of technical proficiency and expertise.

For More Information See the Microsoft Training and Certification Web site at http://www.microsoft.com/traincert/.

You can also send e-mail to mcphelp@microsoft.com if you have specific certification questions.

Acquiring the skills tested by an MCP exam

MOC and MSDN Training can help you develop the skills that you need to do your job. They also complement the experience that you gain while working with Microsoft products and technologies. However, no one-to-one correlation exists between MOC and MSDN Training courses and MCP exams. Microsoft does not expect or intend for the courses to be the sole preparation method for passing MCP exams. Practical product knowledge and experience is also necessary to pass the MCP exams.

To help prepare for the MCP exams, use the preparation guides that are available for each exam. Each Exam Preparation Guide contains exam-specific information, such as a list of the topics on which you will be tested. These guides are available on the Microsoft Training and Certification Web site at http://www.microsoft.com/traincert/.

Facilities

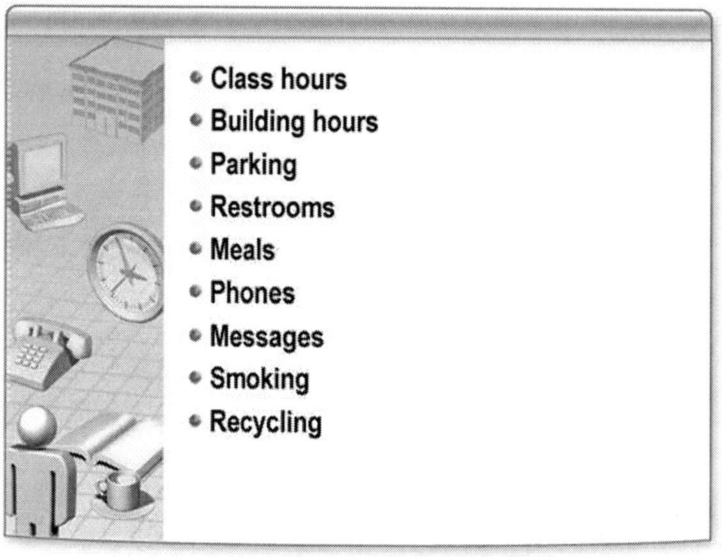
Class hours
Building hours
Parking
Restrooms
Meals
Phones
Messages
Smoking
Recycling

Microsoft®
Training &
Certification

Module 1: Introduction to Designing Security

Contents

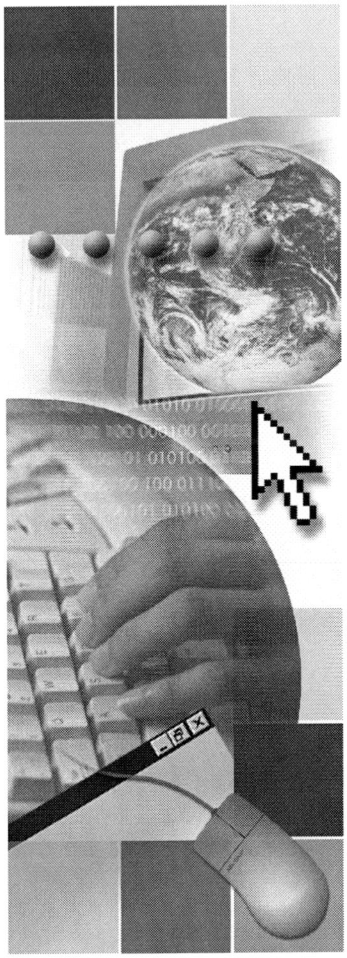

Microsoft®

Overview

- Introduction to Designing Security for Microsoft Networks
- Contoso Pharmaceuticals: A Case Study

Introduction

This module introduces Course 2830, *Designing Security for Microsoft Networks*, and presents general security concepts that are used in the course. This module emphasizes the importance of a network security design in the protection of an organization's assets.

The module also introduces a fictional organization, Contoso Pharmaceuticals, which the labs in the course use as an ongoing case study. You will become familiar with the network security issues that confront Contoso Pharmaceuticals, meet some of its employees, and learn about the lab environment.

Objectives

After completing this module, you will be able to:

- Provide an overview of designing security.
- Describe the components of the case study for this course.

Lesson: Introduction to Designing Security for Microsoft Networks

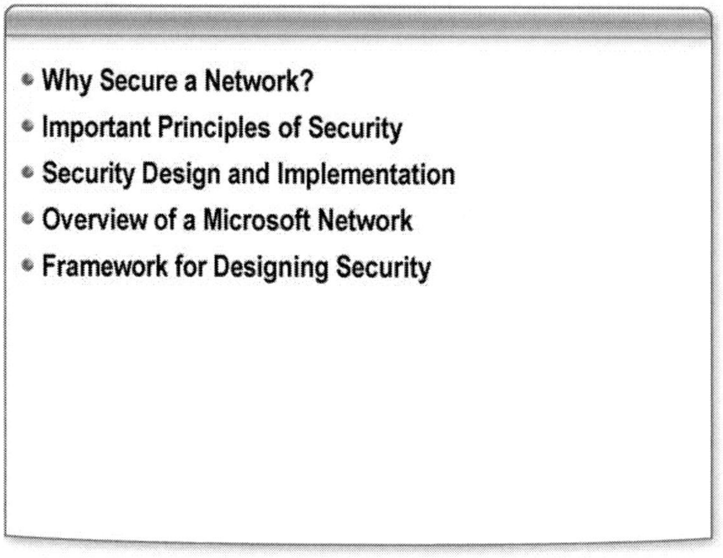

Introduction

A security design is a comprehensive plan that guides the implementation of security policies and procedures for an organization. A security design helps an organization protect its assets so that it can implement security in a consistent and effective manner.

Lesson objectives

After completing this lesson, you will be able to:

- Explain why organizations invest in network security.
- Describe important principles of security.
- Explain the difference between security design and security implementation.
- Describe the areas of a Microsoft network that should be secured.
- Describe the general organization of information in this course.

Why Secure a Network?

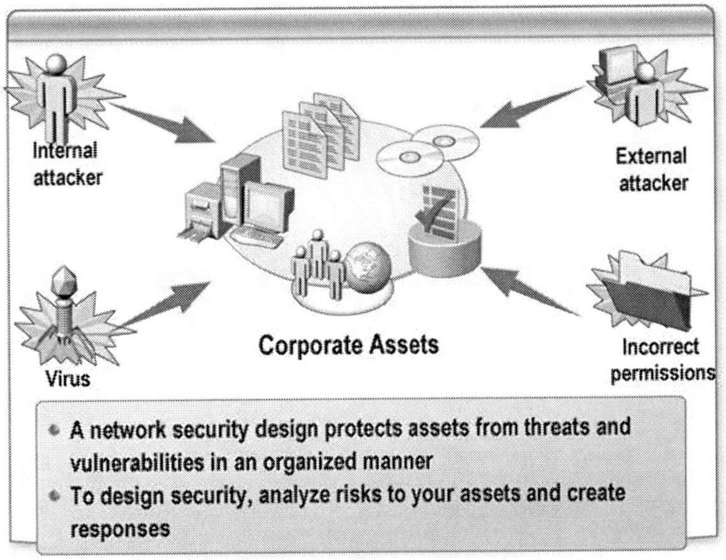

Key points

Organizations invest in network security to protect their assets from threats. Assets on a computer network can include such items as e-mail messages, intellectual property like trade secrets or source code, customer databases, and e-commerce transactions.

A threat is a danger or vulnerability to an asset. Threats to assets include attackers trying to steal information, software applications that lack the latest security updates, and natural disasters such as fires or floods.

A security design uses the concept of risk management to determine appropriate security responses to threats. Risk management is a careful study of criteria, for example, the likelihood of a threat occurring, the impact of the threat, the value of an asset to your organization, and the cost of a security solution. After you perform risk management, you can decide on an appropriate response to a threat. Data collected during risk management is also useful to present to upper management and key stakeholders to persuade them of the importance of network security and its value to your organization.

Important Principles of Security

Principle	Definition
Defense in depth	• Provide multiple layers of protection against threats at multiple points on a network
Least privilege	• Grant the least amount of privileges required for a user or resource to perform a task
Minimized attack surface	• Reduce vulnerable points in a network

Key points

Defense in depth refers to a combination of people, operations, and security technologies. Defense in depth provides multiple layers of protection to a network by defending against threats at multiple points within the network. A single layer is often ineffective against multiple attacks. By using defense in depth, if an attack breaks through one point of defense, other defenses provide additional protection to the asset.

Least privilege refers to consistently granting a user, resource, or application the least amount of privilege or permissions necessary to perform the required task. Practices such as using default or full control permissions on resources, or giving user accounts administrator rights, simplify administration to a dangerous degree. Granting excessive permissions can introduce numerous vulnerabilities that attackers can easily exploit.

The concept of an *attack surface* describes points of entry that an attacker can exploit to penetrate the network. A network that has a minimum of exposed areas or points that are vulnerable to attack has a *minimized attack surface*. In comparison, a network that has several unprotected connections to the Internet has a larger attack surface than a small, isolated network with a single, secured connection to a branch office.

Security Design and Implementation

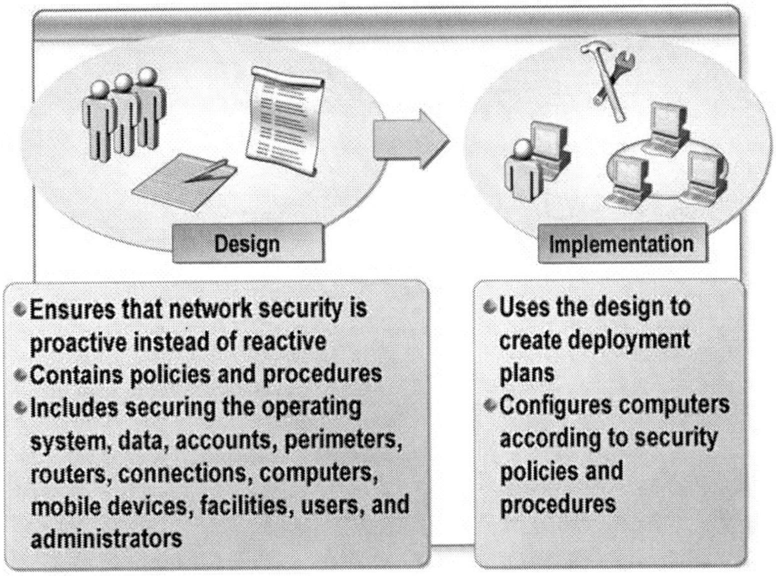

Key points

As a designer of network security, you must understand the difference between security design and security implementation, which are related but different processes.

Security design ensures that an organization has a logical and carefully planned strategy for securing its assets. For example, not all assets are of equal value. In some cases, the cost of protecting an asset may exceed the value of the asset. Security design balances these and other considerations to ensure that security is applied throughout the organization in a controlled and logical manner.

Security design can be a difficult endeavor, particularly in large networks that have distributed administration or various, disconnected interests. Ensure that you include representatives from different departments of your organization in your design.

Security implementation applies the policies and procedures that you created during the design and ensures that they are deployed consistently throughout the organization. For example, security implementation ensures that individual computers receive the appropriate security templates and that computers are correctly configured to achieve the level of security that a specific security policy requires.

Overview of a Microsoft Network

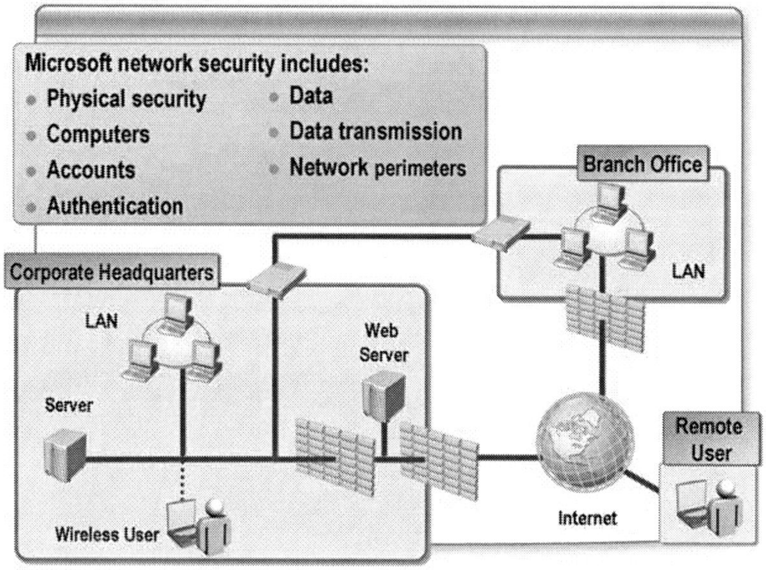

Key points

Assets that require protection are located in many places on a network and in many forms. When you design security for a network, ensure that you create policies and procedures to protect each area of your network from the threats and vulnerabilities that can occur in that area. This course focuses on designing security for the areas in the following table:

Area	Examples of threats and vulnerabilities
Physical security	Poorly secured buildings, data links, theft of hardware
Computers	Attacks during initial installation, incorrectly configured baseline security
Accounts	Incorrect privileges, misuse of Administrator accounts, weak passwords
Authentication	Interception of passwords, incompatibility with software, weak encryption
Data	Configuration of permissions, failure of hardware, corruption of data
Data transmission	Attackers monitoring network, address spoofing, data modification, denial of service
Network perimeters	Exposure of network information, lack of control over infrastructure, exposure of computers to attack

Other Microsoft technologies related to network infrastructure, servers, and services, such as the Microsoft Active Directory® directory service, Microsoft SQL Server™ 2000, Microsoft Exchange 2000, Internet Information Services (IIS), and Microsoft Internet Security and Acceleration (ISA) Server 2000, are covered in detail in separate courses.

Additional reading

For more information about Active Directory, see Course 2154, *Implementing and Administering Microsoft Windows 2000 Directory Services*.

For more information about ISA Server, see Course 2159, *Deploying and Managing Microsoft Internet Security and Acceleration Server 2000*.

For more information about IIS version 5.0, see Course 2295, *Implementing and Supporting Microsoft Internet Information Services 5.0*.

For more information about securing SQL Server 2000, see the white paper, *Microsoft SQL Server 2000 Security*, under **Additional Reading** on the Web page on the Student Materials CD.

For more information about Exchange 2000 security, see *Security Operations Guide for Exchange 2000 Server*, under **Additional Reading** on the Web page on the Student Materials CD.

Framework for Designing Security

Modules	Phase	Tasks
2	• Creating a design team	• Include diverse membership to ensure success and buyoff across organization
3	• Performing threat modeling	• Predict attacks to assets • List vulnerabilities of assets
4	• Performing risk management	• Analyze risk and create risk statements • Prioritize risk
5-11	• Designing security measures	• Based on risk assessment, create policies and procedures to prevent threats from occurring
12	• Detection and reaction	• Detect occurrence of a security incident • Create response to a security incident
A, B, C	• Ongoing use and management of the network	• Define acceptable use by users • Create policies for managing networks • Manage a security operations framework

Key points

The modules in this course present the content in several phases:

- *Creating a security design team.* Ensures that your design is the product of different perspectives so that all vulnerabilities and threats may be discovered. A design team also helps ensure representation of a cross-section of employees in the design and can help ensure compliance with the policies and procedures that the team designs.
- *Performing threat modeling.* Enables you to predict threats to a given asset or resource. Knowing the threats that affect an asset helps you design countermeasures to protect the asset.
- *Performing risk management.* Analyzes likelihood of a threat occurring and the potential damage that a threat may cause. Risk management is a valuable tool that can help you convince management that security measures are necessary to adequately defend a resource against a threat.
- *Designing security measures.* The bulk of this course uses the knowledge and skills from Module 3, "Identifying Threats to Network Security," and Module 4, "Analyzing Security Risks," and applies them to the following areas of a Microsoft network: physical security; computers; accounts; authorization; data; data transmission; and network perimeters. Each module identifies common vulnerabilities to assets in each area and provides recommendations and guidelines for creating security policies that protect each area.
- *Detection and reaction.* Identifies ways to detect intrusions and respond to security incidents in a controlled manner. Early detection of an attack is vital to limiting the damage that the attack may cause. Careful and thoughtful response can make recovery easier and can also prevent mistakes that may make the situation worse.
- *Ongoing use and management of the network.* The appendices in this course also provide information about creating policies for acceptable use, network management, and the secure operation of a network.

Additional reading

For more information about ongoing use and management of the network, see Appendix A, "Designing an Acceptable Use Policy," Appendix B, "Designing Policies for Managing Networks," and Appendix C, "Designing an Operations Framework to Manage Security," in Course 2830, *Designing Security for Microsoft Networks.*

Contoso Pharmaceuticals: A Case Study

- Introduction to Contoso Pharmaceuticals
- Contoso Pharmaceuticals Personnel
- Introduction to the Lab Environment

Introduction

This course presents a case study of a fictional company, Contoso Pharmaceuticals. The labs in each module focus on Contoso's challenges and efforts to design security for its network.

This course uses an interactive lab application to convey scenario-based information for each lab.

Introduction to Contoso Pharmaceuticals

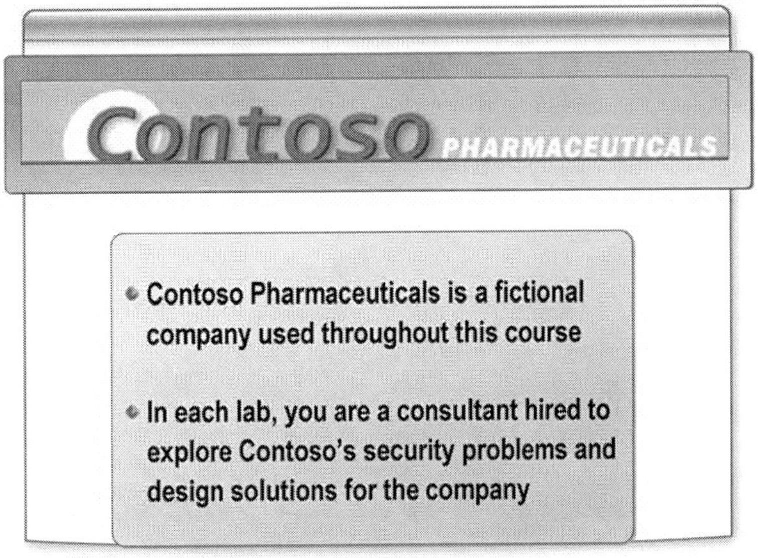

Key points

Contoso Pharmaceuticals produces prescription drugs for a worldwide market. Despite growing into a large company over the years, it has never performed network design in an organized manner. As a result, Contoso Pharmaceuticals has inconsistent—and in some places nonexistent—security on its network.

As part of reforming its Information Technology (IT) department, Contoso has hired a new chief information officer (CIO) to direct security efforts for the company's network. The CIO has hired you as a consultant to help design security for Contoso Pharmaceuticals. In each lab, you will analyze a different scenario that focuses on topics taught in the course.

Contoso Pharmaceuticals Personnel

Key points

Each lab begins with brief video presentations by Contoso Pharmaceuticals employees. The security issues that employees discuss in the videos pertain to the labs. The employees perform various roles and have varying interests. They represent just a few of the roles that security designers work with to create a security design for an organization.

You will hear from the following employees:

- *John Fortune.* As the Chief Executive Officer (CEO) of Contoso Pharmaceuticals, John often provides business motivations for decisions.
- *Ashley Larson.* As the newly hired CIO, Ashley has hired you to assist in designing security for Contoso Pharmaceuticals. In each lab, you will obtain your instructions from Ashley.
- *Helmut Hornig.* Helmut is the Chief Financial Officer (CFO). He provides business information for design decisions that you must make.
- *John Chen.* John is one of Contoso's IT administrators. He offers technical details about the security of the network.
- *Suzan Fine.* Suzan is Vice President (VP) of the research and development department and an executive stakeholder.
- *Lani Ota.* Lani is a business analyst and represents the end user in the organization.

Introduction to the Lab Environment

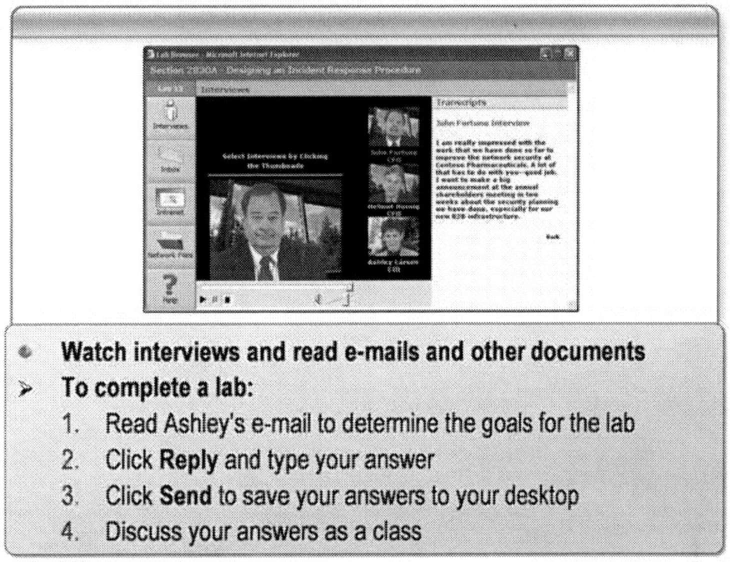

Key points

To begin a lab, on the desktop, click **Internet Explorer**; this opens a Web page that contains links to each lab. Click a link to begin a lab.

Each lab contains the following elements:

- *Interviews*. Company officials describe the scenario and problems with network security at Contoso Pharmaceuticals.
- *E-mails*. Messages contain detailed information for each lab scenario. The e-mails that you receive from Ashley contain the goals.
- *Intranet*. Background information about the company, such as an organizational chart and company history.
- *Network files*. A file server that contains folders with relevant documents that you may need to complete a lab.
- *Help*. Instructions about how to use the interactive lab.

► To complete a lab

1. Read Ashley's e-mail in each lab to determine the goals for the lab.
2. Click **Reply** and then type your answer to Ashley's questions.
3. Click **Send** to save your answers to a folder on your desktop.
4. Discuss your answers as a class.

Microsoft®
Training &
Certification

Module 2: Creating a Plan for Network Security

Contents

Microsoft®

Overview

- Introduction to Security Policies
- Defining a Process for Designing Network Security
- Creating a Security Design Team

Introduction

In this module, you will learn about security policies and procedures for an organization and general strategies for creating policies and procedures. The Microsoft® Solutions Framework (MSF) process model provides a comprehensive framework that you can use to create your security design. To ensure that key stakeholders support your design and that you have the necessary experts together to create a successful design, you will learn how to assemble a security design team.

Objectives

After completing this module, you will be able to:

- Describe common elements of security policies and procedures.
- Create a security design framework by using the MSF process model.
- Create a security design team.

Lesson: Introduction to Security Policies

- What Are Security Policies?
- Types of Security Policies
- Common Reasons That Security Policies Fail
- Guidelines for Creating Policies and Procedures

Introduction

This lesson explains how to use security policies to document and enforce network security in an organization. Included are some common reasons why security policies fail and guidelines for creating successful policies and procedures.

Lesson objectives

After completing this lesson, you will be able to:

- Explain what security policies are.
- Identify types of policies.
- Give reasons why policies fail.
- Explain guidelines for creating policies and procedures.

What Are Security Policies?

Key points

There are three general types of security policies. Each is based on its primary method of enforcement:

- *Administrative policies*. Policies that are enforced by management that cannot be enforced by operating systems, applications, or physical controls. An example is a nondisclosure agreement.
- *Technical policies*. Policies that are enforced by the operating system and applications, such as Security Templates.
- *Physical policies*. Policies that are enforced by implementing physical controls, such as locks.

Additional reading

For more information about security policies, see the white paper, *Best Practices for Enterprise Security: Security Strategies*, at: http://www.microsoft.com/technet/security/bestprac/bpent/sec1/secstrat.asp.

Types of Security Policies

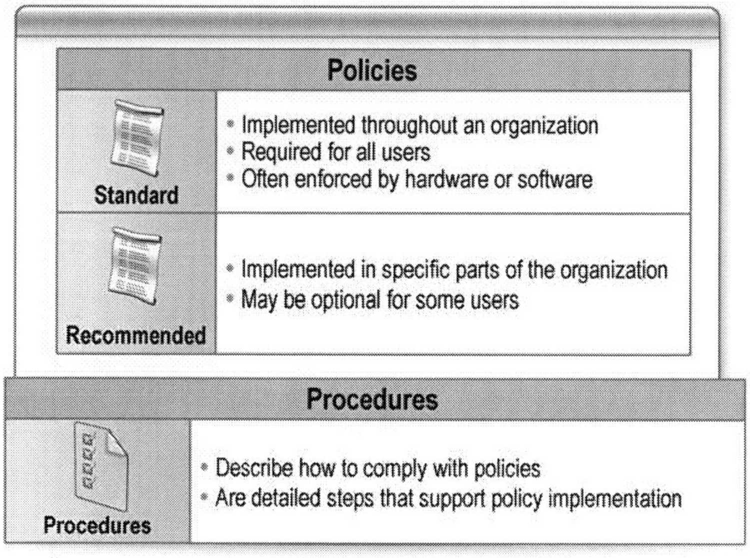

Key points

Ensure that your organization's security policies and procedures reflect:

- Governmental and industry regulations.
- The security requirements of your organization's assets.
- The types of threats to your organization's assets.
- The exposure of your organization's assets to potential attackers.
- Your organization's culture.

Additional reading

For more information about developing security policies and procedures, see *RFC 2196: Site Security Handbook, at:* http://ietf.org/rfc/rfc2196.txt? number=2196.

Common Reasons That Security Policies Fail

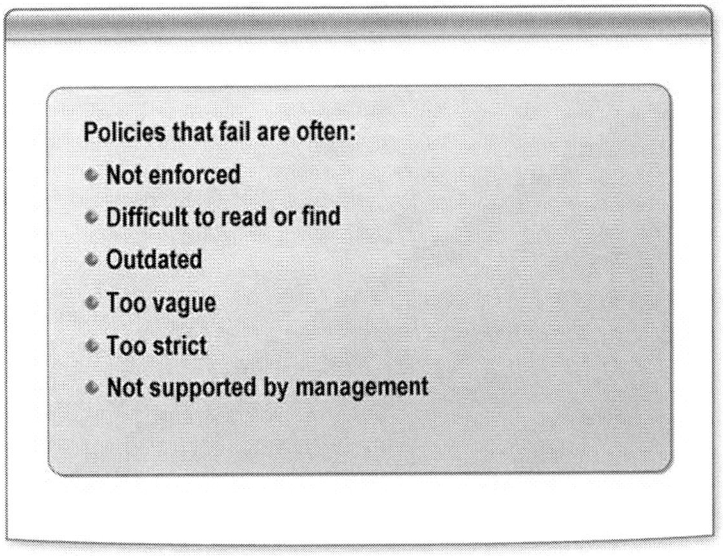

Key points

Security policies fail for many reasons. Anticipate these reasons and ensure that your policies address these concerns.

Examples

Common reasons that policies fail are that they are:

- *Not enforced.* Employees tend to disregard security policies if the policies are not enforced and violators will go unpunished.
- *Difficult to read.* Security policies often contain legal or technical jargon that makes them difficult for employees to understand.
- *Difficult to find.* Security polices that are stored in obscure or inaccessible locations prevent many employees from following them.
- *Outdated.* Security policies that are not kept up to date quickly become obsolete as technologies and business processes change.
- *Too vague.* Security policies that are open to interpretation by employees often result in inconsistent deployment of security in an organization.
- *Too strict.* Security policies that are too strict in their enforcement or their effect on business processes are generally not taken seriously by employees or enforced by management.
- *Not supported by management.* If management does not follow security policies or support their implementation, employees typically do not follow them either.

Guidelines for Creating Policies and Procedures

Guidelines:

- **Create clear and concise policies**
- **Create simple procedures for each policy**
- **Obtain support from all levels of management**
- **Ensure that users can find and use policies**
- **Ensure that policies do not disrupt business continuity**
- **Use technology when possible to enforce policies**
- **Enforce consequences for policy violations**
- **Create incentives for compliance**

Key points

Guidelines for creating policies and procedures include:

- *Clear and concise policies.* Ensure that your security policies serve a clear purpose and are written concisely.
- *Simple procedures.* Whenever possible, write simple procedures and policies that demonstrate how to successfully comply with the policies.
- *Management support.* Obtain management support for the purpose, implementation, and enforcement of security policies.
- *Ease of finding and use.* Distribute your security policies so that employees can refer to them easily. For example, give employees paper copies of policies or post the policies to convenient internal Web sites, and update the policies regularly.
- *Business continuity.* Before implementing security policies, ensure that they do not disrupt business processes. If compliance with security policies conflicts with a business process, work proactively with the owner of the business process to resolve the conflict.
- *Enforcement through technology.* Using technology to enforce security policies helps prevent employees from unwittingly violating security policies. However, remember that technology is not the only method of enforcement.
- *Consequences.* Ensure that the consequences of violating security policy are consistent with the severity of the violation and with your organization's culture. Ensure that managers are empowered to enforce the consequences of violating security policy.
- *Incentives.* Create incentives for following or exceeding security policies. For example, consider making a portion of an employee's bonus contingent on following security polices.

Lesson: Defining a Process for Designing Security

- Introduction to Microsoft Solutions Framework
- The Planning Phase for Network Security
- The Building Phase for Network Security
- The Managing Phase for Network Security
- Practice: Match the Design Task to the MSF Phase

Introduction

Defining a process for network security will help ensure that you create a comprehensive design. Microsoft Solutions Framework (MSF) provides a framework that you can use to design network security.

Lesson objectives

At the end of this lesson, you will be able to:

- Describe the benefits of MSF for developing a network security plan.
- Explain the planning phase for network security.
- Explain the building phase for network security.
- Explain the managing phase for network security.

Introduction to Microsoft Solutions Framework

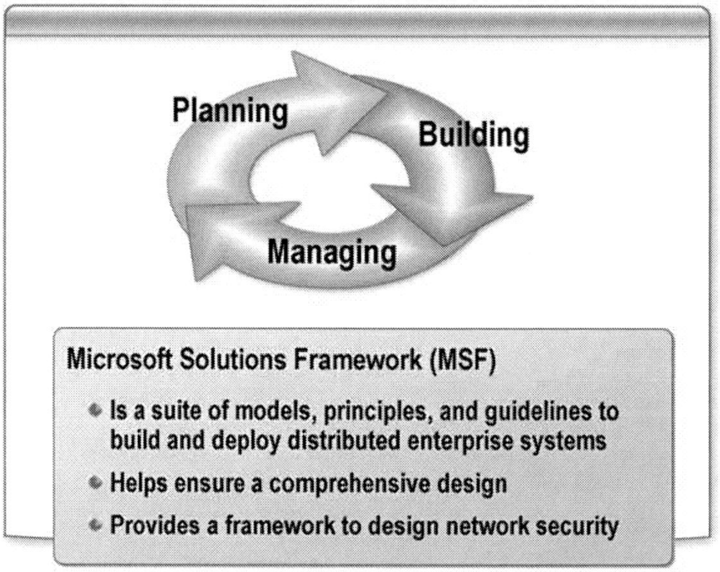

Key points

In any successful IT project, people, processes, and risk management play key roles. To be successful, team members must be able to work and communicate effectively, align technology solutions with business requirements, and manage risk proactively and continuously. These actions are essential to securing an organization's assets; however, they are often the most difficult actions to achieve.

MSF provides a useful framework that consists of three distinct phases for managing these relationships: planning, building, and managing. MSF also includes comprehensive risk management, team, and process models. The following framework helps to ensure an organized and inclusive design.

Additional reading

For more information about MSF, see the white paper, *Overview of MSF*, under **Additional Reading** on the Web page on the Student Materials CD.

For a sample security framework that includes templates, see the *Security Self-Assessment Guide for Information Technology Systems*, from the National Institute of Standards and Technology, at http://csrc.nist.gov/publications/nistpubs/800-26/sp800-26.pdf.

The Planning Phase for Network Security

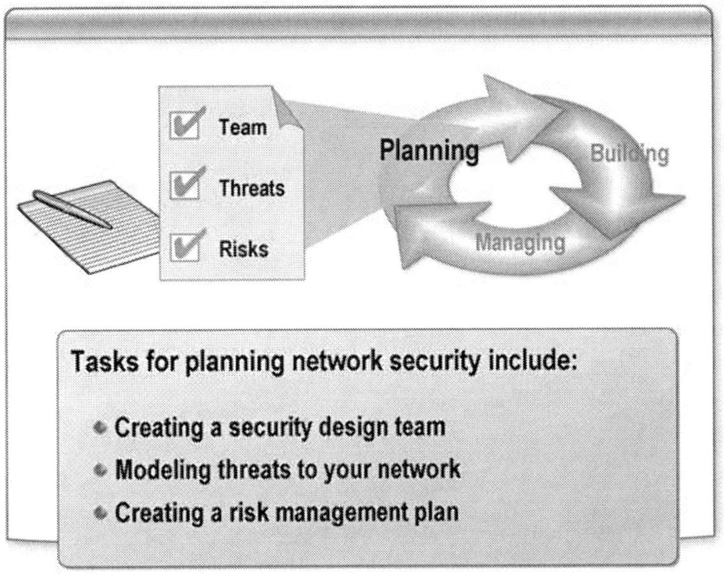

Key points

The goal of the planning phase is to provide the vision for how security will be designed, deployed, and managed. It is essential that your strategic goals contain measurable metrics to determine success.

In the Planning phase, you will:

- *Create a security design team.* The security design team is responsible for creating security policies and envisioning how information will be secured.
- *Model threats.* You will create a living document, called a threat model, to predict security threats that may endanger your network.
- *Create a risk management plan.* An effective security design lessens the financial or business impact of a security incident or reduces the possibility of a security incident occurring. The risk management plan is the foundation of your security design.

Additional reading

For more information about planning for network security, see Course 1517, *Principles of Infrastructure Deployment.*

The Building Phase for Network Security

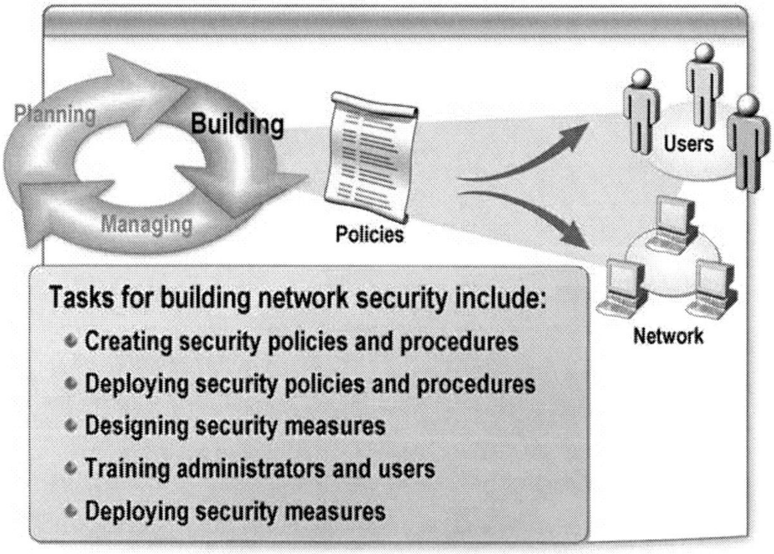

Key points

In the Building phase, you will:

- *Create security policies and procedures.* Your security design team will create new security policies or modify existing ones. The team will work with other departments in your organization, such as human resources (HR) and IT, to develop procedures for compliance with the policies.
- *Deploy security policies and procedures.* After the security design team and the executive sponsor of the project approve the security policies and procedures, you will deploy them across the organization.
- *Design security measures.* During this phase, you will design the technical and physical controls to enforce security policies.
- *Train administrators and users.* Before deploying the security measures, you must train administrators how to deploy and manage the security measures, and then train users how to use the security measures.
- *Deploy security measures.* The last part of the building phase is to test, pilot, and deploy the security measures.

The Managing Phase for Network Security

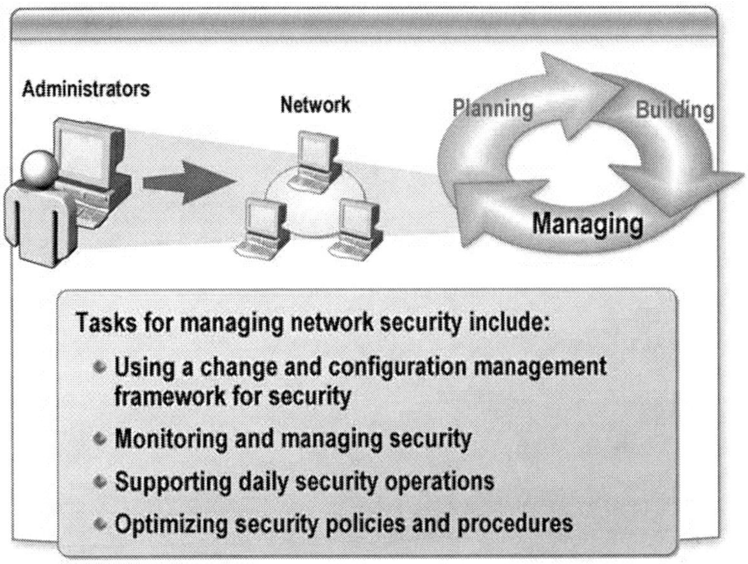

Key points

In the Managing phase, you will:

- *Use a change and configuration management plan.* The purpose of this plan is to ensure that changes to the network do not compromise security.
- *Monitor and manage security.* Administrators in your organization monitor the network for possible security incidents. They also manage the security of the network, including the deployment of security updates.
- *Supporting daily operations.* The help desk and administrators will provide end-user support.
- *Optimizing security policies and procedures.* As administrators monitor, manage, and support security measures and their use by end users, they will find security vulnerabilities and discover better methods to enforce security policies. It is recommended that you use this information to improve and optimize your security policies and procedures.

Additional reading

Appendices A, B, and C of this course contain information about designing policies and procedures for the managing phase of network security.

Practice: Match the Design Task to the MSF Phase

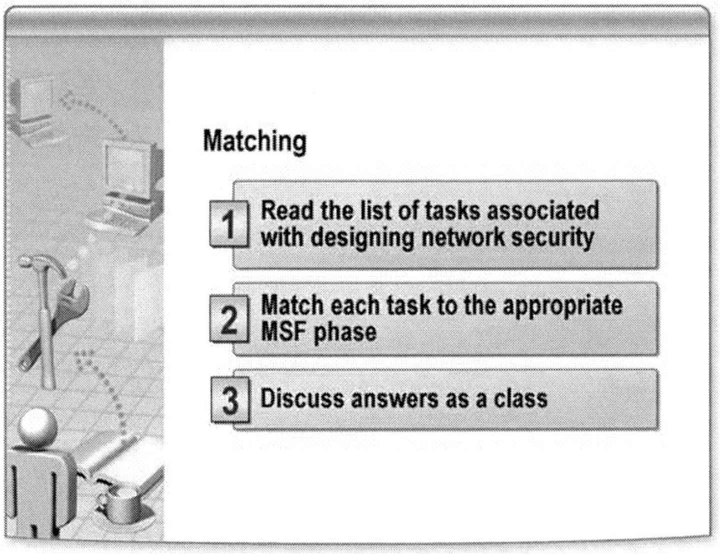

Introduction

Draw a line connecting each task in the left column to its appropriate MSF phase in the right column: Planning, Building, or Managing.

Task	MSF phase
Train administrators and users	Managing
Deploy security policies and procedures	Managing
Optimize security policies and procedures	Building
Model threats	Building
Monitor and manage security	Planning
Design security measures	Building
Support daily operations	Building
Deploy security measures	Planning
Create security policies and procedures	Managing
Create a risk management plan	Managing
Use a change management and configuration plan	Building

Lesson: Creating a Security Design Team

- Core Team Members
- Extended Team Members
- Teams That Deploy and Manage Security
- Guidelines for Creating a Security Design Team
- Practice: Match Role to Responsibility

Introduction

You create a security team to ensure that you have the necessary experts together to create a successful design and that all key stakeholders in your organization support your security design. Support from stakeholders is essential to the success of your design.

The roles presented in this lesson are based on team roles and team structures described in MSF and in the Microsoft Operations Framework (MOF).

Lesson objectives

After completing this lesson, you will be able to:

- Identify core team members.
- Identify extended team members.
- Determine which teams in your organization deploy and manage security.
- Describe guidelines for creating a security design team.

Core Team Members

Role on design team	Responsible for:
Product management	Aligning security with business requirements
Program management	Managing development
Development	Creating and deploying security
Test	Testing and ensuring quality control
User education	Ensuring usability
Logistics management	Managing operations and deployment

Key points

Each role is responsible for a unique part of the security design. Your team does not necessarily require one person per role, but all roles should be assigned to an owner or representative. Recommended roles include:

- *Product management.* Acts as the business advocate for the team. Product managers develop and execute the business case for security and ensure that the security design aligns with the organization's business requirements. They also identify and prioritize risks and facilitate communication among team members and with management.
- *Program management.* Drives the overall project. Program managers manage the strategic goals, budget, schedules, and resources.
- *Development.* Designs, builds, and tests security measures and supports deployment. Developers provide the technical expertise to create security policies.
- *Testing.* Develops test strategy and plans, writes scripts, and pilots testing. Testers also participate in setting metrics to ensure quality control.
- *User education.* Acts as the team advocate to the end user and as the end-user advocate to the team. People who perform this role drive the usability requirements and design and develop administrator and end-user training.
- *Logistics management.* Acts as liaison between team and operations. Logistics managers manage the deployment of security measures and support the design during testing.

Additional reading

For more information about these team roles in the MSF model, see the white paper, *MSF Team Roles*, under **Additional Reading** on the Web page on the Student Materials CD.

Extended Team Members

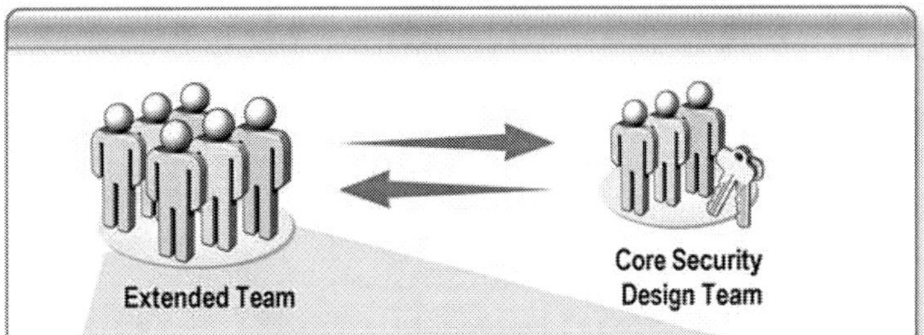

Role	Responsible for:
Executive sponsor	Buyoff and support
Legal	Law and liability
Human resources	Employee rights and responsibilities
Managers	Enforcement
End users	Feedback
Auditors	Reviewing policies, procedures, and practices

Key points

In addition to the core team members of the security design team, you will create an extended team, which must include:

- *Executive sponsor*. Has singular authority to approve or decline recommendations by the security design team. The executive sponsor is also responsible for being the team's advocate with upper management.
- *Legal*. Advises the team about local, national, and international laws and liabilities that may affect the security policies.
- *Human resources*. Ensures that security policies can be enforced and do not conflict with employment laws.
- *Managers*. Enforce security policies. Manager involvement also helps ensure that security policies do not conflict with business processes.
- *End users*. Provide feedback about how to train end users about the security policies and how the policies may affect end users.
- *Auditors*. Ensure compliance with government or industry regulations during the design.

Teams That Deploy and Manage Security

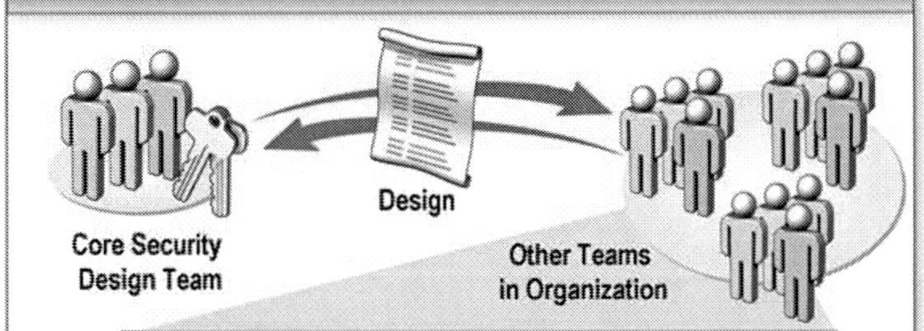

Team	Provides feedback on:
Infrastructure	Release and change management
Operations	Management of desktops and servers
Partner	Additional support and expertise
Release	Management of network infrastructure
Security	Impact on network security
Support	Help desk and support functions

Key points

Between completion of your initial design and deployment, be sure to solicit feedback from the people who will be responsible for deploying, managing, and supporting your design. These individuals may be located throughout your organization.

Additional reading

For more information about teams that deploy and manage different aspects of IT, see the white paper, *MOF Teams*, under **Additional Reading** on the Web page on the Student Materials CD. See also Course 1737, *Microsoft Operations Framework Essentials*.

Guidelines for Creating a Security Design Team

Guidelines:

- **Identify a single executive sponsor**
- **Identify an experienced program manager**
- **Involve teams that will deploy and manage network security in the planning phase**
- **Involve legal and human resources**
- **Ensure that managers and end users participate in the team**
- **Establish clear roles and responsibilities for all team members**
- **Create a communication plan**

Key points

Guidelines for creating a security design team include:

- *A single executive sponsor*. An executive sponsor who can make decisions gives your design authority and helps keep team members focused on the project.
- *An experienced program manager*. Coordinating team members from different parts of your organization is a difficult task. Ensure that you use a program manager who is experienced with personnel and with your corporate culture.
- *Involvement of teams that will deploy and manage network security in the planning phase*. These teams are essential to the success of your design after you have finished it.
- *Legal and human resources*. These departments can ensure that your design is legal and ethical.
- *Participation of managers and end users*. Involving representatives of managers and end users in the design will help ensure that all managers and end users follow your policies.
- *Clear roles and responsibilities for all team members*. Ensure that all members of the security design team understand their responsibilities and the goals of all other roles.
- *A communication plan*. Communicate regularly and clearly to your organization so that people know whom to expect communication from and so that they have time to prepare for your design.

Practice: Match Role to Responsibility

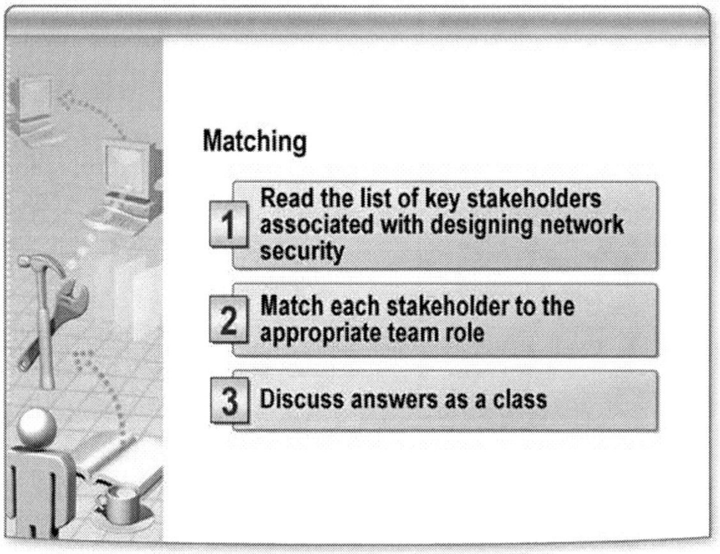

Introduction

Draw a line connecting each key stakeholder role in the core and extended teams in the left column to the appropriate responsibility in the right column.

Role	Responsibility
Core: Program management	Ensure quality control
Core: Product management	Create and deploy security
Core: Development	Ensure usability
Core: Testing	Manage development
Core: User education	Manage operations and deployment
Core: Logistics management	Align security with business requirements
Extended: Executive sponsor	Provide feedback
Extended: Legal	Obtain buyoff and support
Extended: Human resources	Advise about laws and liabilities
Extended: Managers	Ensure policies are enforceable
Extended: End users	Ensure compliance with security policies
Extended: Auditors	Enforce policies

Lab A: Planning a Security Framework

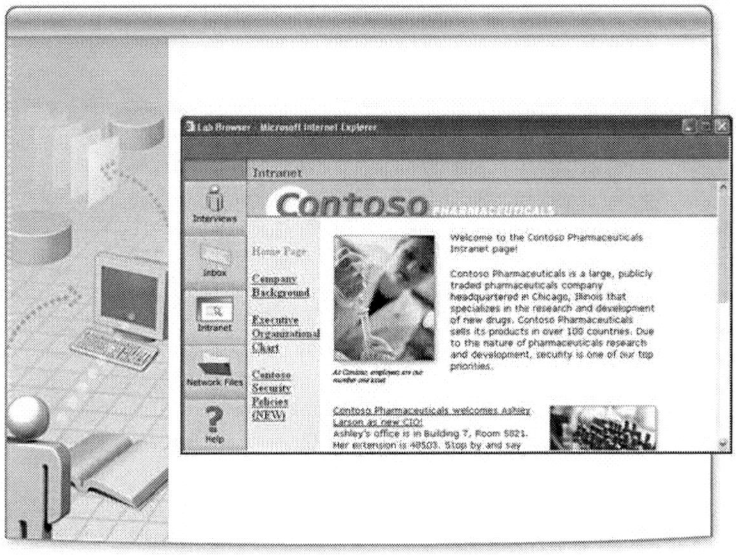

Objectives

After completing this lab, you will be able to:

- Identify reasons why security policies fail.
- Explain the benefits of using MSF to guide security planning.
- Determine members of a security design team.

Scenario

You are a consultant hired by Contoso Pharmaceuticals to help the company design security for its network. Each lab uses an interactive application to convey scenario-based information. Open Internet Explorer to view a Web page that contains links to each lab. Click a link to begin the lab.

Estimated time to complete this lab: 45 minutes

Work with a lab partner or in small teams to perform the lab.

► To complete a lab

1. Read Ashley Larson's e-mail in each lab to determine the goals for the lab.
2. Click **Reply**, and then type your answer to Ashley's questions.
3. Click **Send** to save your answers to a folder on your desktop.
4. Discuss your answers as a class.

Microsoft®
Training &
Certification

Module 3: Identifying Threats to Network Security

Contents

Microsoft®

Overview

- Introduction to Security Threats
- Predicting Threats to Security

Introduction

In this module, you will learn how to identify possible threats to a network and understand common motivations of attackers. The module introduces the STRIDE (Spoofing, Tampering, Repudiation, Information disclosure, Denial of service, Elevation of privilege) threat model as an effective way to predict where threats may occur in an organization.

Objectives

After completing this module, you will be able to:

- Explain common network vulnerabilities and how attackers can exploit them.
- Predict threats to security by using the STRIDE model.

Lesson: Introduction to Security Threats

- Why Network Attacks Occur
- Who Attacks Networks?
- Common Types of Network Vulnerabilities
- How Network Attacks Occur
- Difficulties in Defending Networks

Introduction

A threat describes a danger or vulnerability. Threats can occur from a variety of sources, such as attacks or an incorrectly configured application.

Lesson objectives

After completing this lesson, you will be able to:

- Explain why network attacks occur.
- Describe who attacks networks.
- Describe common types of network vulnerabilities.
- Describe how network attacks take place.
- List the difficulties of defending networks.

Why Network Attacks Occur

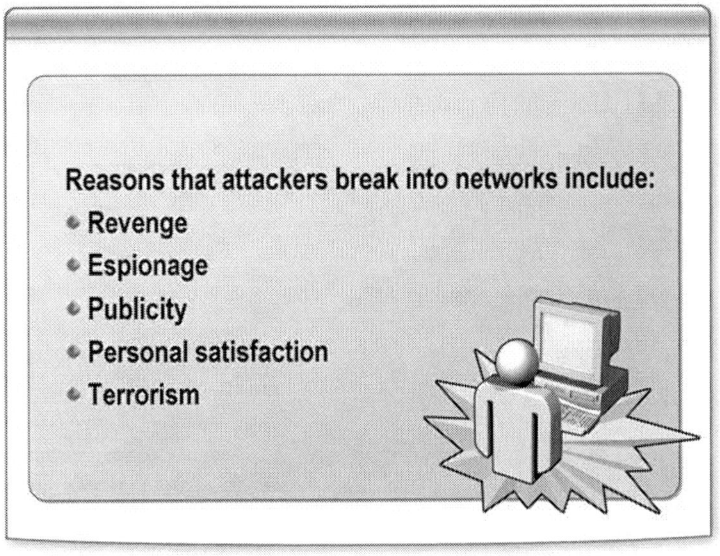

Key points

Attackers attempt to compromise the security of networks and applications for a variety of reasons, including:

- *Revenge.* An attacker may feel slighted by an organization and want to punish it. Sometimes, former employees attack their previous organizations for revenge. This attacker is particularly dangerous due to his in-depth knowledge of the network and his personal motivation for attack.
- *Espionage.* An attacker may spy on an organization or government to obtain secrets. Such an attacker is often motivated by patriotism or monetary gain.
- *Publicity.* An attacker may attack a network or application to seek public notoriety or to advertise her own services. Publicity seekers often report their attacks.
- *Personal satisfaction.* An attacker may attack networks as a hobby, for the challenge, or to boost his ego. This type of attacker is dangerous due to his efforts to attack networks indiscriminately.
- *Terrorism.* An attacker may attack a network as part of a group- or state-sponsored terrorist effort. These are the most serious types of attackers because human life may be at risk.

Who Attacks Networks?

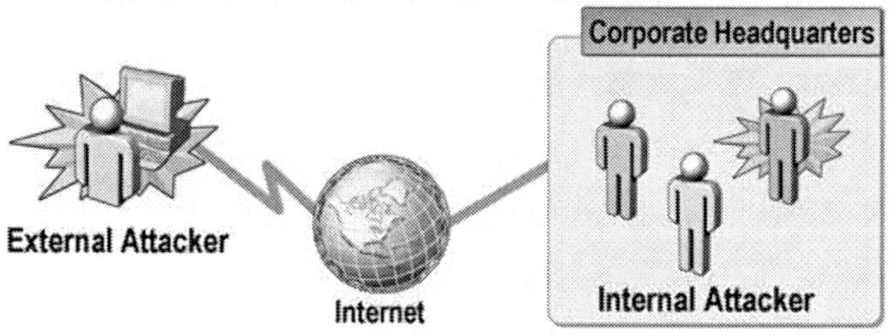

Ability	Characteristics of attackers
Novice	• Possess little programming experience • Use tools that are made by others
Intermediate	• Possess significant programming skills • Automate tools that are created by others
Advanced	• Are expert programmers • Develop tools that others use to attack networks

Key points

Attackers of all abilities and motivations are dangerous to network security in different ways:

- *Novice.* Most attackers have only basic computer knowledge but are still dangerous because they often do not fully understand the consequences of their actions.
- *Intermediate.* Attackers with intermediate skills are often trying to gain respect in attacker communities. Typically, they attack prominent targets or create automated tools for others to attack networks.
- *Advanced.* Highly skilled attackers present a serious challenge to network security because their methods of attack can extend beyond technology into physical intrusion and social engineering, or misleading a user or administrator in order to gain information. Although there are relatively few advanced attackers, their skills and experience make them the most dangerous attackers to a network.

Common Types of Network Vulnerabilities

Vulnerability	Examples
Weak passwords	• Employees use blank or default passwords • Password is predictable
Unpatched software	• Service packs are not maintained • Security hotfixes are not applied
Incorrectly configured hardware and software	• Users have too many privileges • Applications run as the Local System account
Social engineering	• Help desk administrator resets a password without verifying the identity of the caller
Weak security on Internet connections	• Unused services and ports are not secured • Firewalls and routers are used improperly
Unencrypted data transfer	• Authentication packets are sent in clear text • Important data is sent over the Internet in clear text

Key points

Most successful attacks on networks succeed by exploiting common and well known vulnerabilities or weaknesses. Ensure that you train administrators to recognize these vulnerabilities and to become familiar with new ones when they are discovered.

Additional reading

For more information about Microsoft Security Bulletins, see http://www.microsoft.com/technet/security/bulletin/notify.asp.

For the SysAdmin, Audit, Network, Security (SANS) Institute/Federal Bureau of Investigation (FBI) top 20 list of security vulnerabilities, see http://www.sans.org/top20.htm.

How Network Attacks Occur

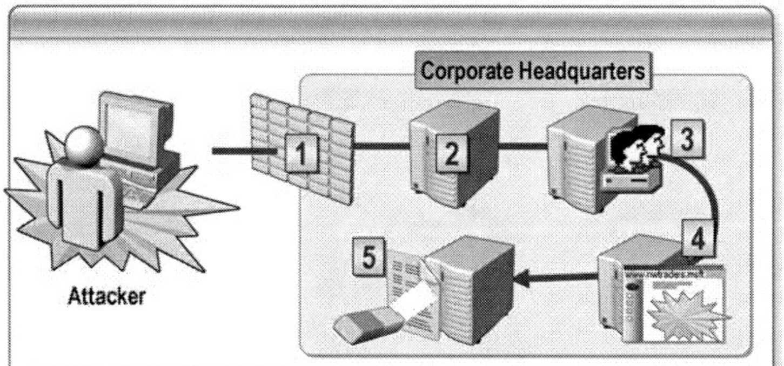

Stages of attack	Examples of attacker actions
1. Footprint	Runs a port scan on the firewall
2. Penetration	Exploits an unpatched Web server
3. Elevation of privilege	Creates an account with administrator rights
4. Exploit	Defaces the Web site
5. Cover-up	Erases the audit trail of the exploit

Key points

Attacks on networks often follow the same pattern. You should design methods for detecting, responding to, or preventing attacks during each of the following stages:

1. *Footprint*. In this stage, the attacker researches the target organization. He may obtain all public information about an organization and its employees and complete port scans on all computers and devices that are accessible from the Internet.
2. *Penetration*. After the attacker has located potential vulnerabilities, she will try to take advantage of a vulnerability. For example, the attacker exploits a Web server that lacks the latest security update.
3. *Elevation of privilege*. After the attacker has successfully penetrated the network, she attempts to obtain administrator or system-level rights. For example, while exploiting the Web server, she gains control of a process running under the LocalSystem security context and uses this process to create an administrator account. Often, poor security as a result of using default settings allows an attacker to obtain network access without much effort.
4. *Exploit*. After the attacker has obtained the necessary rights, he carries out the exploit, or method of breaking into the network. For example, the attacker chooses to deface the organization's public Web site.
5. *Cover-up*. The final stage of an attack is where an attacker attempts to hide his actions to escape detection or prosecution. For example, an attacker erases relevant entries in audit log files.

Additional reading

For more information about how network attacks occur, see *Hacking Exposed: Windows 2000*, by Joel Scambray and Stuart McClure, published by McGraw-Hill Osborne Media.

Difficulties in Defending Networks

Parties	Characteristics
Attackers	• Can attack with very low cost • Only need to understand one vulnerability • Outnumber security personnel • Have unlimited time • Do not follow any set of rules
Security personnel	• Must dedicate time and resources to defend the network against attacks • Must protect end users and managers who may not be vigilant • Must understand all vulnerabilities

Key points

Defending networks has several unique challenges. Attackers as a group possess a nearly infinite ability to attack networks, whereas security professionals have limitations in terms of number, time, and resources. Security professionals must also abide by legal restrictions in terms of how they investigate attackers.

Because of the difficulties in defending networks, it is essential that security personnel are organized, trained, prepared, and vigilant.

Lesson: Predicting Threats to Security

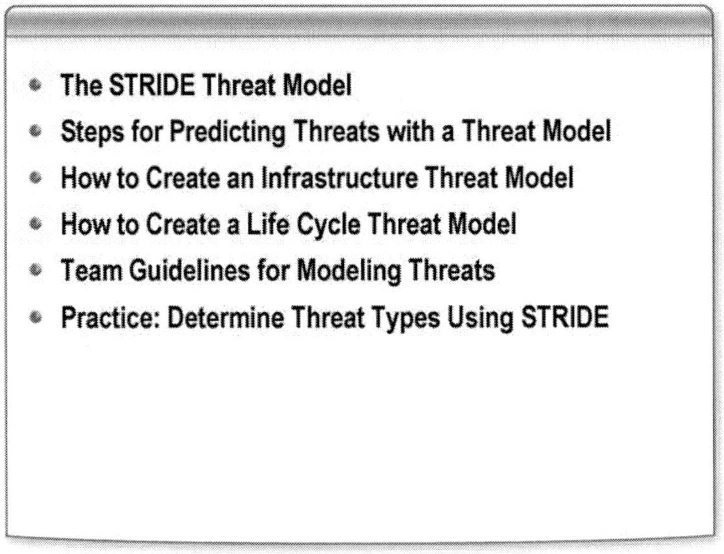

Introduction

The ability to predict threats will help you prioritize how you spend your security resources to protect your network. Threats change every day, depending on changes in technology. Using a technique known as *threat modeling* will help you anticipate where attacks may occur on your network.

Lesson objectives

After completing this lesson, you will be able to:

- Explain the STRIDE threat model.
- Use a threat model to predict threats to a network.
- Create an infrastructure threat model.
- Create a life cycle threat model.
- List guidelines for modeling threats.

The STRIDE Threat Model

Types of threats	Examples
Spoofing	• Forge e-mail messages • Replay authentication packets
Tampering	• Alter data during transmission • Change data in files
Repudiation	• Delete a critical file and deny it • Purchase a product and later deny it
Information disclosure	• Expose information in error messages • Expose code on Web sites
Denial of service	• Flood network with SYN packets • Flood with forged ICMP packets
Elevation of privilege	• Exploit buffer overruns to gain system privileges • Obtain administrator privileges illegitimately

Key points

A threat model is a structured approach that helps you predict potential threats to information security. The potential threats that you discover while performing threat modeling enable you to create an accurate risk management plan. By predicting threats, you can proactively reduce your risk.

The STRIDE model is a simple way to categorize threats according to their characteristics. There are six categories of threats in the STRIDE model. A threat may belong to more then one category.

Additional reading

For more information about the STRIDE model, see Chapter 3, "Public Enemy #1: the Buffer Overrun," in *Writing Secure Code*, by Michael Howard and David LeBlanc, published by Microsoft Press.

Steps for Predicting Threats with a Threat Model

Steps:

1. **Define the hardware and software to evaluate**
2. **Create a team to model threats**
3. **Predict ways that the targets may be attacked**

Key points

To use a threat model, such as STRIDE, follow these steps:

1. *Define the scope.* Decide what hardware and software you will evaluate during the threat modeling exercise. By defining the hardware and software, you can focus exclusively on the object of the threat modeling, such as a Web server or a branch office, rather than the entire network.
2. *Create a team.* The team should include a variety of technical skills and experience. Ideally, each team member can think about the object of the threat modeling exercise from many perspectives, including those that may be far-fetched or illegal. To preserve objectivity, choose team members that have a limited stake in the object of the threat modeling.
3. *Predict threats.* Meet in a room with white boards, flipcharts, and relevant documentation to discuss the possible ways that the object could be attacked. Keep the sessions short and schedule several sessions so that team members have time to think about the object. Ask someone to document the findings of the team.

How to Create an Infrastructure Threat Model

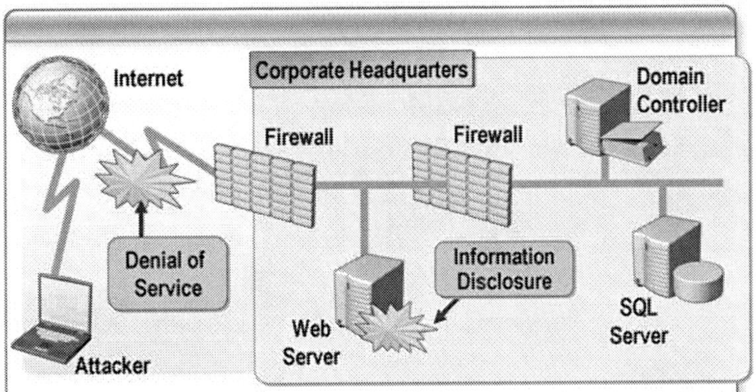

Type	Threat	Probability	Impact
Denial of service	Automated attack prevents legitimate traffic from flowing	High	Medium - high
Information disclosure	An SA account is used in SQL query strings	Medium	Critical

Key points

One approach to threat modeling is to apply the STRIDE model to a well-defined section of network infrastructure. For example, you may want to isolate a Web server for threat modeling.

When you perform threat modeling on infrastructures, ensure that you have all of the relevant documentation, including:

- Network diagrams.
- Hardware and software configurations.
- Data flow diagrams.
- Custom source code.

Additional reading

For more information about infrastructure threat models, see *Designing Secure Web-Based Applications for Microsoft Windows 2000*, by Michael Howard, published by Microsoft Press.

How to Create a Life Cycle Threat Model

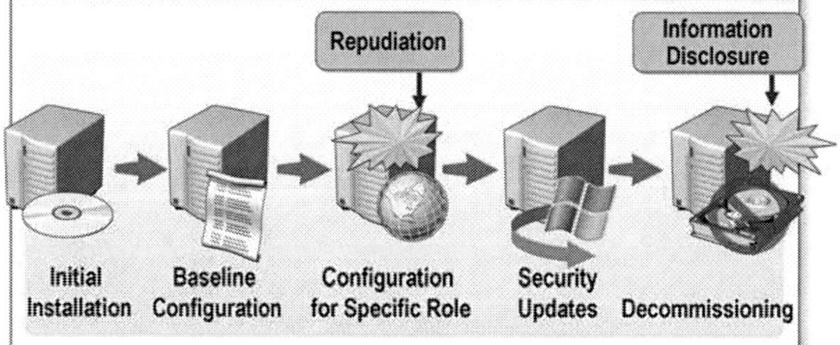

Type	Threat	Probability	Impact
Repudiation	Auditing not enabled during configuration of Web server	Medium	Medium-high
Information disclosure	Data remains on the hard disk	Medium	High

Key points

Another approach to threat modeling is to apply the STRIDE model to the life cycle of a device or application. For example, you can predict threats to computers that are deployed on your network. As shown in the slide, a computer's vulnerability to different threats depends on its life cycle stage.

Team Guidelines for Modeling Threats

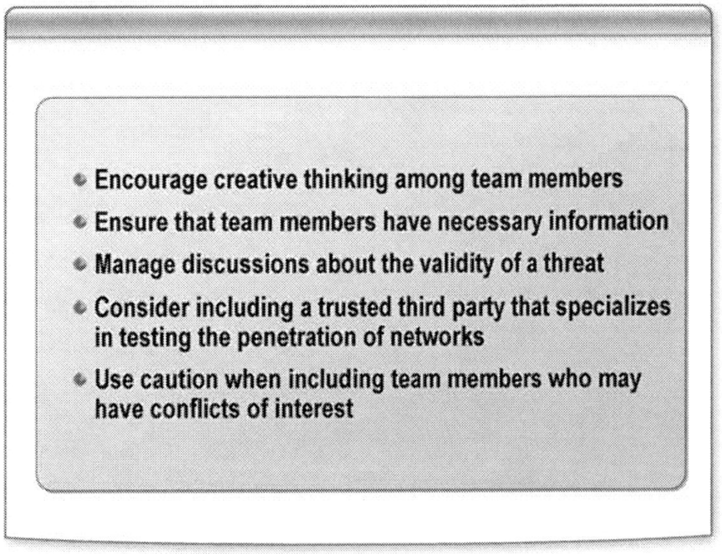

Guidelines

- Encourage creative thinking among team members. Some suggestions, however unrealistic, may prompt others to discover additional valid threats.
- Ensure that team members have all of the information that they need, such as network diagrams or application source code.
- Manage discussions about the validity of a threat to focus on threats to the network and to avoid disagreements about minor differences of opinion.
- When assembling your team, consider including a trusted third party that specializes in network penetration testing.
- Use caution when including team members who may have conflicts of interest. For example, a developer who wrote the code in the application being assessed, or a manager who funded the project to create the application may overestimate the ability of the application to withstand an attack, or may be too familiar with it to be objective about its assessment.

Practice: Determine Threat Types Using STRIDE

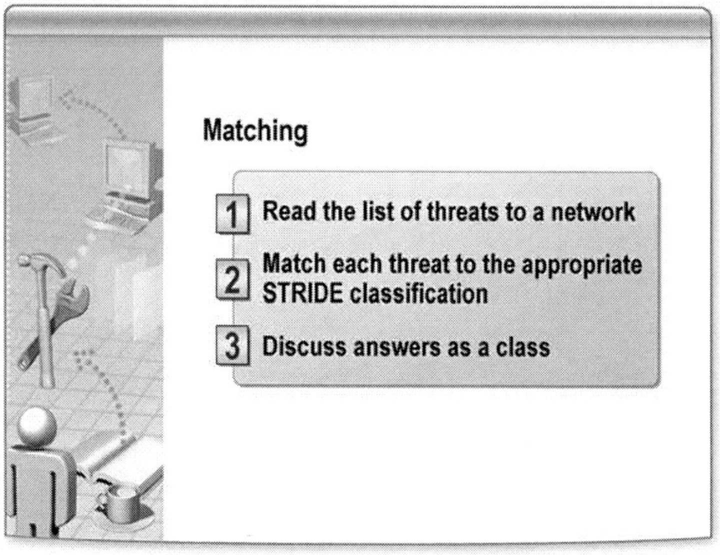

Introduction

For each threat, list the appropriate part of the STRIDE classification:

- Spoofing
- Tampering
- Repudiation
- Information disclosure
- Denial of service
- Elevation of privilege

Threat	STRIDE classification
Password sent in plain text from a client computer to a database	
Poorly coded Web site allows a cross-site scripting attack	
Attacker can gain physical access to servers	
Security updates that prevent buffer overruns are not applied to servers	

Lab A: Identifying Threats to Network Security

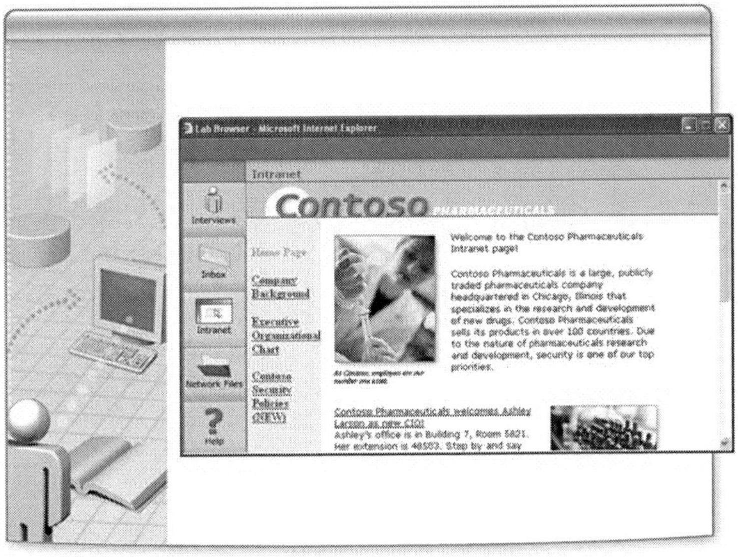

Objectives

After completing this lab, you will be able to predict threats to a network by using the STRIDE (Spoofing, Tampering, Repudiation, Information disclosure, Denial of service, Elevation of privilege) threat model.

Scenario

You are a consultant hired by Contoso Pharmaceuticals to help the company design security for its network. Each lab uses an interactive lab application to convey scenario-based information. To begin a lab, on the desktop, click **Internet Explorer**; this opens a Web page that contains links to each lab. Click a link to begin a lab.

Estimated time to complete this lab: 45 minutes

Work with a lab partner to perform the lab.

► **To complete a lab**

1. Read Ashley Larson's e-mail in each lab to determine the goals for the lab.
2. Click **Reply**, and then type your answer to Ashley's questions.
3. Click **Send** to save your answers to a folder on your desktop.
4. Discuss your answers as a class.

Important In this lab, you do not need to send e-mail to Ashley Larson. Instead, open the Microsoft Excel spreadsheet named Threat Model Worksheet.xls, and add information to it. Rename the file and save it to the Lab Answers folder on your desktop for discussion.

Microsoft®
Training &
Certification

Module 4: Analyzing Security Risks

Contents

Microsoft®

Overview

- Introduction to Risk Management
- Creating a Risk Management Plan

Introduction

In this module, you will learn how to determine what resources in your organization require protection and how to prioritize those resources based on their value. You will then develop a risk management plan, based on the Microsoft Operations Framework (MOF) risk model, to identify and analyze risks proactively and to determine an appropriate level of protection for each resource.

Objectives

After completing this module, you will be able to:

- Explain the purpose and operation of risk management.
- Draft the elements of a risk management plan.

Lesson: Introduction to Risk Management

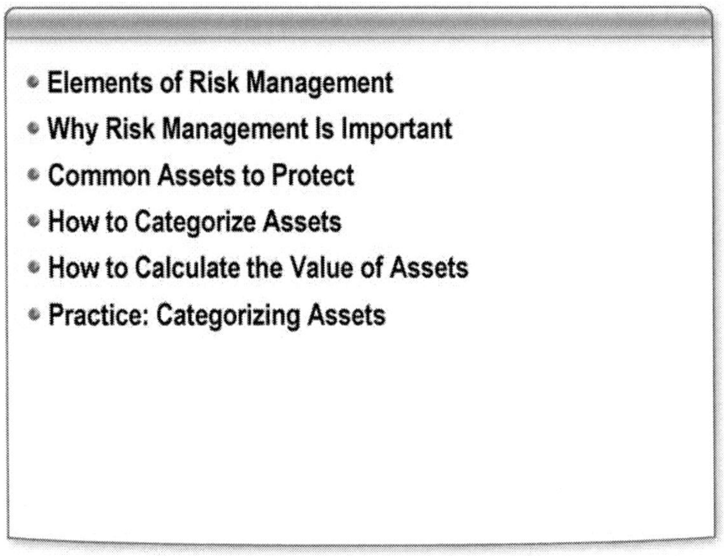

Introduction

Risk management is the act of examining the relative value of your assets and then allocating your security resources based on the likelihood of the risk occurring and the value of the asset. Risk management helps you prioritize your efforts and spending to secure your network.

Lesson objectives

After completing this lesson, you will be able to:

- Describe the different elements of risk management.
- Explain why risk management is important.
- Identify common assets to protect.
- Categorize assets according to type.
- Calculate the value of an asset.

Elements of Risk Management

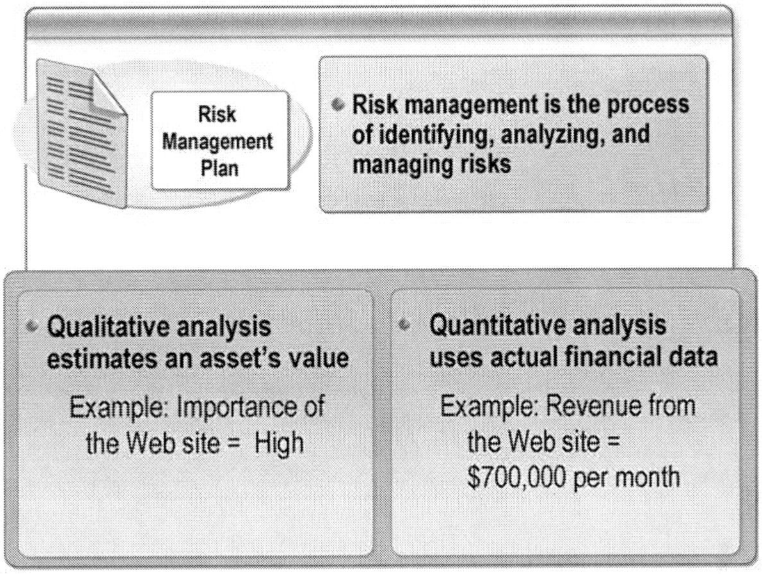

Key points

A risk is the possibility of suffering a loss, and the impact or extent of damage that would result if the loss occurs. Risk management is the process of identifying risks, analyzing the risks, and creating a plan to manage the risks.

There are two types of risk analysis:

- *Qualitative*. Ranks risks according to their relative impact on business operations. Qualitative analysis often requires you to estimate the probability of a threat and the impact of the threat occurring on a scale of 1 to 10. You then multiply the two numbers for the probability and impact and use the product to rank the risk relative to other risks.
- *Quantitative*. Places actual values on the probability and impact of threats to determine how to allocate security resources. Although quantitative risk analysis uses advanced financial accounting skills, it remains an inexact science.

Note Neither qualitative nor quantitative risk analysis is necessarily superior to the other. Both are essential parts of a risk management strategy.

Additional reading

For more information about managing risk, see:

- *Risk Management Guide for Information Systems*, from the National Institute of Standards and Technology (NIST), at http://csrc.ncsl.nist.gov/publications/nistpubs/800-30/sp800-30.pdf.
- The Microsoft white paper, *Risk Model for Operations*, under **Additional Reading** on the Web page on the Student Materials CD.

Why Risk Management Is Important

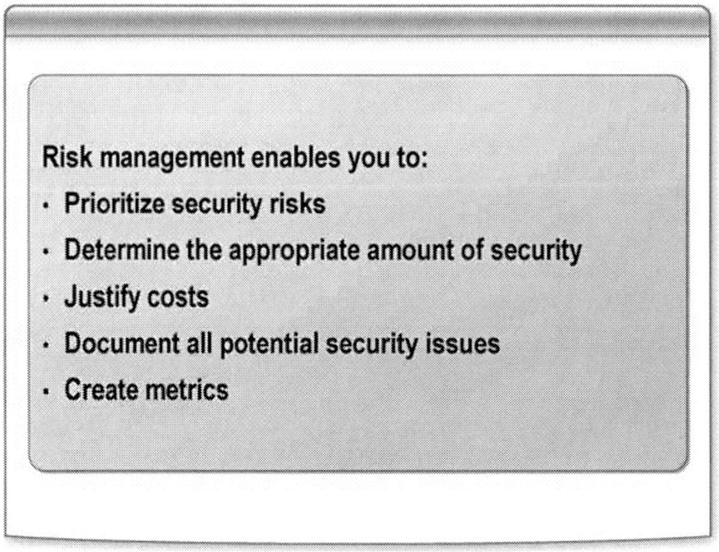

Key points

Risk management helps ensure that your security plan is rational and that you apply your resources to maximize results. By assessing risks and creating a risk management plan, you can:

- *Prioritize security risks*. You can rank security risks to your organization relative to other risks. This helps your organization determine how to allocate resources to secure the network.
- *Determine the appropriate amount of security*. You can discover the point at which incremental improvements to security become inefficient and costly.
- *Justify costs*. You can use a quantitative risk analysis to justify the expense of security personnel, hardware, and software.
- *Document all potential security issues*. Risk management requires a thorough assessment of threats to your network and their potential impacts. An organization that chooses to respond to security threats randomly may overlook critical security issues on its network.
- *Create metrics*. Risk management uses metrics that help you judge the success of your security plan. You can also use metrics to prepare compensation plans for executives and security personnel.

Additional reading

For more information about risk management, watch the 25-minute presentation, *Building a Business Case for IT Investments using REJ*, at: http://www.microsoft.com/seminar/mmcfeed/mmcdisplay.asp?lang=en&product=103346&task=100006.

Also see the white paper, *Rapid Economic Justification*, at: http://www.microsoft.com/technet/ittasks/plan/sysplan/wwww.asp.

Common Assets to Protect

Type	Examples
Hardware	• Desktop and portable computers • Routers and switches • Backup media
Software	• Software installation CDs • Operating system images • Custom software code
Documentation	• Security policies and procedures • Network diagrams and building plans
Data	• Trade secrets • Employee information • Customer information

Key points

In addition to protecting physical assets listed in the table, a large part of the role of security is protecting public confidence and the trust of business partners. In Generally Accepted Accounting Practices (GAAP), this type of asset is known as *goodwill*, which can be placed on financial statements when a company is sold.

Consider, for example, that an attacker defaced your organization's Web site. You notify customers that the attacker has stolen the private information of the Web site's users, including their addresses and credit card numbers. In addition to incurring direct financial losses from lost business, your organization also suffers a loss of goodwill because the company's image is tarnished.

How to Categorize Assets

Type	Examples	What is at risk?
Public	• Public Web sites • Press releases	• Trust • Sales
Private	• Intranet Web site • E-mail with partners	• Proprietary information • Partnerships
Confidential	• Payroll information • Customer information	• Revenue • Internal operations
Secret	• Trade secrets • Products in development	• Intellectual property • Closely-held business plans

Key points

After you identify all of the assets in your risk management plan, organize the assets into discrete categories, such as public, private, confidential, or secret, according to their security requirements.

Categorizing assets helps you prioritize assets and assign owners. Assigning ownership ensures that someone is ultimately responsible for the security of the asset. It also ensures that you assign similar levels of protection to assets that have similar security requirements. By categorizing assets, you will avoid giving minor information, such as cafeteria menus, the same degree of protection as information critical to the success of your business, such as the source code to an enterprise accounting application.

How to Calculate the Value of Assets

To determine the value of an asset:

- **Quantify the asset's overall value to your organization**
- **Calculate the direct financial impact of losing the asset**
- **Calculate the indirect business impact of losing the asset**

Example

Asset	Value of asset	Exposure factor	Direct impact	Indirect impact
E-commerce Web site	$17,520,000 per year	Six hours per year = .000685%	Value x exposure factor = $12,000	Advertising + customer defection = $27,520

Key points

Determining the monetary value of an asset is an important part of risk management. Business managers often rely on the value of an asset to guide how much money and resources to spend securing it. Many organizations maintain a list of asset values as part of their disaster recovery plans.

To assign a value to an asset appropriately, determine three main factors:

- *The overall value of the asset to your organization.* Calculate or estimate the asset's value in direct financial terms. For example, if you have an e-commerce Web site that generates an average of $2,000 per hour in revenue from customer orders, you can state with confidence that the annual value of the Web site in terms of sales revenue is $17,520,000.
- *The immediate financial impact of losing the asset.* If the Web site were unavailable for six hours, the calculated exposure is .000685 percent a year. By multiplying this number by the annual value of the asset, you can predict the directly attributable losses to be $12,000.
- *The indirect business impact of losing the asset.* In this example, you estimate that your company would spend $10,000 in advertising to counteract the negative publicity that the incident caused. You also estimate a loss of .01 of 1 percent of annual sales, or $17,520. By combining the extra advertising expenses and the loss in annual sales revenue, you can predict a total of $27,520 in indirect losses.

Also consider the value of the asset to your competitors. For example, if your competitors were able to acquire the customer information from your Web site, you may estimate that you would lose $5 million in revenue to your competitor.

Practice: Categorizing Assets

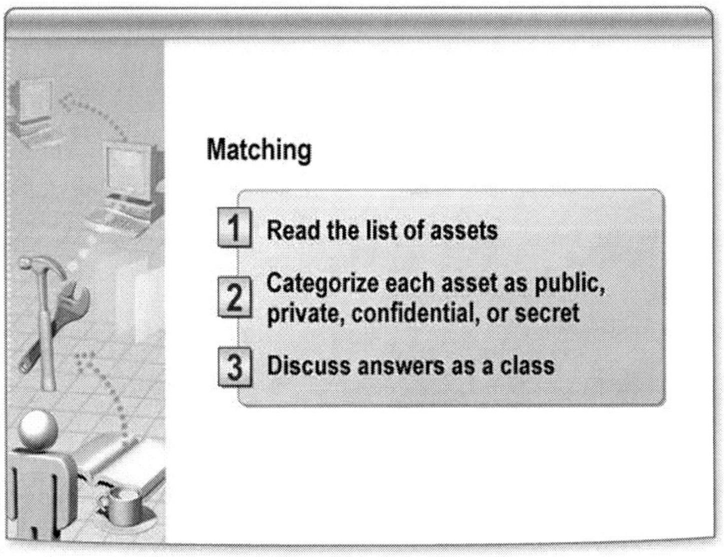

Introduction

In the table below, draw a line connecting each asset in the left column to its type in the right column: public, private, confidential, or secret.

Asset	Type
Health insurance records for employees	Secret
Business-to-business (B2B) Web site	Public
Informational Web site	Confidential
Research and development notes	Private
Customer purchases	Secret
Press releases	Confidential
Merger plans	Public

Lesson: Creating a Risk Management Plan

- Overview of the MOF Risk Management Process
- How to Identify Risks to Assets
- How to Analyze Risks to Assets
- How to Plan for the Management of Risks
- How to Track Changes to a Risk Management Plan
- Risk Management Controls
- Guidelines for Creating a Risk Management Plan
- Practice: Analyzing a Risk Management Plan

Introduction

The final segment of the Planning phase of the Microsoft Solutions Framework (MSF) focuses on risk management. This lesson uses another Microsoft framework, the Microsoft Operations Framework (MOF), to teach a structured approach to performing risk management.

Your risk management plan will determine the level of protection that you apply to the assets in your organization. It will also provide you with a single source of information that can be highly valuable for justifying costs to senior executives and business managers.

Lesson objectives

After completing this lesson, you will be able to:

- Explain the MOF framework as it applies to risk management.
- Describe the five phases of the MOF risk management process.
- List guidelines for creating a risk management plan.

Overview of the MOF Risk Management Process

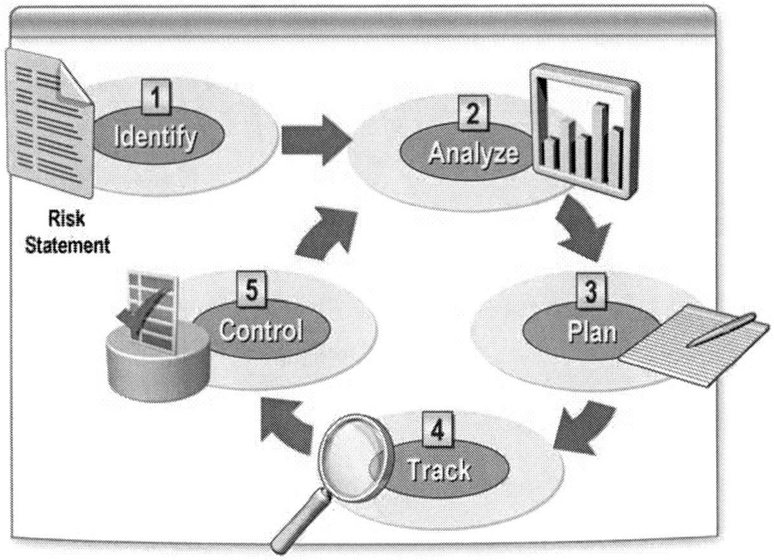

Key points

MOF outlines five stages of risk management. Each phase requires you to complete several tasks. Risk management is an ongoing task. Changes to assets, their exposure to threats, and the impact of risks that occur require you to revisit your risk plan regularly.

The five stages of managing risk are:

1. Identify risks.
2. Analyze risks.
3. Plan for the management of risks.
4. Develop methods to track changes to risks.
5. Respond to risk management controls.

Additional reading

For more information about MOF and risk management, see the white paper, *MOF Risk Management*, under **Additional Reading** on the Web page on the Student Materials CD.

How to Identify Risks to Assets

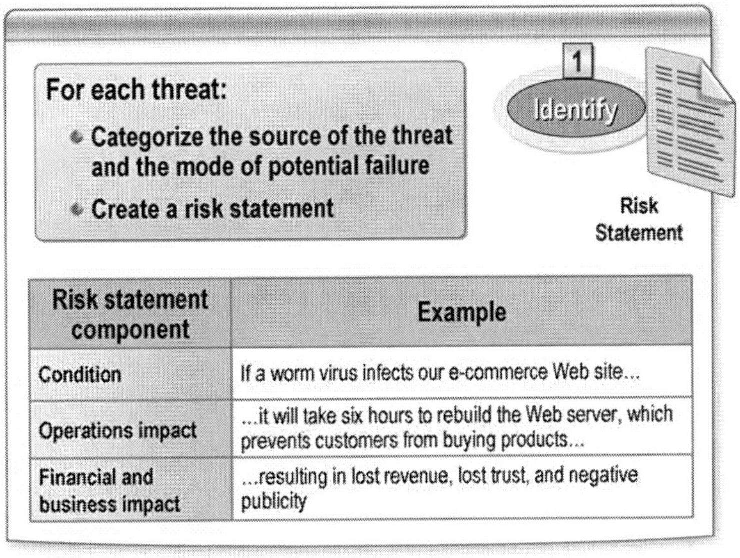

Key points

To identify threats to assets, you perform threat modeling. For each threat that you identify, create a *risk statement*. Risk statements combine information about a threat with information about the impact of the threat occurring.

Risk statements help you clearly state the risks that threaten your assets and the consequences of a threat occurring so that you can design appropriate security measures to reduce the risks. A single asset may have many risk statements associated with it.

A risk statement contains three parts:

- *Condition*. Generally an "if" clause about what happens if a threat occurs.
- *Operations consequence*. Describes the effects on IT operations of a threat that occurs to an asset. The effects are also known as the *mode of failure*.
- *Financial and business impact*. Describes the effects on the organization of a threat that occurs to an asset.

How to Analyze Risks to Assets

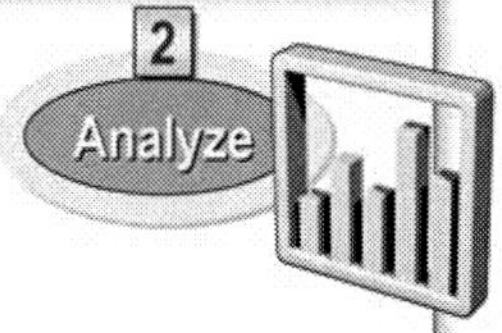

- Estimate the cost per year of a risk occurring
- Use the result to guide your risk management strategy

Determine	Definition	Example
1. Single loss expectancy	Total loss in a single incident of the risk	Financial impact: \$12,000 + Business impact: \$27,520 = \$39,520
2. Annual rate of occurrence	Number of times per year that you expect the risk to occur	Twice per year
3. Annual loss expectancy	Amount of financial loss the risk can cause per year	Total loss: \$39,520 x 2 = \$79,040

Qualitative analysis

After you create risk statements for each risk, you can analyze the impact of each risk in greater detail. Qualitative risk analysis uses a general ranking of probability and impact to determine a relative rank of a risk. The following table offers an example.

Threat	Probability	Impact	Relative rank
Information disclosure: attacker obtains password	5	9	45
Denial of service: automated attack on a B2B Web site	7	5	35

In this example, the threat of information disclosure is medium, but with a high impact. By estimating probability and impact on a scale of 1 to 10 and multiplying the two numbers, a relative rank of 45 is obtained. This information can help security designers prioritize threats, although the value placed on probability and impact is subject to debate.

Quantitative analysis

A quantitative risk analysis yields more precise results than a qualitative analysis, but it is more difficult to calculate.

In a quantitative risk analysis, you analyze risk by determining:

1. *Single Loss Expectancy (SLE)*. The total amount of revenue that is lost from a single occurrence of the risk. You calculate the SLE by adding direct and indirect losses. The SLE is similar to the impact of a qualitative risk analysis.
2. *Annual Rate of Occurrence (ARO)*. The number of times that you reasonably expect the risk to occur during one year. To estimate the ARO, draw on your past experience and consult risk management experts and security and business consultants. The ARO is similar to the probability of a qualitative risk analysis.
3. *Annual Loss Expectancy (ALE)*. The total amount of money that your organization will lose in one year if nothing is done to mitigate the risk. You calculate this value by multiplying the SLE and the ARO. The ALE is similar to the relative rank of a qualitative risk analysis.

How to Plan for the Management of Risks

For each risk:

- **Create a risk management strategy**
- **Create contingency plans and triggers**

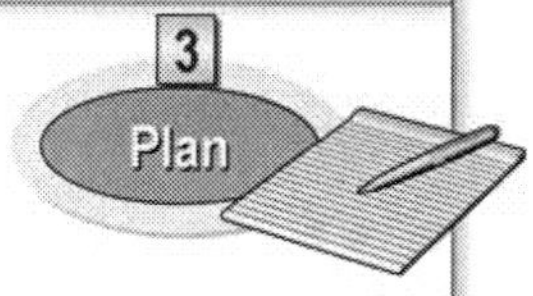

Strategy	Definition	Example
Accept	Acknowledge that the risk exists	Do nothing proactive
Mitigate	Proactively change the asset's exposure to the risk	Use virus protection software
Transfer	Partially shift the responsibility for the risk to another party	Use an external vendor to host the Web site
Avoid	Eliminate the source of risk or exposure to risk	Remove the Web site from the Internet

Key points

To manage a risk, you can apply one of four general strategies:

- *Accept.* You accept risk and do nothing proactive, with the exception of making contingency plans. Consider acceptance if the ALE for an asset is less than the value of the asset, and if the business impact is low.
- *Mitigate.* You mitigate risk by proactively changing the asset's exposure to the risk or your organization's reliance on the asset. Consider a risk mitigation strategy if the ALE is less than the value of the asset, and you can take proactive actions in advance. Mitigation is the primary risk management strategy.
- *Transfer.* You transfer risk by partially shifting the responsibility for the risk to another party, such as an insurance or managed services company. Transfer is becoming an increasingly important strategy for security.
- *Avoid.* You avoid risk by eliminating the source of the risk or the asset's exposure to the risk. This is an extreme reaction to risk and should only be done when the severity of the impact of the risk outweighs the benefit that is gained from the asset.

How to Track Changes to a Risk Management Plan

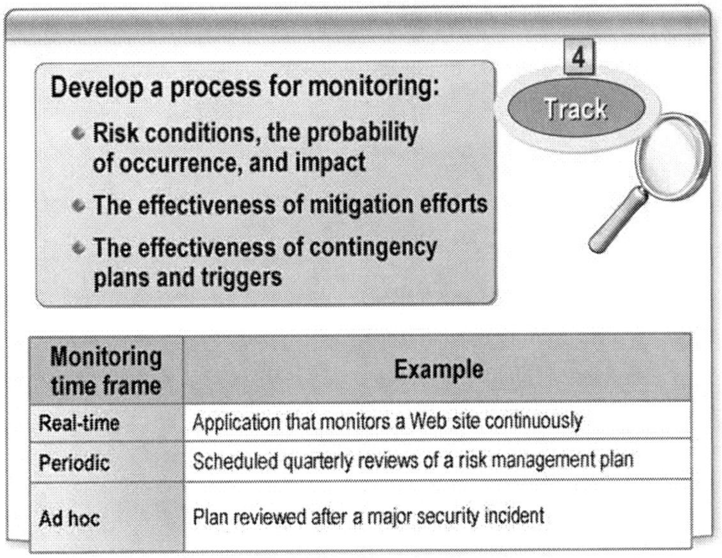

Key points

For each risk, monitor:

- *Risk conditions, the probability of occurrence, and impact.* Changed conditions, such as increased probability of a risk occurring or decreased financial impact of a risk, will require you to update the risk management plan.
- *Effectiveness of the mitigation effort.* You may find that your mitigation efforts are ineffective. Often, this occurs when a technical policy that you implement conflicts with business processes. Employees sometimes subvert the technical policy by working around it to achieve their business goals.
- *Effectiveness of contingency plans and triggers.* Over time, security risks that are identified in the risk management plan will occur. After the security incident, determine how effective the contingency plans were, and whether the triggers for initiating a response were effective.

You can monitor security risks in three time frames:

- *Real-time.* Use applications such as intrusion detection software to continuously monitor computers and network devices and to make predetermined decisions based on the risk.
- *Periodic.* Evaluate risk on a regularly scheduled basis, such as bimonthly or quarterly.
- *Ad hoc.* Evaluate risk at nonscheduled intervals. Ad hoc monitoring is often done in response to a major security incident or change to the network.

Risk Management Controls

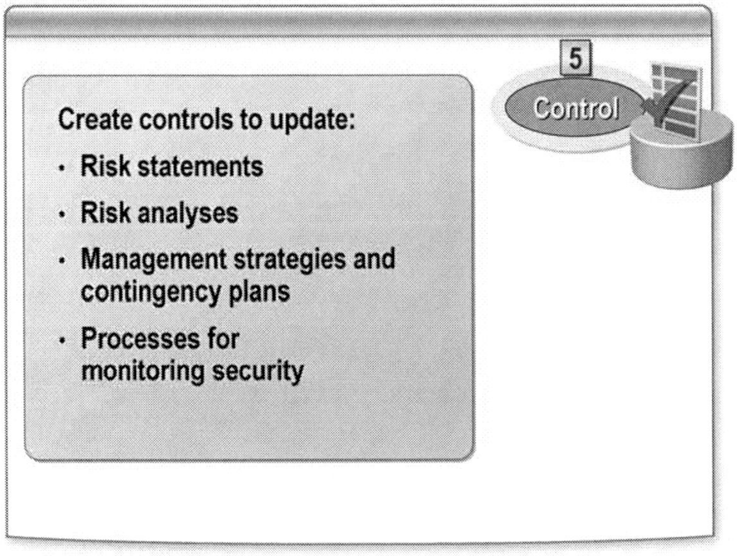

Key points

Risk management controls define when and how you will update the risk management plan. Tracking changes enables you to identify reasons to change your plan, and controls define what to change and how. By creating controls during the design phase, you can help ensure that your organization's risk management plan does not become obsolete.

For example, you may create a control that states that each quarter you will update the risk management plan to take into account changes in technology. Another control may state that after each security incident that costs more than $2,500 in damages, you will assess and revise the risk management plan for that category of asset.

Using controls helps to ensure that changes to the risk management plan occur incrementally, which results in a more efficient use of resources over time.

Use design controls to update:

- Risk statements.
- Risk analyses.
- Risk management strategies.
- Contingency plans.
- Processes for monitoring security.

Guidelines for Creating a Risk Management Plan

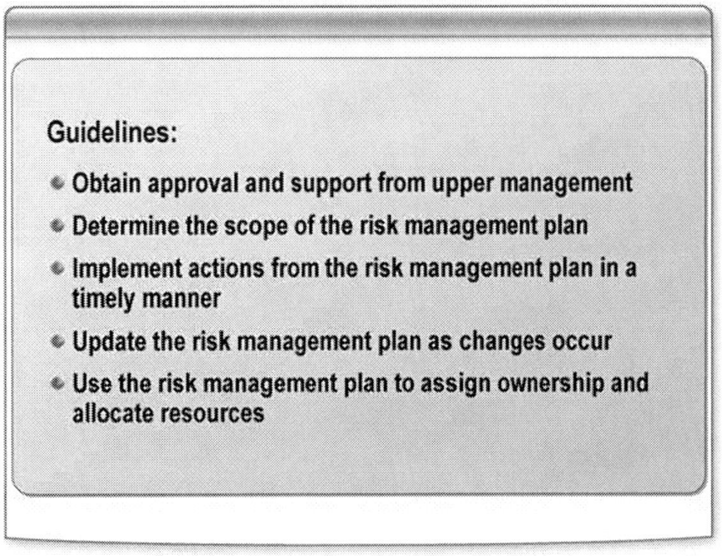

Key points

Guidelines include:

- *Obtain approval and support from upper management.* As in most projects, approval and support from management is a key component to success. Support from a single executive sponsor, if possible, is even more valuable.
- *Determine the scope of the risk management plan.* Determining scope early in the design helps to ensure that your efforts remain focused on your plan's objectives.
- *Implement actions from the risk management plan in a timely manner.* The data that you compile during your analysis may change, so it is important to act on that information as quickly as possible.
- *Update the risk management plan as changes occur.* As your network resources change, the risks to those resources may change. Be sure to update your risk management plan accordingly.
- *Use the risk management plan to assign ownership and allocate resources.* The risk management plan can act as a guide so that each risk has an owner, and you can track how much you spend to manage each risk.

Practice: Analyzing a Risk Management Plan

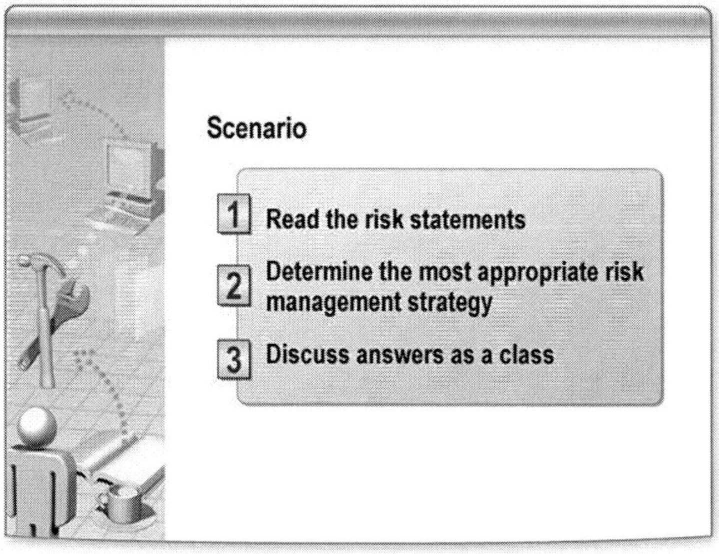

Instructions

Read each risk statement and determine the most appropriate risk management strategy: accept, mitigate, transfer, or avoid.

1. If an attacker physically compromises a domain controller, he could enumerate all domain accounts and passwords. If the incident is detected, it would be necessary to change all passwords. If the incident is not detected, it could result in the compromise of all company resources.

2. If an attack on the customer Web site compromises your customer database, the attacker could steal your customer lists and sell them to other criminals or to your competitors.

Lab A: Analyzing Security Risks

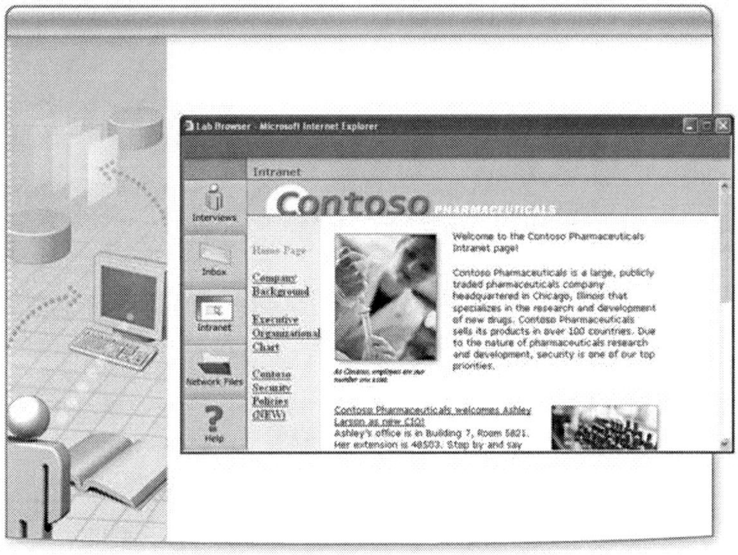

Objectives

After completing this lab, you will be able to perform risk management by applying qualitative and quantitative risk analysis concepts to threats.

Scenario

You are a consultant hired by Contoso Pharmaceuticals to help the company design security for its network. Each lab uses an interactive application to convey scenario-based information. To begin a lab, on the desktop, click **Internet Explorer**; this opens a Web page that contains links to each lab. Click a link to begin a lab.

Estimated time to complete this lab: 45 minutes

Work with a lab partner to perform the lab.

► **To complete a lab**

1. Read Ashley Larson's e-mail in each lab to determine the goals for the lab.
2. Click **Reply**, and then type your answer to Ashley's questions.
3. Click **Send** to save your answers to a folder on your desktop.
4. Discuss your answers as a class.

Important As part of the answer for this lab, you will open the Excel spreadsheet named R&D Portable Computer Threat Model.xls, and add information to it. You may use this spreadsheet in subsequent labs. Rename the file, and save it to the Lab Answers folder on your desktop for discussion.

Microsoft®
Training &
Certification

Module 5: Creating a Security Design for Physical Resources

Contents

Microsoft®

Overview

- Determining Threats and Analyzing Risks to Physical Resources
- Designing Security for Physical Resources

Introduction

In this module, you will determine threats and analyze risks to physical resources in an organization. You will then learn how to design security for facilities, computers, mobile devices, and hardware. You will also learn about implementing disaster recovery as a way to protect physical resources.

This module focuses on access to and protection of physical resources. Other modules will focus on access to and protection of data.

Objectives

After completing this module, you will be able to:

- Determine threats and analyze risks to physical resources.
- Design security for physical resources.

Lesson: Determining Threats and Analyzing Risks to Physical Resources

- Physical Resources to Protect
- Why Physical Security Is Important
- Common Threats to Physical Security
- Practice: Analyzing Risks to Physical Security

Introduction

If an attacker can gain access to physical resources, such as computers, buildings, and server closets, he can easily penetrate your network and access your organization's confidential or secret information. Securing physical access requires diligence and awareness of threats that an attacker can easily perform on unsuspecting employees.

Lesson objectives

After completing this lesson, you will be able to:

- Describe physical resources to protect.
- Explain why physical security is important.
- List threats to physical security.

Physical Resources to Protect

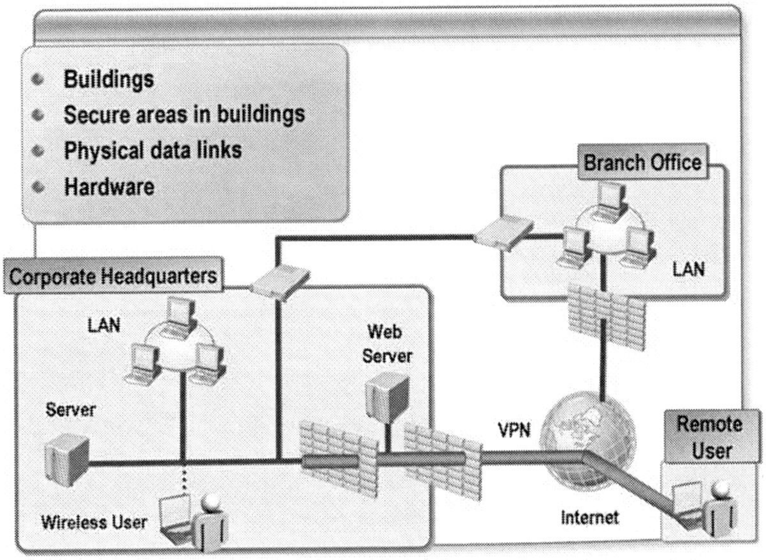

Key points

The key to securing physical resources is to secure access to those resources. Most of the protection on a computer or network is provided by software. If an attacker can gain physical access to a computer or network, there is generally little stopping the attacker from penetrating your network.

You should physically secure access to your organization for:

- Buildings.
- Secure areas in buildings.
- Physical data links.
- Hardware.

Additional reading

For more information about security, see the white paper, *The Ten Immutable Laws of Security*, at: http://www.microsoft.com/technet/columns/security/essays/10imlaws.asp.

For more information about physical security, see the white paper, *Basic Physical Security*, at: http://www.microsoft.com/technet/columns/security/5min/5min-203.asp.

Why Physical Security Is Important

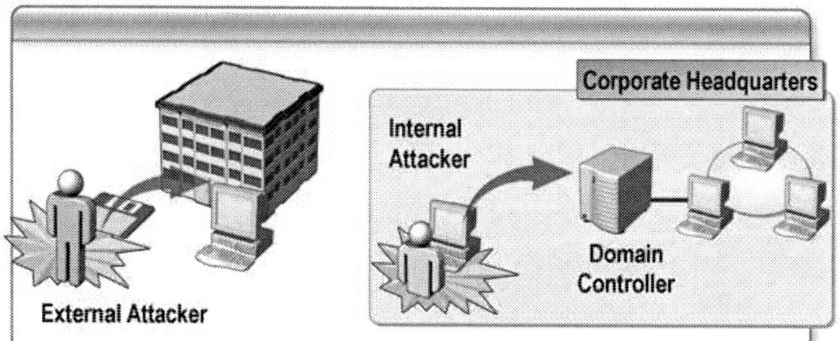

Attacker	Threat	Example
External	Trojan attack on an unsecured workstation	An attacker enters the facility unnoticed and loads a Trojan horse that sends all passwords to an FTP site
Internal	Theft of a password from a server	An attacker enters an unlocked server room, exports the passwords from a domain controller, and accesses confidential data

External attacker scenario

Without proper physical security of a building, an external attacker could enter a facility unnoticed, locate an unattended computer, and load a Trojan horse application that sends keystrokes, including passwords, to a location on the Internet.

Internal attacker scenario

Without proper physical security of a server room, an internal attacker could enter the room and extract an account database from a server by using a boot startup disk or CD. The attacker could then perform a brute force attack on the password hashes in the database and access confidential data from user accounts.

Common Threats to Physical Security

Resource	Threat
Buildings	• Unauthorized entry or exit • Remote surveillance
Secure areas in buildings	• Unauthorized access to sensitive computers • Theft of disposed data and equipment
Physical data links	• Installation of eavesdropping hardware or software • Sabotage of infrastructure
Hardware	• Theft of computers • Installation of Trojan horses or viruses

Key points

In addition to the common threats listed in the slide, consider places where the physical security of your network is not under your direct control. For example, wireless networks often expand the physical control of your data link for up to one mile from the location of the access point. Or, your organization may share space for data wiring with other organizations, or share entrances and exits to your offices, such as in leased office buildings.

Practice: Analyzing Risks to Physical Security

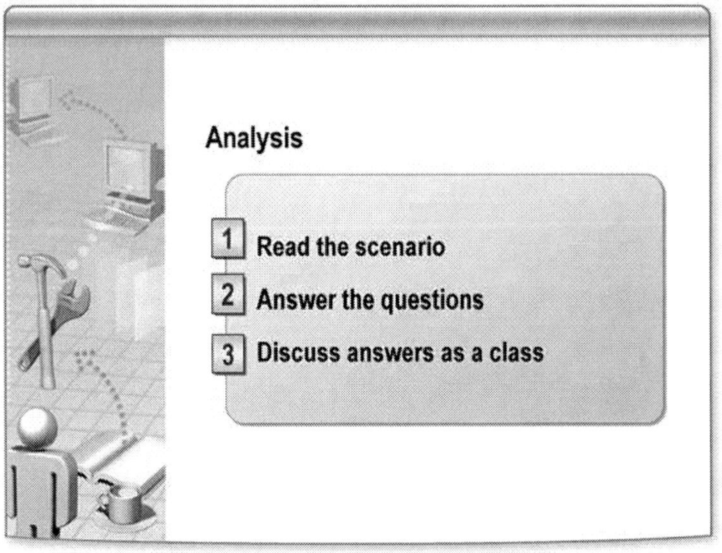

Introduction

Your company has issued to the sales staff 50 portable computers with confidential information. The sales staff uses the portable computers at customer sites and trade shows. Because the sales staff rarely has Internet access at these locations, they must maintain the information on their hard disks.

The replacement cost of a lost or stolen portable computer is $3,000. The cost that is associated with disclosure of information on a portable computer is estimated to be $12,000, and the loss of productivity from a stolen portable computer is estimated to be $5,000. Based on statistics from previous years, the company projects that four portable computers will be stolen next year.

Senior management has proposed two risk management strategies:

- *Install hardware alarms.* Each alarm will cost $175 per portable computer and is estimated to reduce by one the number of computers stolen.
- *Educate users about how to secure their portable computers.* Training will cost $350 per user and is estimated to reduce by two the number of computers stolen.

Implementing both strategies will reduce by three the number of stolen portable computers.

Questions

1. Based on the previous information, what is the Single Loss Expectancy (SLE), or total amount of revenue that is lost from a single occurrence of the risk?

2. What is the Annual Loss Expectancy (ALE), or total amount of money that your organization will lose in one year if nothing is done to mitigate the risk?

3. Subtract the cost of each risk management strategy from its estimated savings. Based on the results, which of the risk management strategies would you recommend?

4. What are some other considerations when choosing either of the risk management strategies?

Lesson: Designing Security for Physical Resources

- Methods for Securing Facilities
- Methods for Securing Access to Computers
- Methods for Securing Portable Computers and Mobile Devices
- Considerations for Disaster Recovery Planning
- Practice: Risk and Response
- Security Policy Checklist

Introduction

To secure physical resources, you must secure the computers on your network and the access to them from your office or facility. Portable computers in particular require special consideration due to their vulnerability to theft or misplacement. You must also consider how your organization will recover network operations from a physical disaster, such as a fire or flood.

Lesson objectives

After completing this lesson, you will be able to:

- Describe methods for securing facilities.
- List methods for securing access to computers.
- Explain methods for securing portable computers and mobile devices.
- List considerations for recovering from disaster.

Methods for Securing Facilities

To secure	Consider
 Entrances to and exits from facilities	• Hiring security guards • Requiring identification badges • Installing video surveillance • Installing fences and parking lot gates • Permitting entry and exit only from main entrances
 Information in buildings	• Requiring the secure disposal of sensitive data and equipment • Securing data cables from wiretapping • Positioning monitors and keyboards away from windows • Erasing whiteboards in meeting rooms

Key points

Many methods exist for securing access to facilities. Balance the cost of each method with the security that it provides. To protect entrances, for example, you can require employees to use either keys or electronic badges. Electronic badges are more expensive than keys, but they provide much greater security. Electronic badges are very difficult to copy, you can centrally manage the security level of electronic badges, and you can review detailed access reports.

In addition to securing entrances and exits of facilities, ensure that you protect access to information inside facilities. An internal attacker who finds an unused or forgotten network connection could potentially obtain information about your internal network. If data cables are accessible, attackers can tap into them or attach listening devices that gather network data.

Not all information is electronic. For example, an attacker could read valuable information from whiteboards in conference rooms by looking through windows or entering the room after a meeting has ended. Although the probability of this occurring may be low, the cost of erasing the whiteboards is minimal.

Methods for Securing Access to Computers

To secure	Consider
 Access to computers	• Regulating the removal of computers from facilities • Regulating the movement of computers within a facility • Removing floppy disk drives and CD-ROM drives • Installing device locks on computers
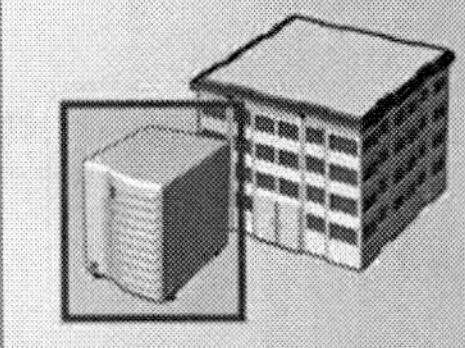 Access to computers in sensitive areas	• Controlling entry points to server rooms and data closets • Requiring authorization for access to server rooms and data closets • Restricting LAN access from lobbies and reception desks

Key points

You can secure access to computers and sensitive areas within facilities by using a variety of methods. You must balance the cost of each method with the level of security that it provides.

For example, an attacker who gains access to the facility could obtain information on a computer by removing the computer from the facility and attacking it offline. An attacker could use removable boot media, such as a CD-ROM or floppy disk, to restart the computer and reset the local administrator password on the computer. Securing the computer by removing its media drives or by securing the room where the computer is stored will provide more protection than only securing the entrances and exits to the building.

Note You can use the BIOS of a computer to disable the use of floppy disks, Universal Serial Bus (USB) ports, and CD-ROM drives, thereby making it more difficult for an attacker to restart the computer. If you disable these items, you will need to create a BIOS password to protect access to the BIOS. You can also use the BIOS to prompt users to enter passwords before the computer begins the boot process.

Additional reading

For more information about attacks on computers, see the white paper, *Analysis of Alleged Vulnerability in Windows 2000 Syskey and the Encrypting File System*, at: http://www.microsoft.com/technet/security/topics/efs.asp.

Methods for Securing Portable Computers and Mobile Devices

Key points

Portable computers and mobile devices, such as handheld personal computers and mobile phones, require special security due to their portability. Increasingly, users are connecting such devices to corporate networks or the Internet. Even if users do not store sensitive data on these devices, the devices often contain the user's authentication information, which an attacker can exploit. Mobile devices are also often equipped with 802.11 wireless network interfaces. Wireless connections, if not properly secured, are vulnerable to exploitation in public areas such as airports.

On portable computers that run Microsoft® Windows NT® version 4.0 or later, you can use the System Key (SYSKEY) in modes 2 or 3 to require a password from a user before the computer will restart. The password is used to decrypt the account database and Local Security Authority (LSA) secrets.

Additional reading

For more information about using SYSKEY to protect portable computers, see Q143475, *Windows NT System Key Permits Strong Encryption of the SAM.*

For more information about security for handheld devices, see the white paper, *Pocket PC Security*, at: http://www.microsoft.com/technet/itsolutions/mobile/maintain/mblsecur.asp.

Also see the white paper, *The Road Warrior's Guide to Laptop Protection*, at: http://www.microsoft.com/technet/columns/security/5min/5min-205.asp.

Considerations for Disaster Recovery Planning

Disasters can be:

- Natural
- Caused by people

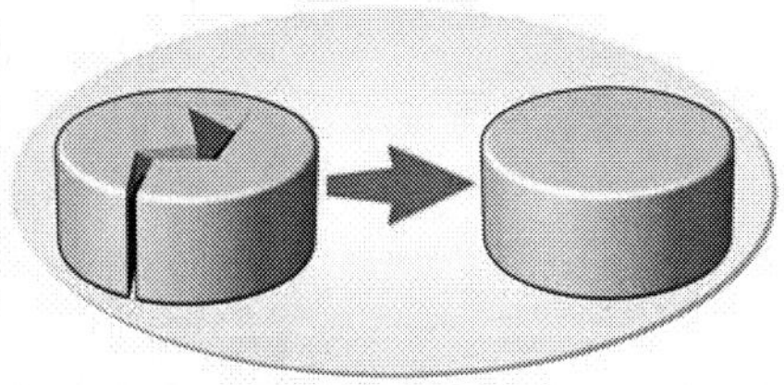

Disaster recovery method	Detail
Store backup media off-site	• Backup tapes are taken to a secure facility • Backup is performed over the network to a remote location
Maintain cold spares and facilities	• Hardware that is readily available • Partially-equipped facility that is ready on short notice
Maintain hot spares and facilities	• Fully redundant hardware that is ready for immediate use • Fully equipped facility that is ready for immediate use

Key points

Physically securing a network includes recovering from natural disasters such as tornados and hurricanes, and disasters caused by people such as unintentional or accidental acts, and intentional acts like vandalism and terrorism.

To plan for disaster recovery, consider using or maintaining:

- *Off-site storage of backup media.* Storing backups of your critical data off-site protects your data if a disaster damages or destroys the data at your primary facility.
- *Spare servers.* If you lose a server in an emergency, spare servers enable you to restore services. Spare servers are either online or offline and are sometimes referred to as *hot* or *cold spares*. An online spare is similar to a redundant or failover server. It can be brought online quickly with a minimum of configuration to limit disruption to business operations. An offline server can be configured and added to a network quickly. An online spare costs more to maintain but provides less disruption to operations.
- *Spare facilities.* Consider maintaining alternate facilities that you can use in the event of an emergency. Like spare servers, spare facilities are either online or offline and are sometimes referred to as a *hot* or *cold facilities*. An online facility contains the necessary equipment to resume operations quickly. An offline facility may comprise access to a business facility where you could restore operations (but not as quickly as at an online facility).

Additional reading

For more information about disaster recovery, see *Data Security and Data Availability in the Administrative Authority – Part 2*, at: http://www.microsoft.com/technet/treeview/default.asp?url=/technet/security/bestprac/bpent/sec3/datasec.asp.

Also see Chapter 14, "Data Center Availability: Facilities, Staffing, and Operations," in the Microsoft SQL Server™ 2000 Resource Kit, at: http://www.microsoft.com/technet/prodtechnol/sql/reskit/sql2000/part4/c1461.asp.

Practice: Risk and Response

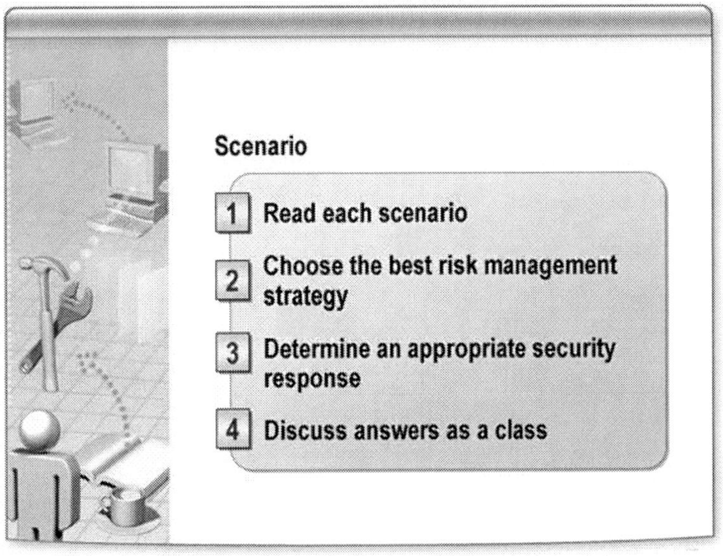

Introduction

For each scenario, choose whether to accept, mitigate, transfer, or avoid the risk that is presented, and enter an appropriate security response.

Scenario	Risk strategy	Security response
Users leave portable computers unattended in public places		
Computers connected to the internal network are located in the building lobby		
Password-protected backup media is transported to an off-site storage facility by a courier service		
You rent office space in a building that houses data and telephone wiring for the building in a common, secure room		
Mission-critical data servers are located in a secure data center in your organization		

Security Policy Checklist

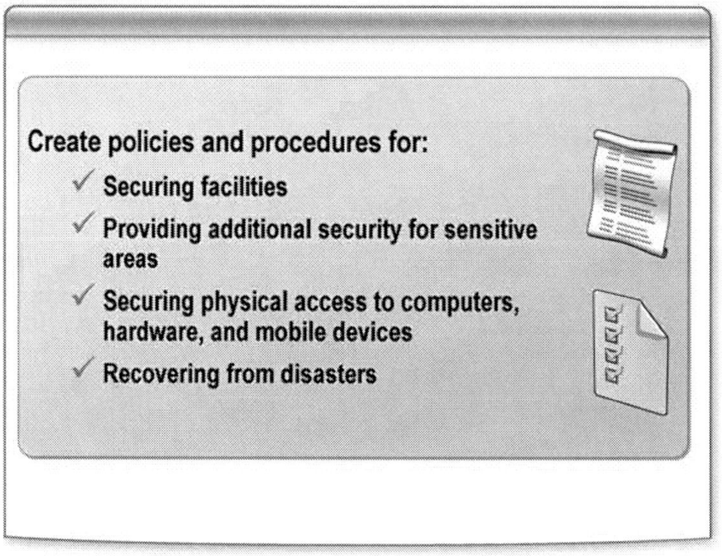

Checklist

Use the following checklist to guide your security design for physical resources.

Phase	Task	Details
Planning	Model threats	STRIDE (Spoofing, Tampering, Repudiation, Information disclosure, Denial of service, Elevation of privilege) and life cycle threat models
	Manage risks	Qualitative and quantitative risk analysis

Phase	Task	Details
Building	Create policies and procedures for:	Securing facilities
		Providing additional security for sensitive areas
		Securing physical access to computers, hardware, and mobile devices
		Recovering from disasters

Lab A: Designing Security for Physical Resources

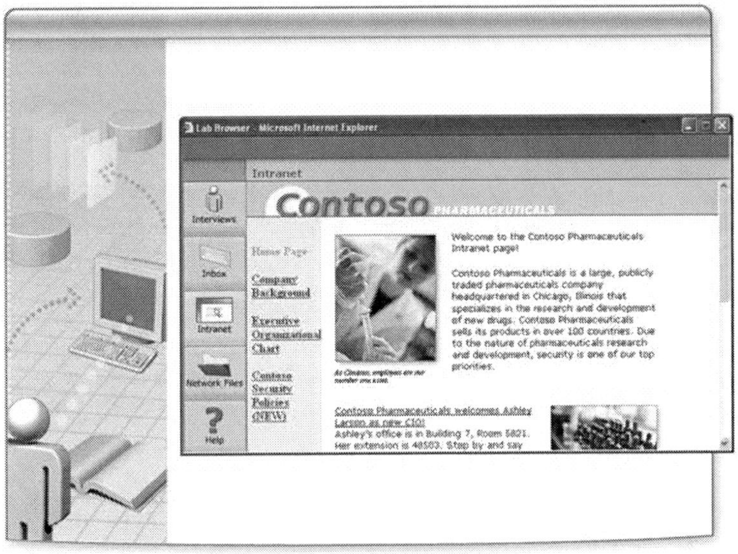

Objectives

After completing this lab, you will be able to apply security design concepts to physical security of resources.

Scenario

You are a consultant hired by Contoso Pharmaceuticals to help the company design security for its network. Each lab uses an interactive application to convey scenario-based information. To begin a lab, on the desktop, click **Internet Explorer**; this opens a Web page that contains links to each lab. Click a link to begin a lab.

Estimated time to complete this lab: 45 minutes

Work with a lab partner to perform the lab.

► To complete a lab

1. Read Ashley Larson's e-mail in each lab to determine the goals for the lab.
2. Click **Reply**, and then type your answer to Ashley's questions.
3. Click **Send** to save your answers to a folder on your desktop.
4. Discuss your answers as a class.

Microsoft®
Training &
Certification

Module 6: Creating a Security Design for Computers

Contents

Microsoft®

Overview

- Determining Threats and Analyzing Risks to Computers
- Designing Security for Computers

Introduction

In this module, you will learn how to determine threats and analyze risks to computers in an organization. You will also learn how to design security for computers throughout their life cycles, from initial purchase to decommissioning.

Objectives

After completing this module, you will be able to:

- Determine threats and analyze risks to computers.
- Design security for computers.

Lesson: Determining Threats and Analyzing Risks to Computers

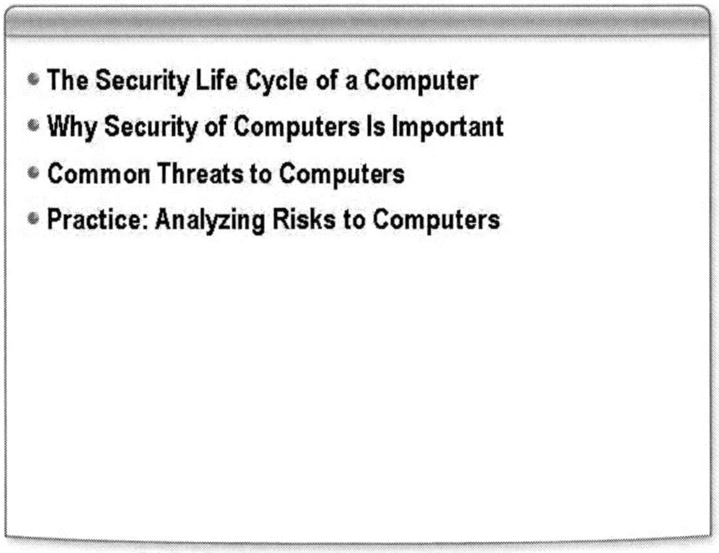

Introduction

The computers on your network present many opportunities for attackers to access your organization's data. Ensuring that your computers are secured and updated throughout their operational lives is essential to maintaining a secure network.

Lesson objectives

After completing this lesson, you will be able to:

- Describe the security life cycle of a computer.
- Explain why securing computers is important.
- Describe common threats to computers.

The Security Life Cycle of a Computer

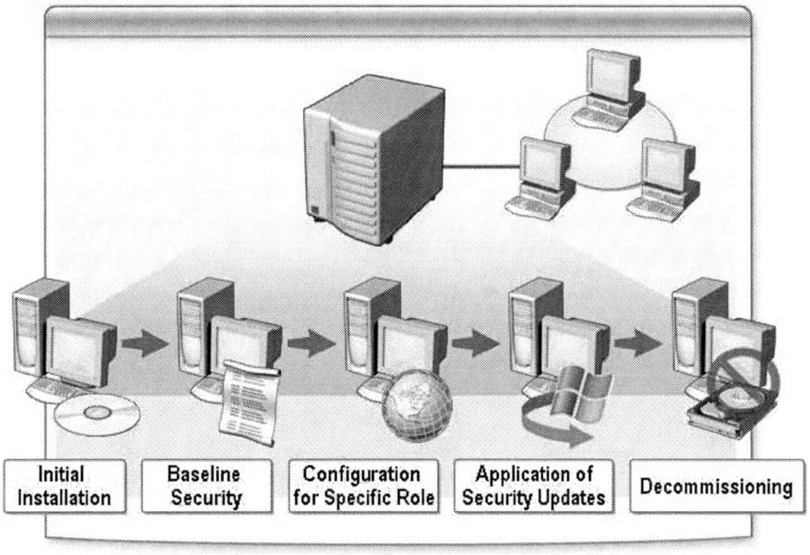

Key points

The security life cycle of a computer includes the following phases:

- *Initial installation*. During the initial installation of an operating system and applications, viruses and configuration errors can compromise the security of a computer. Be sure to set the password for the built-in Administrator account during the initial installation.
- *Baseline configuration*. After initial installation, configure the baseline configuration settings for security that your organization requires for computers.
- *Role-specific security*. Computers that have specific roles, such as Web servers, require additional configuration beyond the baseline security configuration to ensure that they are protected against threats that are specific to the computer's role.
- *Application of security updates*. During the computer's lifetime, service packs and security updates for the operating system and applications will be released. To maintain the baseline security configuration, install the service packs and security updates.
- *Decommissioning*. At the end of a computer's operational lifetime, dispose of it in a way that makes it impossible for attackers to obtain information on the hard disk or media devices.

Why Security of Computers Is Important

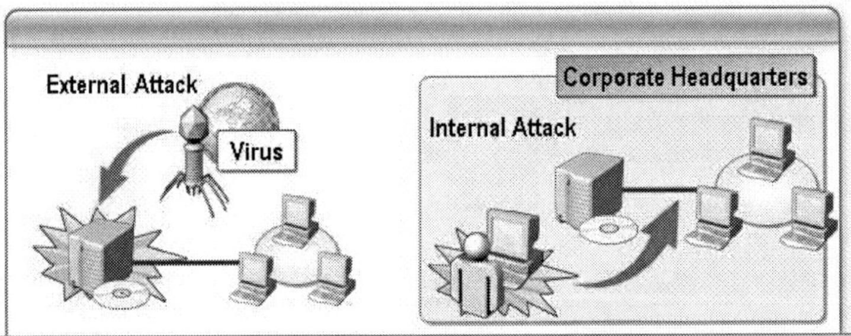

Attacker	Threat	Example
External	A virus exploits a known vulnerability in the operating system	A worm virus attacks new computers before security updates are installed. The virus installs a Trojan horse application. The compromised computers are deployed with the Trojan horse application.
Internal	Exposure of the Administrator password	A local Administrator password is sent in plaintext during a network installation. An attacker uses the password to view data on his manager's computer.

External attacker scenario

When a network administrator installs software on new computers for the Sales department, a virus infects the computers before the administrator can install a service pack that protects against the virus. The virus exploits a known vulnerability and installs a Trojan horse application. The administrator deploys the computers to users without realizing that the computers have been compromised by an external attacker.

Internal attacker scenario

During an unattended installation of an operating system over the network, the local Administrator account's password is configured and sent in plain text over the network. An internal attacker who is sniffing packets on the network intercepts the password. The attacker discovers that the password also works with the Administrator account on his manager's computer. He uses the account to access confidential data on his manager's computer.

Common Threats to Computers

Phase	Threat
Installation	• Administrator password is exposed during installation • Virus infects a computer before virus protection software is installed • Operating system is configured incorrectly
Baseline and configuration	• Baseline security is not deployed uniformly • Computer is not secured properly for its role • Security configuration is not updated when a computer's role changes
Security updates	• Service packs and hotfixes are applied inconsistently • Service pack and hotfix installations are not audited • Hotfixes are not reapplied after a service is added
Decommissioning	• Sensitive data remains on hard disks and other storage media when the computer is decommissioned

Key points

Although technical security measures are essential for securing computers in your organization, the majority of threats to computers are from people and flawed processes. For example, an attacker physically attacks a computer's hard disk, or a process in an organization omits the application of service packs before deployment.

Additional reading

For more information about change management, see Appendix C, "Designing an Operations Framework to Manage Security."

Practice: Analyzing Risks to Computers

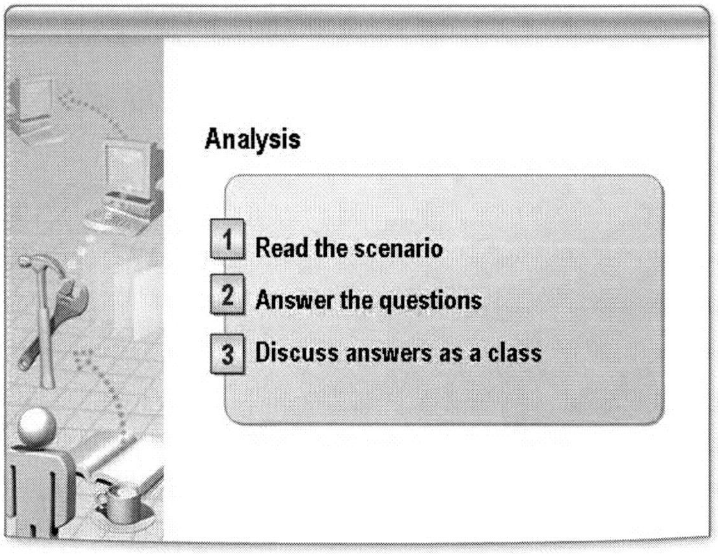

Introduction

Northwind Traders recently signed a contract with a government agency to perform confidential research for a national security project. The government will supply Northwind Traders with 100 government computers that the agency has collected from various internal departments.

Northwind Traders proposes to hire Consolidated Messenger, a publicly held shipping company, to pick up the computers from a secure government facility and ship them to the Northwind Traders headquarters. The IT staff at Northwind Traders will install antivirus software and the research application that is required for the project.

Northwind Traders' research facility is still under construction and will be ready in three weeks. In the interim, Consolidated Messenger will store the computers at a warehouse that Northwind Traders shares with Coho Vineyard.

Questions

1. What are the potential threats to the computers and to Northwind Traders?

2. Do these threats pose a significant risk?

3. What actions would you recommend that Northwind Traders take to secure the computers?

Lesson: Designing Security for Computers

- Common Methods for Performing an Initial Installation Securely
- How to Create a Secure Baseline Configuration
- How to Design Security for Specific Computer Roles
- Common Methods for Applying Security Updates
- Common Methods for Assessing the Security of Computers
- How to Decommission Computers Securely
- Practice: Risk and Response
- Security Policy Checklist

Introduction

Every computer on your network goes through various stages in its life cycle. Your security design must manage security for each stage in the life cycle, and also ensure that computers stay secure as they move from stage to stage.

Lesson objectives

After completing this lesson, you will be able to:

- Secure an initial installation.
- Create a secure baseline configuration.
- Design security for specific computer roles.
- Explain methods for applying security updates.
- Assess the security of computers.
- Decommission computers securely.

Common Methods for Performing an Initial Installation Securely

Method	Details
Isolated network	• Protects computers from attackers before security measures are installed and configured
Updated media	• Ensures that all security updates and service packs are installed during the initial installation
Custom scripts	• Ensures that only required services are installed for the computer's role • Enables the configuration of secure default settings
Hard disk imaging	• Uses a copy of a secure installation, including the installation and configuration of applications and security measures
RIS	• Centrally manages the installation of custom scripts and hard disk images over the network

Key points

When you perform the initial installation of an operating system and applications on a computer, do the following:

- Implement secure default configurations of the operating system and applications.
- Install only required services and applications for the computer's role.
- Configure default accounts and passwords securely.
- Ensure that you use uncompromised files to install the operating system and applications.
- Use trusted personnel to perform initial installations.

You can use several methods to perform an initial installation, including isolated networks, updated media, custom scripts, hard disk imaging, and Remote Installation Services (RIS). You can combine methods to achieve the level of security that you require. For example, you can create a custom installation script for all Web servers and install the operating system on an isolated network by using installation media that is updated with the latest security updates and service packs.

One of the most important tasks that you perform during the initial installation is creating the password for the built-in Administrator account. When you install the operating system by using unattended installation scripts, the password for this account in stored in plain text. To protect the password, only use unattended text files on isolated networks.

Performing the initial installation on an isolated network also helps ensure that the computer does not become exposed to known viruses on your network until after you have installed virus protection software and the latest service packs and hotfixes.

Additional reading

For more information about performing an initial installation securely, see:

- *Microsoft Windows 2000 Guide to Unattended Setup*, under **Additional Reading** on the Web page on the Student Materials CD.
- *Hotfix Installation and Deployment Guide*, under **Additional Reading** on the Web page on the Student Materials CD.
- The white paper, *Technical Guide to Remote Installation Services*, at: http://www.microsoft.com/technet/treeview/default.asp?url=/technet/prodtechnol/windows2000serv/deploy/remosad.asp.

How to Create a Secure Baseline Configuration

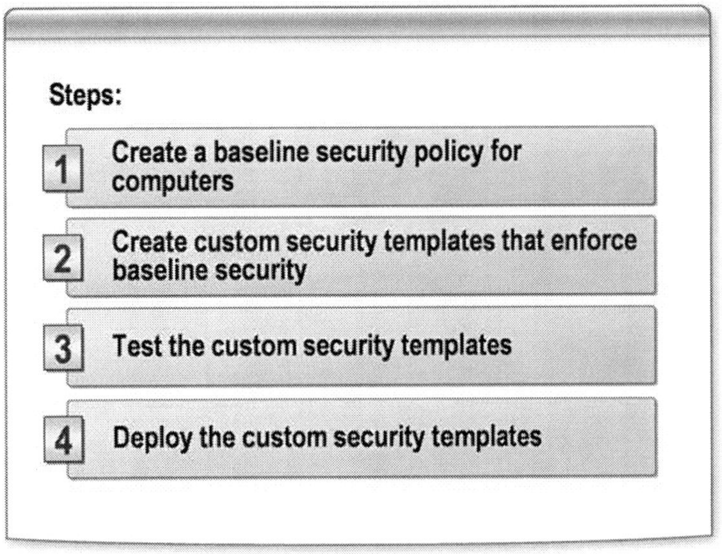

Key points

Before you deploy computers to your organization, define the baseline security configuration for computers. You can implement a baseline either during or after the initial installation of the operating system. In Microsoft® Windows® 2000 and Microsoft Windows XP, you can create and deploy security templates to computers that have similar security requirements.

To create a secure baseline for computers:

1. *Create a baseline security policy for computers.* This policy contains all business and technical requirements for the computer, operating system, and applications. For example, the policy may dictate that all operating systems be protected against SYN-ACK (synchronize acknowledge) denial of service (DoS) attacks. A good policy also describes the role that the computer performs.
2. *Create custom security templates that enforce baseline security.* Based on information that you include in the baseline security policy, create custom security templates that enforce the baseline security configuration. For example, to protect the operating system against SYN-ACK attacks, consider adding registry values and settings to a security template to alter the behavior of the TCP/IP stack on the computer to prevent an attack.
3. *Test the custom security templates.* Test each template to verify that it performs as intended and does not adversely affect other operating system services or applications. Also consider performing a limited pilot deployment to further ensure that the security template does not break other services or applications.
4. *Deploy the custom security templates.* You can deploy security templates manually by using the **secedit** command-line tool or automatically by using Group Policy.

Additional reading

For more information about security templates, see:

- The white papers, *Security Configuration Tool Set* and *Using Software Restriction Policies in Windows XP and Windows .NET Server 2003 to Protect Against Unauthorized Software*, under **Additional Reading** on the Web page on the Student Materials CD.
- Chapter 3, "Managing Security with Windows 2000 Group Policy," in *Security Operations Guide for Windows 2000 Server*, under **Additional Reading** on the Web page on the Student Materials CD.
- Q214752, *Adding Custom Registry Settings to Security Configuration Editor.*

How to Design Security for Specific Computer Roles

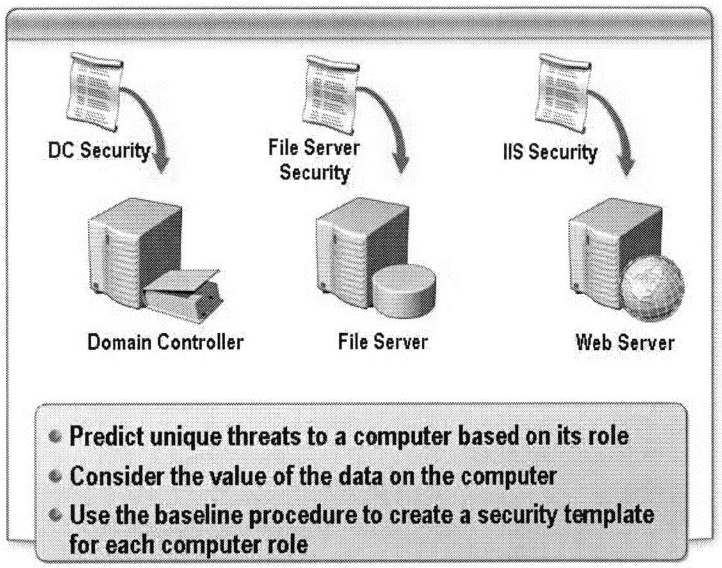

Key points

The services and applications that you install on a computer depend on the role that the computer performs. Similarly, computers use different threat models according to their role. As a result, computers have different security requirements beyond baseline security. For example, a Web server that runs Internet Information Services (IIS) is exposed to the Internet and is accessed by thousands of untrusted users every day, whereas a file server does not run IIS and will be only accessible by internal users.

Designing security for computers with specific roles often requires detailed knowledge and experience with the services or applications that run on the computers. For example, a Windows 2000 administrator may not possess the database knowledge and experience necessary to fully secure a computer that runs Microsoft SQL Server™ 2000, even if the computer runs Windows 2000.

Ensure that the individuals who design the security for a computer's role have the resources or expertise required to meet the organization's security requirements. Also, ensure that your organization has policies in place to manage security on computers when they change roles, for example, a file server that is redeployed as a Web server.

Additional reading

For more information about designing security for computers with specific roles, see:

- Chapter 4, "Securing Servers Based on Role," in *Security Operation Guide for Windows 2000 Server*, under **Additional Reading** on the Web page on the Student Materials CD.
- The white paper, *Microsoft SQL Server 2000 Security*, under **Additional Reading** on the Web page on the Student Materials CD.
- *Security Operations Guide for Exchange Server 2000*, under **Additional Reading** on the Web page on the Student Materials CD.
- The white paper, *Secure Internet Information Services 5 Checklist*, at: http://www.microsoft.com/technet/prodtechnol/iis/tips/iis5chk.asp.
- The IIS Lockdown Tool Web page, at http://microsoft.com/technet/security/tools/tools/locktool.asp.

Common Methods for Applying Security Updates

Tool:	Use for:	Deploys:
Windows Update	Home computers and small offices	Operating system service packs and security updates to individual computers
Office Update	Home computers and small offices	Office 2000 and Office XP service packs and security updates to individual computers
Group Policy	Computers running Windows 2000 or Windows XP in Active Directory	.msi-packaged service packs and security updates by using software installation policies
Microsoft Software Update Services	Computers running Windows 2000 or Windows XP	Security updates based on Group Policy settings
SMS Update Services Feature Pack	All SMS client computers on networks managed by using SMS	Service packs and security updates by using a special add-in interface for SMS

Key points

You can use several methods to apply security updates to computers on your network, including:

- *Windows Update*. Scans individual computers to ensure that the latest security updates, Windows components, and device drivers are installed. Windows Update also recommends and installs security updates. You must be a local administrator to use Windows Update.
- *Office Update*. Scans individual computers to ensure that the latest Microsoft Office security updates and other updates are installed. Office Update also recommends and installs security updates. You must be a local administrator to use Office Update.
- *Group Policy*. Installs security updates to computers centrally by using the Active Directory® directory service. Users do not need to perform any actions when Group Policy deploys security updates.
- *Microsoft Software Update Services (SUS)*. Acts as a local distribution server for security updates to computers on your network. You can configure computers to automatically download and install security updates or download security updates at prescheduled times.
- *Microsoft Systems Management Server (SMS) Update Services Feature Pack*. Includes wizards for packaging and deploying security updates and installation by using Software Inventory. The feature pack manages security updates on your network by using SMS.

Additional reading

For more information about security update methods, see:

- The Microsoft Windows Update Web site, at: http://windowsupdate.microsoft.com.
- The Microsoft Office Product Updates Web site, at: http://office.microsoft.com/ProductUpdates/default.aspx.
- The white paper, *Software Update Services Deployment*, under **Additional Reading** on the Web Page on the Student Materials CD.
- The white paper, *Windows 2000 Group Policy*, under **Additional Reading** on the Web page on the Student Materials CD.
- The white paper, *Securing IT with Systems Manager*, at: http://www.microsoft.com/smserver/evaluation/overview/secure.asp.
- The Web page, *Software Update Services Feature Pack*, at: http://www.microsoft.com/smserver/evaluation/overview/featurepacks/suspack.asp.

Multimedia: Microsoft Software Update Services

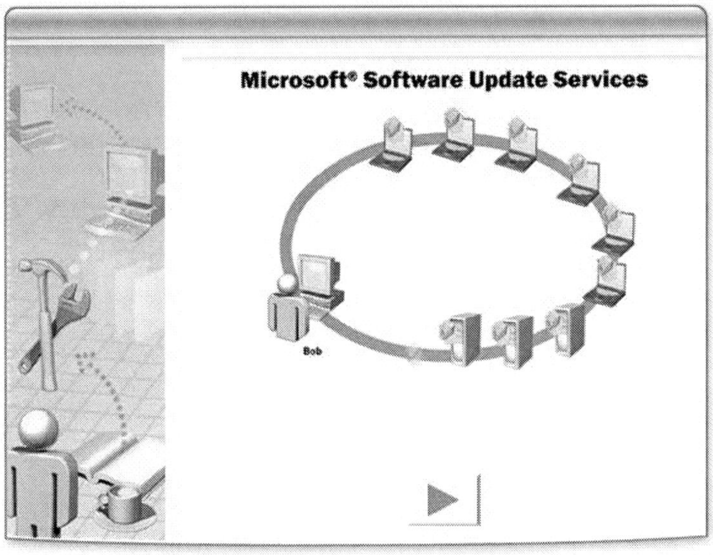

Key points

This animation shows how SUS provides an automated solution for managing and distributing critical Windows patches.

Additional reading

The animation is located in the **Media** folder on the Web page on the Student Materials CD.

Common Methods for Assessing the Security of Computers

Methods	Details
Security configuration and analysis tools	▪ Compares the security configuration on a computer to a security template ▪ Supports Windows 2000 and Windows XP
Microsoft Baseline Security Analyzer	▪ Scans computers on a network for common security vulnerabilities ▪ Supports Windows NT 4.0, Windows 2000, and Windows XP
Third-party software for testing vulnerabilities	▪ Scans computers, applications, and network devices for security vulnerabilities ▪ Can be expensive
Vulnerability assessment or penetration testing	▪ Attempts to compromise a network to locate security vulnerabilities ▪ Requires significant expertise

Key points

Assess the security of computers on your network regularly to ensure that all computers have the security they require.

There are many methods for assessing the security of computers, including:

- *Security Configuration and Analysis MMC.* You can use this snap-in or the **secedit** command to compare the security configuration of a computer running Windows 2000 or Windows XP with a security template. The snap-in and command both reveal any changes to the computer's baseline or security configuration for its specific role.
- *Microsoft Baseline Security Analyzer* (MBSA). You can use MBSA to scan computers running Microsoft Windows NT® version 4.0, Windows 2000, or Windows XP. MBSA determines common security vulnerabilities to the operating system, including IIS; common applications, such as Microsoft Office and Microsoft Internet Explorer; and server applications such as SQL Server 2000.
- *Third-party software that tests for vulnerabilities.* Vulnerability testing software from a security assessment company or other third party assesses the security of your Windows-based computers, network devices, and computers running non-Microsoft operating systems. Vulnerability testing software is often very expense and requires specific expertise to use.
- *Vulnerability or penetration testing.* The most complex type of assessment is vulnerability or penetration testing that is conducted by members of your own organization or a third party. This type of testing not only reveals vulnerabilities, it also shows you how to better protect your network from attackers.

Important Before performing any type of penetration testing, obtain written approval from management.

Additional reading

- For more information about the Security Configuration and Analysis MMC snap-in, see the white paper, *Security Configuration Tool Set*, under **Additional Reading** on the Web page on the Student Materials CD.
- For more information about MBSA, see the white paper, *Baseline Security Analyzer*, at: http://www.microsoft.com/technet/security/tools/tools/mbsawp.asp.
- For a list of Security Solutions Partners, see: http://www.microsoft.com/isaserver/partners/solutionproviders.asp.
- For more information about security assessments, see *Microsoft QuickStart for Security Operations Assessment*, at: http://www.microsoft.com/education/?ID=OperationsAssessment.
- For more information about assessment tools, see *Automated Security Self-Evaluation Tool (ASSET)* from the Computer Security Resource Center, at the National Institute of Standards and Technology, at: http://csrc.nist.gov/asset.

How to Decommission Computers Securely

Resource	Recommendations
Computers	• Destroy all data stored in Flash RAM, proprietary ROM modules, and hard disks
Storage devices	• Remove media from all removable media drives, including CD-ROM, tape, and floppy disk drives
Media	• Ensure that data and data artifacts have been destroyed on storage media, including hard disks, CD-ROMs, floppy disks, and backup tapes • Or, destroy the media itself
Documentation	• Remove printer ribbons from printers • Destroy all documentation that may be useful for an attacker, such as security configuration data

Key points

Decommissioning is the disposal of a computer or related accessory that your organization no longer uses. If you fail to decommission these items securely, you may disclose confidential information.

Create procedures to securely decommission:

- *Computers.* Many components of a computer, including Flash RAM, proprietary ROM modules, and hard disks, contain information that is stored persistently. You must destroy the data that these components store to ensure that attackers cannot retrieve confidential information.
- *Storage devices.* Careless employees may leave compact discs, floppy disks, or other removable media in a drive when they dispose of a computer. Ensure that you remove media from storage devices before disposal.
- *Media.* All data and data artifacts on storage media should be removed before you dispose of the storage media. If the information that was stored on the media is highly sensitive, consider physically destroying the media after you erase or format the data on the media.
- *Documentation.* Printer ribbons can reveal what was printed on them. If your printers print confidential information, consider destroying these items before you dispose of the hardware. Also ensure that you dispose of printed confidential information in a secure manner, for example, by shredding.

Additional reading

For more information about securely disposing of hardware, see "Section 8-306. Maintenance" in the United States Department of Defense's *National Industrial Security Program Operating Manual (NISPOM)*, at: http://www.dss.mil/isec/nispom.htm.

Practice: Risk and Response

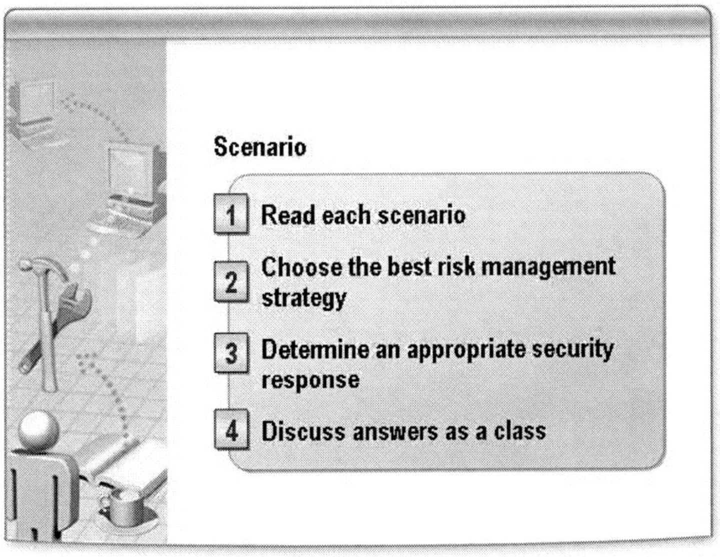

Introduction

For each scenario, choose whether to accept, mitigate, transfer, or avoid the risk that is presented, and then enter an appropriate security response.

Scenario	Risk strategy	Security response
After computers are used for three years, the organization donates them to a charity, which resells the computers.		
Users are responsible for installing security updates on their computers.		
An organization uses the factory preinstallation of software as the baseline security configuration for all computers.		

Security Policy Checklist

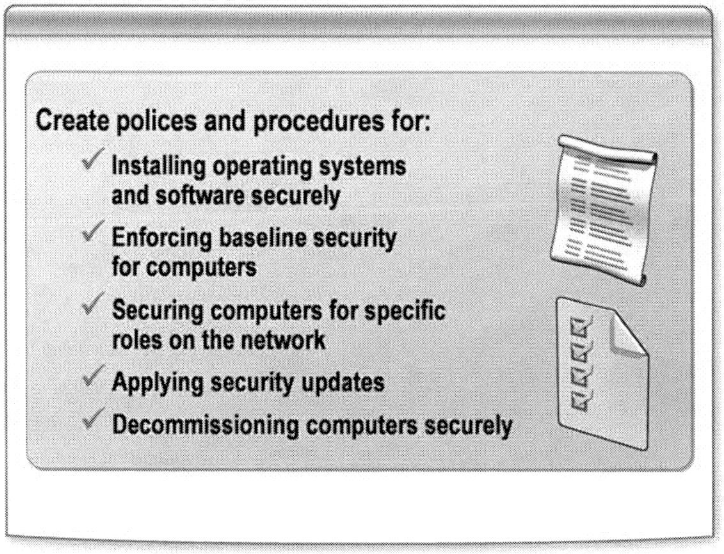

Checklist

Use the following checklist to guide your security design for computers.

Phase	Task	Details
Planning	Model threats	STRIDE (Spoofing, Tampering, Repudiation, Information disclosure, Denial of service and Elevation of privilege) and life cycle threat models
	Manage risks	Qualitative and quantitative risk analysis

Phase	Task	Details
Building	Create policies and procedures for:	Installing operating systems and software securely
		Enforcing baseline security for computers
		Securing computers for specific roles on the network
		Applying security updates
		Decommissioning computers securely

Lab A: Designing Security for Computers

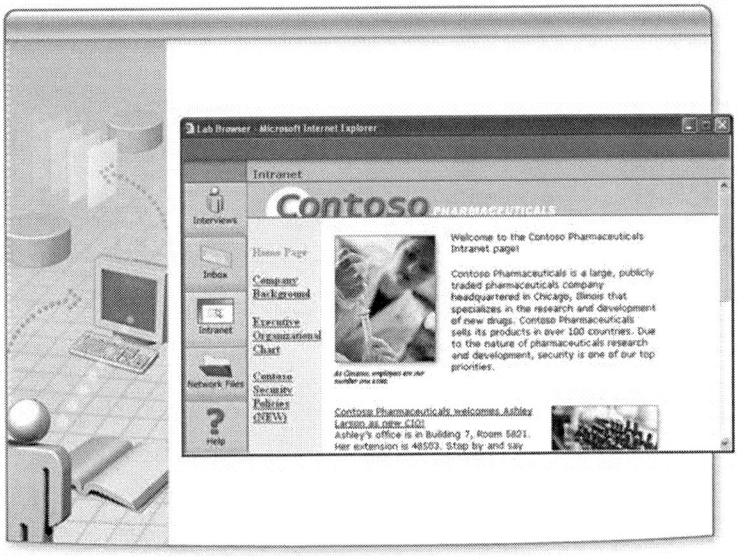

Objectives

After completing this lab, you will be able to apply security design concepts to computer security.

Scenario

You are a consultant hired by Contoso Pharmaceuticals to help the company design security for its network. Each lab uses an interactive application to convey scenario-based information. To begin a lab, on the desktop, click **Internet Explorer**; this opens a Web page that contains links to each lab. Click a link to begin a lab.

Estimated time to complete this lab: 30 minutes

Work with a lab partner to perform the lab.

► **To complete a lab**

1. Read Ashley Larson's e-mail in each lab to determine the goals for the lab.
2. Click **Reply**, and then type your answer to Ashley's questions.
3. Click **Send** to save your answers to a folder on your desktop.
4. Discuss your answers as a class.

Microsoft®
Training &
Certification

Module 7: Creating a Security Design for Accounts

Contents

Microsoft®

Overview

- Determining Threats and Analyzing Risks to Accounts
- Designing Security for Accounts

Introduction

In this module, you will learn how to determine threats and analyze risks to accounts in an organization. You will also learn how to design security for accounts, including determining security requirements, creating password policies, and designing strategies to manage account security.

Objectives

After completing this module, you will be able to:

- Determine threats and analyze risks to accounts.
- Design security for accounts.

Lesson: Determining Threats and Analyzing Risks to Accounts

- Account Types and Their Security Requirements
- Why Account Security Is Important
- Common Vulnerabilities of Accounts
- Practice: Analyzing Risks to Accounts

Introduction

Computer networks use accounts to grant users access to the information on a network. If an attacker gains access to an account that has excessive privileges, or breaks the password that is associated with an account, the attacker can obtain authorized access to a network.

Lesson objectives

After completing this lesson, you will be able to:

- Describe security requirements of different account types.
- Explain why account security is important.
- List common vulnerabilities to accounts.

Account Types and Their Security Requirements

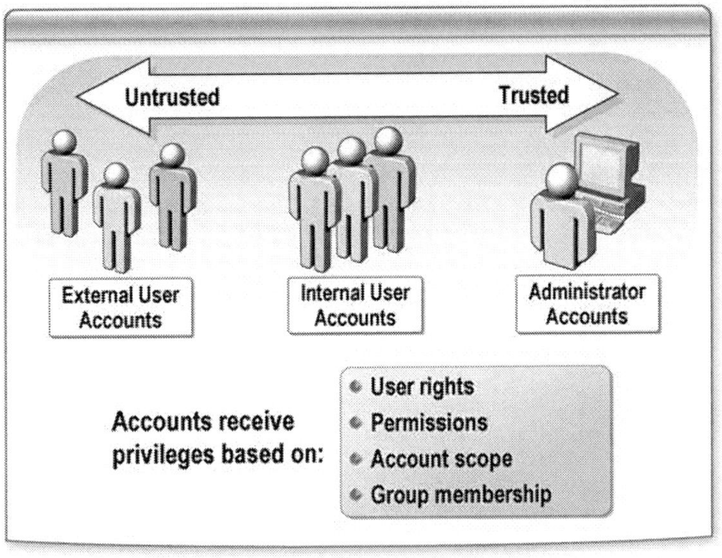

Key points

User accounts define the actions that a user can perform. Accounts require different security based on who uses them.

Type of account	Level of trust	Examples
External users	Low	Anonymous Web users, authenticated Web users, business partners
Internal users	Medium	Contract employees, full-time employees, accounts used by testers
Administrators	High	Users with administrator rights, service accounts used by applications, data administrators, service administrators

Accounts receive their authority from the following sources:

- *User rights.* These rights authorize users to perform specific actions on a computer, such as backing up files and directories that do not have NTFS (NTFS file system) permissions. User rights also include logon rights, such as the ability to log on to a system interactively.
- *Permissions.* Discretionary access control lists (DACLs) control permissions to Active Directory® directory service objects and NTFS folder and file objects. DACLs are comprised of access control entries (ACEs), which define the protections that apply to an object and its properties.
- *Account scope.* Microsoft® Windows® 2000 and Microsoft Windows XP use local and domain accounts to define the scope of an account's authority. Local accounts have authority only on the local computer. Domain accounts have authority throughout the domain or forest.

- *Group membership*. Security groups enable you to assign the same security permissions to large numbers of user accounts in a single operation, which ensures consistent security permissions across all members of a group. By using security groups to assign permissions, rather than assigning permissions to individual accounts, you can easily manage and audit permissions.

Additional reading

For more information about accounts, see the white paper, *Active Directory Users, Computers, and Groups*, at: http://www.microsoft.com/technet/prodtechnol/ad/windows2000/maintain/adusers.asp.

Why Account Security Is Important

Attacker	Threat	Example
External	Dictionary attack on weak password	An attacker performs a dictionary attack on the Administrator account, discovers a weak password, and then uses the Administrator account to gain access to the network
Internal	Extraction of account information from LSA	An attacker extracts a service domain account password that is stored as an LSA secret, then uses the account to gain access to other computers

External attacker scenario

An external attacker attempts a dictionary attack on the built-in Administrator account by continually attempting to log on to the organization's File Transfer Protocol (FTP) server. The attacker eventually discovers that the password for the Administrator account is "password." The attacker then logs on to the company's Remote Access Service (RAS) server by using the account and password.

Internal attacker scenario

An internal attacker uses known tools to extract the Local Security Authority (LSA) secrets from his computer at work and then obtains the passwords that the service accounts use. The computer uses an enterprise backup utility that runs as a service, and uses a domain account that has backup and restore privileges. The attacker uses the password for the backup service account to circumvent NTFS security and access other computers on the network.

Common Vulnerabilities of Accounts

Vulnerable area	Example
Passwords	• Weak passwords • Use of the same password in multiple accounts • Passwords that are stored on computers • Sharing or writing down of passwords by users
Account privileges	• Users who have local Administrator privileges • Services that do not run as the System account • Accounts with unnecessary user rights • User or service accounts with permissions to private files, folders, and registry keys
Account use and management	• Use of an Administrator account for nonadministrative tasks • User accounts with account management rights • Active accounts that are no longer used

Key points

Because the logon account is the central unit of security on Microsoft networks, you must ensure that your organization uses and manages accounts securely. Although you can implement technical security policies to protect accounts, two vulnerabilities exist that rely solely on trust: users and administrators. You must trust users to create strong passwords and keep them secret and trust your administrators to use their rights and permissions for legitimate purposes.

Practice: Analyzing Risks to Accounts

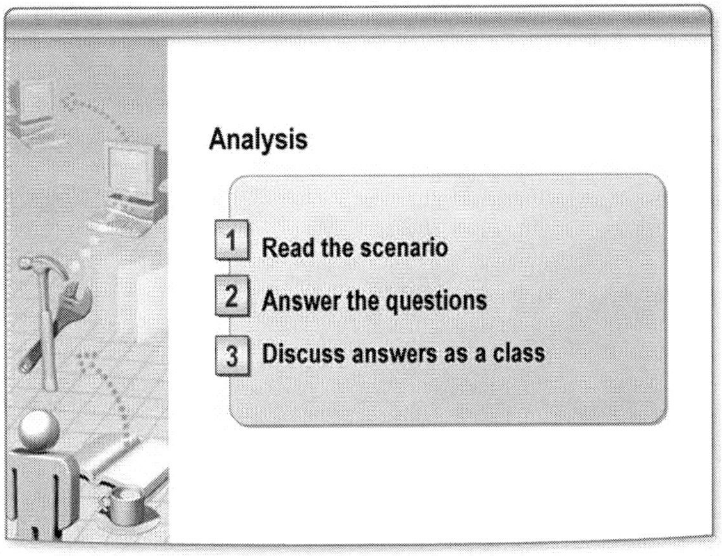

Scenario

Weak passwords on the Northwind Traders network are vulnerable to attack. If an attacker guesses a weak password that a user account uses, the company estimates a loss of $10,000. Northwind Traders estimates that under current conditions, this type of compromise occurs an average of five times per year.

Management has asked you to evaluate three proposed solutions:

- Option 1 creates a security policy that requires the use of complex passwords and the implementation of a password complexity filter to technically enforce the creation of strong passwords. The IT staff estimates that it would cost $2,000 to implement the filter. Option 1 would reduce the number of compromised passwords by 1.5.
- Option 2 adds training for users and administrators to option 1. Total cost is estimated at $10,000. Option 2 would reduce the total number of compromised passwords by 3.
- Option 3 adds an account lockout policy to option 1. The IT staff estimates that it would cost $30,000 to resolve support issues that relate to lockouts. Option 3 would reduce the number of compromised passwords by 3.5.

Questions

1. What is the annual loss expectancy (ALE) of the threat?

2. Subtract the cost of each risk management strategy from its estimated savings. Based on the results, which risk management options save Northwind Traders the most money?

3. What are some other considerations when choosing one or more of these risk management strategies?

Lesson: Designing Security for Accounts

- Guidelines for Granting Rights and Permissions
- Considerations for Using and Managing Accounts
- Guidelines for Using Administrative and Service Accounts
- How Account Passwords Are Stored
- Considerations for Designing Password Policies
- Practice: Risk and Response
- Security Policy Checklist

Introduction

Securing accounts means ensuring that accounts have the appropriate level of permissions and rights associated with them. Your security design must also manage other vulnerabilities, such as the misuse of accounts and improper storage and use of passwords.

Lesson objectives

After completing this lesson, you will be able to:

- Explain how to grant rights and permissions.
- Describe considerations for using and managing accounts.
- List guidelines for using administrative and service accounts.
- Explain how account passwords are stored.
- Describe considerations for designing password policies.

Guidelines for Granting Rights and Permissions

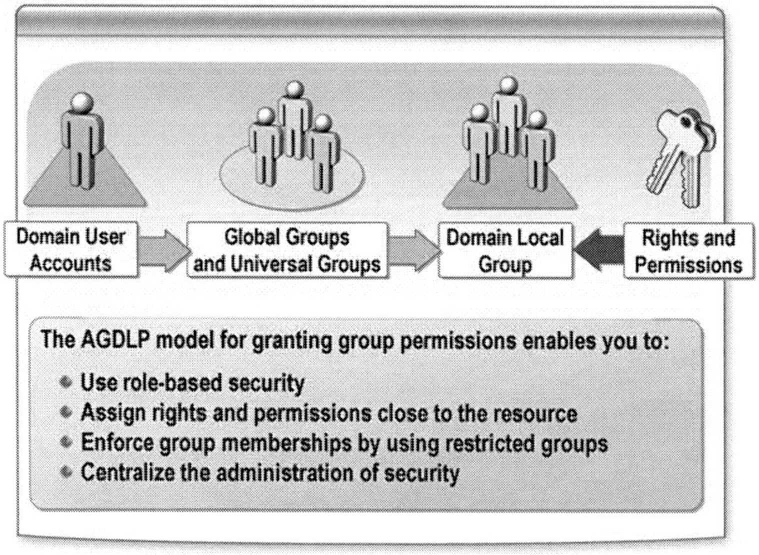

Key points

AGDLP (account, global group, domain local group, permissions) refers to an access control model that is used for placing accounts in groups, placing the groups in domain local groups, and then assigning permissions to the domain local groups. Using AGDLP to grant rights and permissions enables you to:

- *Use role-based security*. When you assign security to user groups that are based on roles, rather than assigning security to actual user accounts, you ensure that when a user's role changes, the security also changes. For example, when you replace one employee with another, you only have to change the group membership of the two employees, rather then change the permissions on resources.
- *Assign rights and permissions close to the resource*. You can use AGDLP to closely associate the rights and permissions to a resource, such as a file, on the file itself, rather than on the user account. This means that rights and permissions to resources remain stable if and when the security requirements of the organization change.
- *Enforce group memberships by using restricted groups*. By using a structured group model like AGDLP, you can implement technical security policies that enforce the assignment of rights and permissions. In Windows 2000 and Windows XP, you can accomplish this enforcement with Restricted Groups in Group Policy.
- *Centralize the administration of security*. In AGDLP, managing rights and permissions is a function of group management, which centralizes the assignment and revocation of rights and permissions to security group administrators.

Note Domain local groups are only valid in their home domain. Because the Schema and Configuration containers and the Global Catalog are replicated throughout the Active Directory forest, you must use the group model AGUP (account, global group, universal group, permissions) to ensure that the permissions will function correctly when users from other domains attempt to access the objects and attributes stored in the Schema container, the Configuration container, or the Global Catalog.

Considerations for Using and Managing Accounts

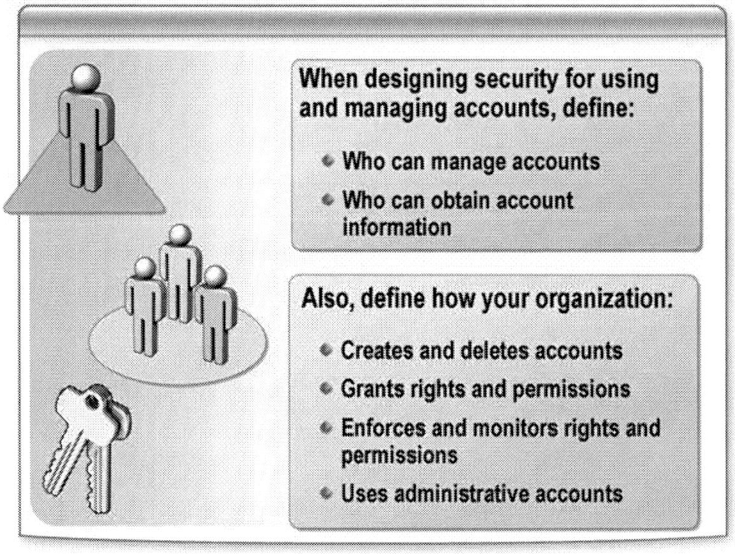

Key points

When designing security for using and managing accounts, you need to define levels of trust for the individuals who administer your network. To protect account information, define:

- *Who can manage accounts and passwords.* Anyone who can manage an account can change the rights and permissions of the account or disable its use. Anyone who can manage a password to an account can, at any time, access all of the information that the account can access.
- *Who can obtain account information.* Account information often includes personal data, such as home addresses, birthdates, and telephone numbers. Each account uses metadata that includes the password policy for the account. An attacker can use account information to identify the footprint of a network.

Additionally, you must develop processes for:

- *Creating and deleting accounts.* Monitor the creation of new accounts and ensure that unused accounts are locked out and promptly deleted. You must also create procedures for creating and distributing account passwords.
- *Granting rights and permissions to accounts.* Ensure that clear policies exist for granting rights and permissions. For example, you may require a user's manager to use a secure Web site to submit a request to change permissions for the user.
- *Enforcing and monitoring rights and permissions.* Use Restricted Groups to enforce group membership. Enable auditing of account management events, and review audit log files frequently.
- *Using administrative accounts or administrative access.* Use administrative accounts only when necessary. Ensure that administrators receive proper training about how to comply with the policies and procedures.

Additional reading

For more information about restricting access to account information, see:

- Q246261, *How to Use the Restrict Anonymous Registry Value in Windows 2000.*
- Q166992, *Standard Security Practices for Windows NT.*

For more information about enforcing group membership, see:

- Q228496, How to Use Restricted Groups in Windows 2000.
- The Web page, What's new in Windows XP, at: http://www.microsoft.com/technet/prodtechnol/winxppro/proddocs/sag_SCErestrictgroups.asp.

Guidelines for Using Administrative and Service Accounts

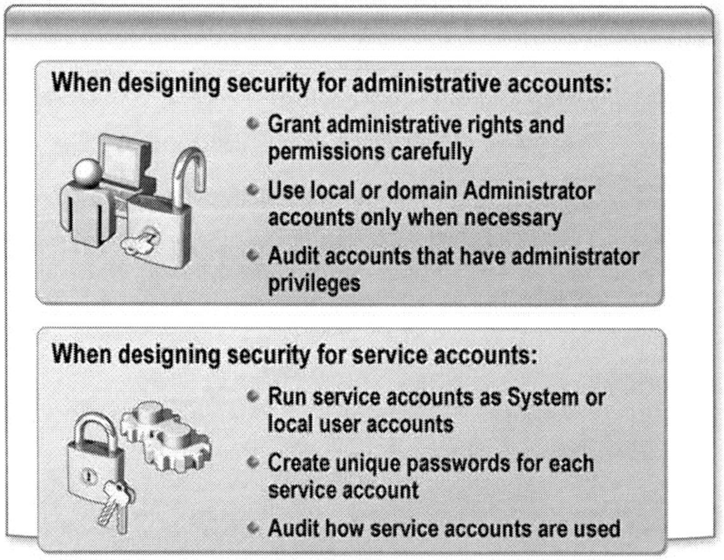

Key points

When designing security for administrative accounts:

- *Grant administrative rights and permissions carefully.* You cannot secure a resource against its administrator. You must be able to trust that your administrators will use their authority legitimately.
- *Use local or domain Administrator accounts only when necessary.* Using Administrator accounts unnecessarily increases the vulnerability of a network. Instead, when you require administrative rights, use Terminal Services in Remote Administration mode, or log on with a normal user account and use the *runas* service with Administrator credentials.
- *Audit accounts that have administrator privileges.* Review the audited actions of administrative accounts to create a record of how the accounts are used.

When designing security for service accounts:

- *Run service accounts as System or local user accounts.* Service account passwords for non-System accounts are stored as LSA secrets, which an attacker can extract. If the account is a domain account, an attacker who extracts the password from a computer can then log on to the domain.
- *Create unique passwords for each service account.* If many computers use the same service account name and password, a compromise of one computer can lead to the compromise of all of the computers.
- *Audit how service accounts are used.* You can review audit logs for the use of service accounts by auditing both logon events and account logon events. If a service account is used in a nonservice account logon session, you will know that the account is not being used for its designated purpose.

Additional reading

For more information about delegating administrative control, see *Step-by-Step Guide to Using the Delegation of Control Wizard*, at: http://www.microsoft.com/technet/prodtechnol/windows2000serv/howto/delestep.asp.

For more information about auditing service accounts, see Q274176, *Security Event for Associating Service Account Logon Events*.

How Account Passwords Are Stored

Password location	Details
Kerberos and NTLM	• Active Directory stores entire passwords as one hash value
LAN Manager	• Passwords are divided into two 7-character upper case passwords before the hash is created Success92! → SUCCESS + 92!
Service accounts	• Passwords are stored in plaintext as LSA secrets
Cached credentials	• Neither the password nor a representation of the password is stored persistently

Key points

The following table lists common password storage locations and details.

Password location	Storage format details
Kerberos	Stored in Active Directory as part of the user's long-term key
NTLM	Stored as an MD4 hash value of the password
LAN Manager	Stored as the concatenation, or linking, of the two 7-character halves of the password that are used to encrypt a constant using Data Encryption Standard (DES)
Service account	Stored in plaintext as an LSA secret
Cached logon credentials	Not stored persistently

An attacker who has physical access to a computer can extract NTLM and LAN Manager password hash values from the Security Accounts Manager (SAM) database and attack the hashes offline by using commonly available tools. To prevent the compromise of these passwords, remove LAN Manger password hashes from the computer if you are not using the LAN Manager authentication protocol, and then implement strong passwords.

Additional reading

For more information about Kerberos version 5 authentication protocol, see the white paper, *Kerberos Authentication in Windows 2000*, under **Additional Reading** on the Web page on the Student Materials CD.

For more information about how LAN Manager passwords are stored, see Q147706, *How to Disable LM Authentication on Windows NT*.

Considerations for Designing Password Policies

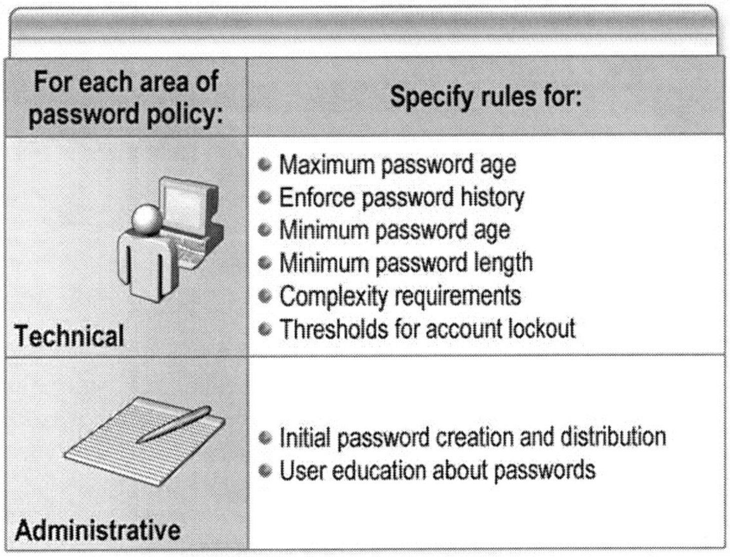

Key points

In Windows 2000 and Windows XP, you can configure the following technical password policy settings:

- *Maximum password age*. The number of days that a password can be used before the user must change it. Regularly changing passwords helps prevent the compromise of passwords.
- *Enforce password history*. The number of unique, new passwords that must be associated with a user account before an old password can be reused. When used with minimum password age, this setting prevents constant reuse of the same password.
- *Minimum password age*. The number of days that a password must be used before the user can change it. The default value is zero, but it is recommended that this be reset to a few days. When used in conjunction with similarly short settings in enforce password history, this restriction prevents constant reuse of the same password.
- *Minimum password length*. The minimum number of characters that a user's password can contain. The default value is zero. Seven characters is a widely used minimum, and ten characters is a recommended minimum for enhanced security.

- *Passwords must meet complexity requirements.* The default password filter (Passfilt.dll) that is included with Windows 2000 Server and Windows XP Professional requires that a password have the following characteristics:
  - Does not contain your name or user name
  - Contains at least six characters
  - Contains characters from three of the following four groups:
    - Uppercase letters [A...Z]
    - Lowercase letters [a...z]
    - Numerals [0...9]
    - Special, nonalphanumeric characters, such as!@#)(*&^%
- *Account lockout.* Account lockout thresholds stipulate that accounts become inoperable after a certain number of failed logon attempts during a certain amount of time. Account lockout policies are intended to detect and prevent brute force attacks on account passwords. However, account lockout policies can increase the number of support incidents on a network when legitimate users forget their passwords after changing them or going on vacation. Strict account lockout policies can also be exploited to create denial of service (DoS) incidents. A better way to detect and prevent brute force attacks is to create long, complex passwords and employ a comprehensive auditing strategy.

You must also develop administrative policies and processes for:

- *Creating and distributing passwords.* If you create or distribute passwords carelessly, an attacker can use them to attack the network. For example, if the initial password for new accounts is "password," and for some reason an account is never used, you now have an account on the network that has a very predictable password, which means the account can be easily compromised.
- *Educating users about how to create strong passwords.* Even if you enable the password complexity filter, users can still create passwords that are easily guessable, such as "Windows2000." Although the password meets the technical complexity requirements, it is not a strong password.

Practice: Risk and Response

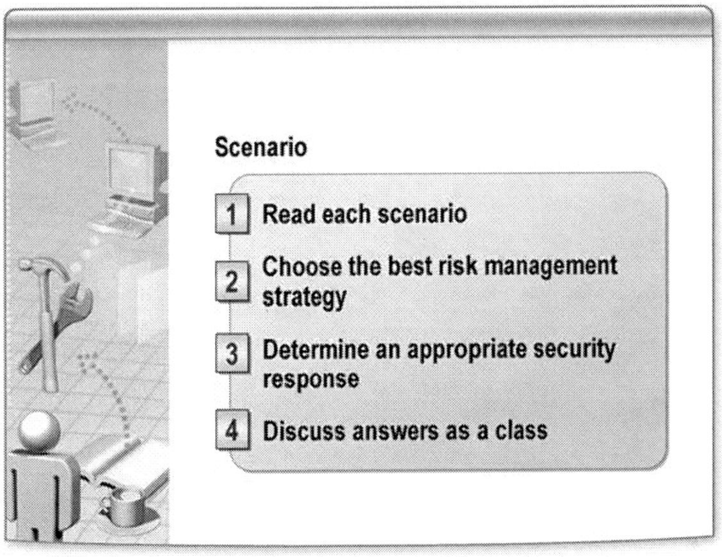

Introduction

For each scenario, choose whether to accept, mitigate, transfer, or avoid the risk that is presented, and then enter an appropriate security response.

Scenario	Risk strategy	Security response
Attacker who has physical access to a computer can extract LSA secrets and obtain service account passwords of domain service accounts		
Attacker can use brute force to easily break LAN Manager password hashes		
Administrators may not be trustworthy		
Users may not create complex passwords		
Administrators can change the password of an account, and then access data by using a user's security context		

Security Policy Checklist

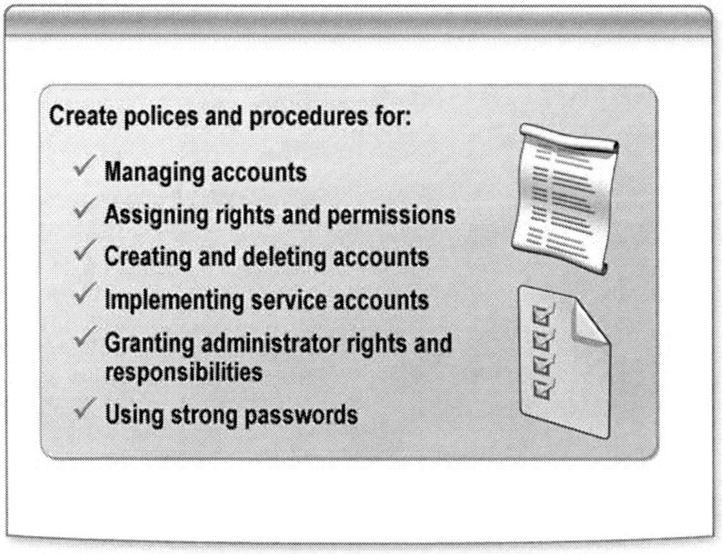

Checklist

Use the following checklist to guide your security design for accounts.

Phase	Task	Details
Planning	Model threats	STRIDE (Spoofing, Tampering, Repudiation, Information disclosure, Denial of service and Elevation of privilege) and life cycle threat models
	Manage risks	Qualitative and quantitative risk analysis

Phase	Task	Details
Building	Create policies and procedures for:	Managing accounts
		Assigning rights and permissions
		Creating and deleting accounts
		Implementing service accounts
		Granting administrator rights and responsibilities
		Using strong passwords

Lab A: Designing Security for Accounts

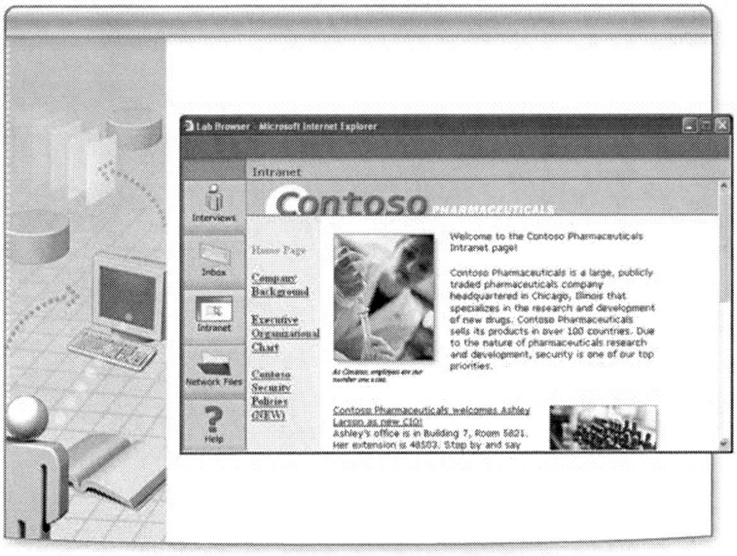

Objectives

After completing this lab, you will be able to apply security design concepts to account security.

Scenario

You are a consultant hired by Contoso Pharmaceuticals to help the company design security for its network. Each lab uses an interactive application to convey scenario-based information. To begin a lab, on the desktop, click **Internet Explorer**; this opens a Web page that contains links to each lab. Click a link to begin a lab.

Estimated time to complete this lab: 30 minutes

Work with a lab partner to perform the lab.

► **To complete a lab**

1. Read Ashley Larson's e-mail in each lab to determine the goals for the lab.
2. Click **Reply**, and then type your answer to Ashley's questions.
3. Click **Send** to save your answers to a folder on your desktop.
4. Discuss your answers as a class.

Microsoft®
Training &
Certification

Module 8: Creating a Security Design for Authentication

Contents

Microsoft®

Overview

- Determining Threats and Analyzing Risks to Authentication
- Designing Security for Authentication

Introduction

In this module, you will learn how to determine threats and analyze risks to authentication. You will learn how to design security for authenticating local users, remote users, and users who access your network across the Internet. You will also learn when to choose multifactor authentication for additional security.

Objectives

After completing this module, you will be able to:

- Determine threats and analyze risks to authentication.
- Design security for authentication.

Lesson: Determining Threats and Analyzing Risks to Authentication

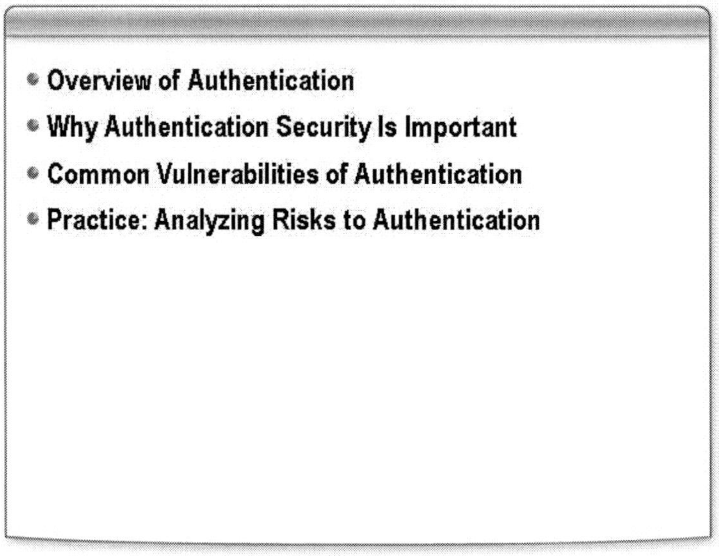

Introduction

Authentication validates that a user possesses the correct credentials that are associated with an account. In a Microsoft® Windows® network, the authentication methods that are used to verify logon credentials are based primarily on how and where an account is accessing the network. If incorrect configurations or incompatibilities with applications exist, attackers may be able to intercept or impersonate authentication information.

Lesson objectives

After completing this lesson, you will be able to:

- Describe authentication in general terms.
- Explain why authentication is important.
- List common vulnerabilities of authentication.

Overview of Authentication

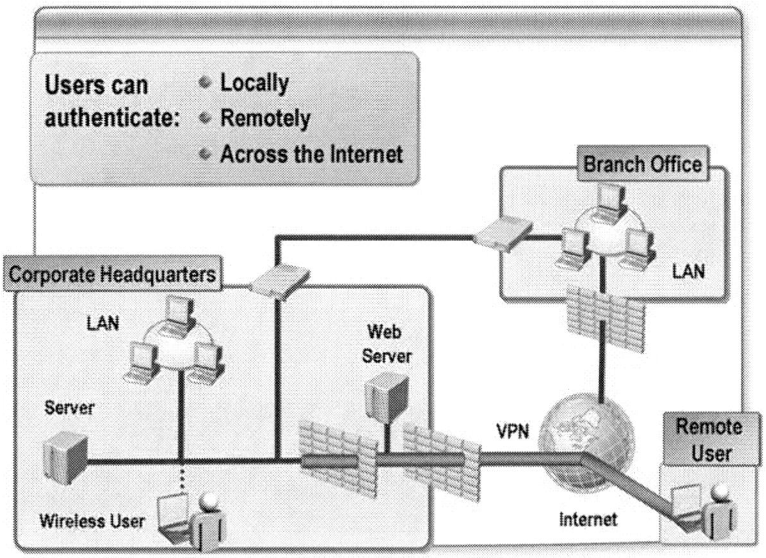

Key points

When designing security for authentication, consider all types of authentication that your network uses, including applications that use their own authentication protocols. On a Microsoft network, different authentication methods are used, depending on whether a user is directly connected to the local area network (LAN), accessing the network remotely, or accessing the network over the Internet.

Why Authentication Security Is Important

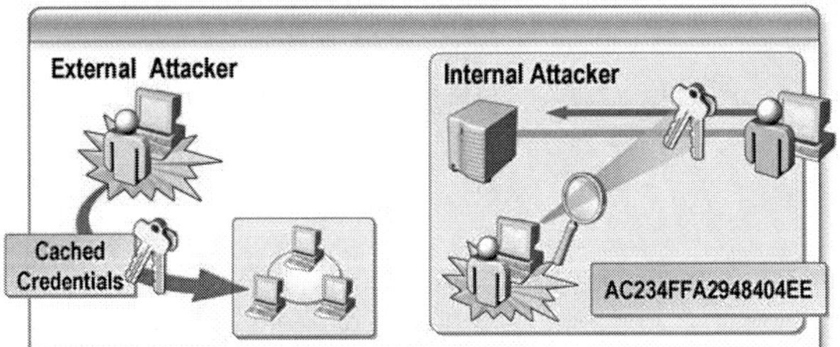

Attacker	Threat	Example
External	Spoofing	Attacker uses a friend's home computer and gains remote access to the network by using cached credentials
Internal	Network monitoring	Attacker intercepts password hashes used by an earlier authentication protocol and performs a brute force attack to reveal the password

External attacker scenario

While using a friend's home computer, an external attacker discovers that the computer has Remote Access Service (RAS) credentials to the internal network that are persistently stored on the computer. The attacker successfully authenticates to the network using the credentials, and then gains access to network resources.

Internal attacker scenario

An internal attacker installs network monitoring software that operates in promiscuous mode to intercept authentication packets. After intercepting packets in an authentication sequence, the attacker performs a brute force attack on the password hash that is retrieved from a packet and determines the user's password. The attacker later uses the intercepted account name and password to access the network.

Common Vulnerabilities of Authentication

Vulnerability	Example
Passwords	• Passwords are transmitted in plaintext • Password hashes are transmitted over the network • Passwords are intercepted by Trojan horse applications
Compatibility	• Older software uses weak authentication methods • Authentication protocols are weakened for use with other applications • Incompatibility with non-Microsoft operating systems
Encryption	• An application uses weak encryption • Older operating systems use weak encryption methods • An attacker intercepts and replays authentication packets

Key points

After an attacker penetrates a network, one of the first things that he will do is attempt to obtain domain logon credentials. Ensure that you design an authentication strategy that minimizes exposure to vulnerabilities of passwords, compatibility with older or non-Microsoft software, and encryption.

After an account is successfully authenticated, it is very difficult—in some cases impossible—to detect whether the person using the account is the user who has been assigned that account or an attacker. Often, you can only make the determination after the attacker has caused damage.

Practice: Analyzing Risks to Authentication

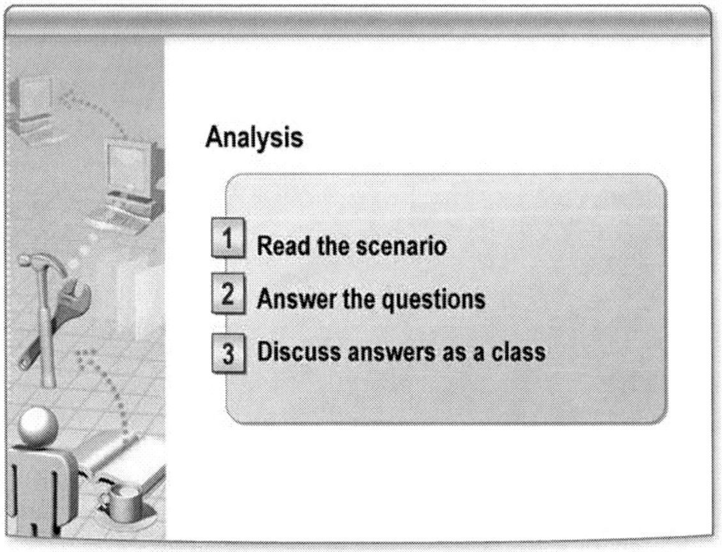

Introduction

Northwind Traders has 10,000 users who work in a single office complex. Everyone uses computers running Microsoft Windows NT® version 4.0 or Windows 2000 that are members of an Active Directory® directory service domain. Hubs connect the network. The account lockout policy threshold is set to 10 incorrect logon attempts. Administrators must use smart cards to be authenticated.

Management has asked you to perform a qualitative risk analysis of items in the table. For each threat, assign a probability and impact value between 1 and 10, and then multiply the two values to compute the relative risk. Then, answer the question.

Threat	Probability	Impact	Relative risk
1. Attacker intercepts packets that contain password hashes and attempts to break them offline			
2. Attacker intercepts authentication packets and attempts to replay them			
3. Attacker installs a Trojan horse application to record keystrokes, including passwords			
4. Attacker exploits authentication protocols that are designed for use with older operating systems			
5. Attacker looks over the shoulder of a user as she enters her password			

(*continued*)

Threat	Probability	Impact	Relative risk
6. Attacker steals the smart card of an administrator and succeeds in guessing the PIN (personal identification number)			
7. Attacker performs a brute force attack on a user account by using a script			

Question

What two threats present the greatest relative risk? Why?

Lesson: Designing Security for Authentication

- Steps for Determining Authentication Requirements
- LAN Authentication Protocols
- Considerations for Authenticating Accounts on a LAN
- Considerations for Authenticating Web Users
- Considerations for Authenticating RAS Users
- What Is Multifactor Authentication?
- Considerations for Authenticating Applications and Network Devices
- Practice: Risk and Response
- Security Policy Checklist

Introduction

To secure authentication, you secure user access to the network from local, remote, and Web-based clients. Authentication security also depends on the types of computers and software on your network. For example, a network of similar or heterogeneous clients that all use the same operating system has different requirements than a network made up of several different operating systems or different versions of the same operating system.

Lesson objectives

After completing this lesson, you will be able to:

- Determine authentication requirements for your network.
- Describe LAN authentication protocols and considerations for authenticating accounts on a LAN.
- Describe considerations for authenticating Web users.
- Describe considerations for authenticating RAS users.
- Explain multifactor authentication.
- Describe considerations for authenticating applications and network devices.

Steps for Determining Authentication Requirements

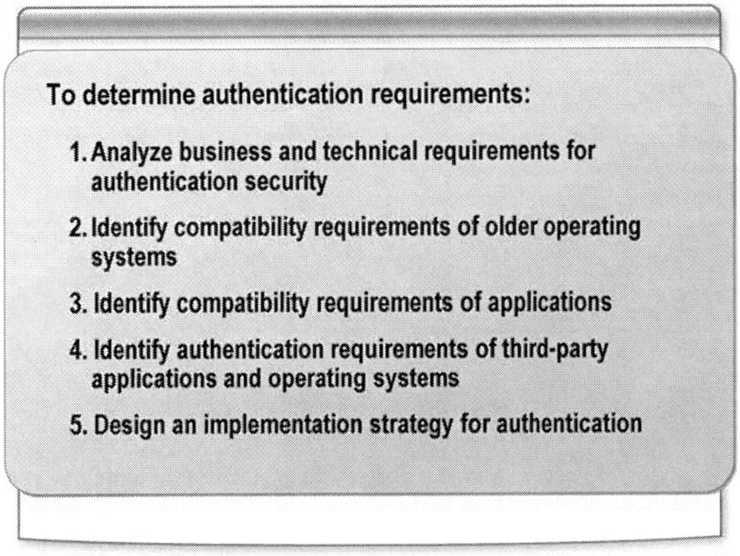

Key points

To determine authentication requirements:

1. *Analyze business and technical requirements for authentication security.* Your organization may have specific authentication requirements, such as compliance with government regulations or protection against exposure to unique threats. Your organization may also have different requirements for various types of accounts, such as Administrator accounts.
2. *Identify compatibility requirements of older operating systems.* If you do not use older operating systems, such as MS-DOS®, Windows 95, or Windows 98, disable any authentication protocols that are used only for older operating systems. In general, these protocols are weaker than newer protocols.
3. *Identify compatibility requirements of applications.* Enterprise applications and other line-of-business applications may have their own authentication protocols or specific authentication requirements.
4. *Identify authentication requirements of third-party applications and operating systems.* You must ensure authentication compatibility with non-Microsoft applications and operating systems. Also consider how accounts on network devices are authenticated.
5. *Design an implementation strategy for authentication.* After gathering the information in steps 1 through 4, you will be able to design an implementation strategy to authenticate accounts securely.

LAN Authentication Protocols

Protocol	Considerations
LAN Manager	• Used by older Microsoft operating systems • Uses a basic challenge and response exchange • Not a secure authentication protocol
NTLM	• Used by default in Windows NT 4.0 and for local accounts in Windows 2000 and later operating systems • Uses a basic challenge and response exchange
NTLMv2	• Supported by Windows 95 and later operating systems • Improves security of NTLM by adding session security and encryption • Mutually authenticates client and server
Kerberos	• Used by default in Windows 2000 and later operating systems in Active Directory domains • Mutually authenticates client and server • Supports the use of smart cards

Key points

Windows 2000 and Windows XP support several methods for authentication on a LAN. As part of your security design, you must determine which authentication methods to support. Generally, newer authentication methods are stronger but may not be compatible with older applications or operating systems.

In Windows 2000 and Windows XP, the Security Support Provider Interface (SSPI) determines which of the following authentication protocol to use to validate authentication credentials:

- *LAN Manager*. Older Microsoft operating systems use the LAN Manager authentication protocol, which is the least secure challenge and response authentication protocol in Windows 2000 and Windows XP. Use LAN Manager authentication if computers must connect to files stored on computers running MS-DOS, Windows 95, or Windows 98.
- *NTLM*. This improved version of LAN Manager stores passwords more securely. NTLM is the default authentication protocol in Microsoft Windows NT 4.0 domains and for local accounts in Windows 2000 and Windows XP.
- *NTLM version 2 (NTLMv2)*. The most secure of the LAN Manager-based authentication protocols in Windows 2000 and Windows XP is NTLM v2. It is also available for earlier operating systems if you install the Active Directory client extensions for Windows 95, Windows 98, or Windows NT 4.0. NTLMv2 performs mutual authentication and can be further secured by adding session security.

- *Kerberos version 5 authentication protocol.* This is the default authentication protocol in computers running Windows 2000 and Windows XP that are in Active Directory domains. It is compliant with RFC (Request for Comments) 1510. The Kerberos protocol is considered the strongest authentication protocol in Windows 2000 and later operating systems when it is used with strong passwords. The Kerberos protocol in Windows 2000 supports Kerberos extensions for use with smart cards for multifactor authentication.

Additional reading

For more information about LAN authentication methods in Windows 2000 and Windows XP, see the following resources:

- The white paper, *Security Support Provider Interface*, under **Additional Reading** on the Web page on the Student Materials CD.
- The white papers under *Microsoft Provided SSP Packages*, at: http://msdn.microsoft.com/library/en-us/security/security/Microsoft_provided_ssps.asp.
- The white paper, *Windows 2000 Kerberos Authentication*, under **Additional Reading** on the Web page on the Student Materials CD.
- The white paper, *Kerberos Explained*, at: http://www.microsoft.com/TechNet/prodtechnol/windows2000serv/maintain/kerberos.asp.
- Q217098, *Basic Overview of Kerberos Authentication in Windows 2000.*
- Q239869, *How to Enable NTLM 2 Authentication for Windows 95/98/2000/NT.*

For more information about Active Directory client extensions, see the white paper, *Active Directory Client Extensions for Windows 95, Windows 98 and Windows NT 4.0*, at: http://www.microsoft.com/windows2000/server/evaluation/news/bulletins/adextension.asp.

Considerations for Authenticating Accounts on a LAN

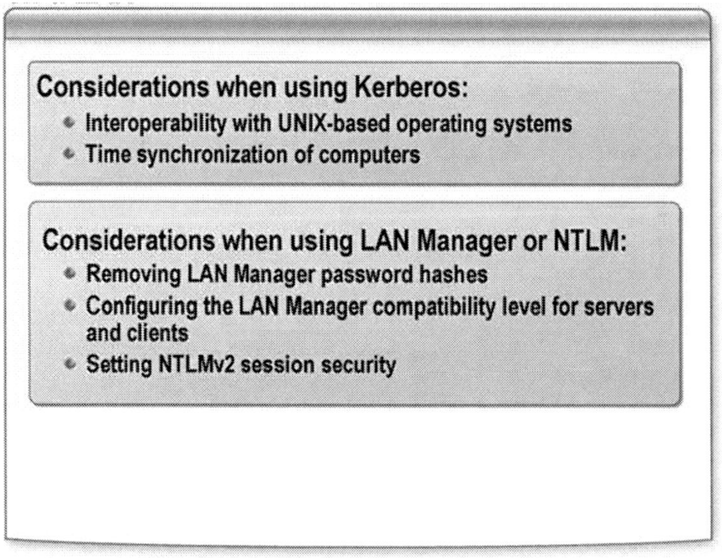

Key points

When using the Kerberos version 5 authentication protocol, consider:

- *Interoperability with Kerberos realms.* If your organization operates UNIX-based computers, consider integrating the Kerberos realm, which is similar to a domain in Active Directory, with Active Directory in Windows 2000. First, enable the **Use DES encryption types** setting for all UNIX accounts, because the default implementation of the Kerberos protocol in Windows 2000 uses RC4 for the encryption of Kerberos messages. Also, set the Service Principal Name (SPN) for all UNIX resources. You may also need to enable the **Do not require Kerberos preauthentication** setting to interoperate with UNIX-based computers.
- *Time synchronization.* To prevent the replay of Kerberos authentication messages and tickets, the Kerberos protocol requires that all computers have their time synchronized within a defined threshold. In Active Directory, this threshold is five minutes. However, times may become unsynchronized, due to such things as administrators resetting times, or conflicts with other Windows 2000 forests or UNIX-based computers. Domain computers running Windows 2000 and Windows XP automatically synchronize their system clocks with the domain controller that authenticates them by using the Windows Time service.

When using LAN Manager and NTLM authentication protocols, consider:

- *Removing LAN Manager password hashes.* LAN Manager password hashes are sent along with NTLM authentication messages for compatibility with older operating systems. Because an attacker can easily crack LAN Manager password hashes, remove them from the account databases if your network does not require them. You can remove LAN Manager password hashes for all accounts on a computer by using a setting in Group Policy, or you can remove the hashes for an individual account by using a password greater then 14 characters in length.

- *Configuring the LAN Manager compatibility level for servers and clients.* You can configure how computers use LAN Manager and NTLM authentication protocols by configuring the LAN Manager compatibility registry value or Group Policy setting. In the Group Policy settings in this context, the client refers to the computer that is trying to gain authentication, and the server is the computer that is validating the authentication. As the following table indicates, choose the highest level that maintains compatibility with other systems and applications, particularly applications that rely on NTLM.

  For all computers:

Level	Result
Level 0	Clients use LAN Manager and NTLM authentication and never use NTLMv2 session security
Level 1	Clients use LAN Manager and NTLM authentication and use NTLMv2 session security if the server supports it
Level 2	Clients use only NTLM authentication and use NTLMv2 session security if the server supports it
Level 3	Clients use NTLMv2 authentication and use NTLMv2 session security if the server supports it

  For domain accounts that are stored in Active Directory and local accounts that are stored in SAM (Security Accounts Manager) databases, you must set the level higher than 3 to have any effect, as the following table indicates.

Level	Result
Level 4	Clients use NTLM authentication and use NTLMv2 session security if the server supports it; domain controllers refuse LAN Manager authentication and accept NTLM and NTLMv2
Level 5	Clients use NTLMv2 authentication and use NTLMv2 session security if the server supports it; domain controllers refuse NTLM and LAN Manager authentication and only accept NTLMv2

  Note There is no way to completely disable NTLM-based authentication methods in Windows 2000 and Windows XP.

- *Setting NTLMv2 session security.* NTLMv2 supports additional security for authentication messages. You can configure NTLMv2 session security by editing the registry or by using Group Policy. If you configure NTLMv2 session security, you must ensure that the NTLMv2 security settings for client and server are compatible.

Additional reading

For additional information about configuring LAN authentication protocols, see:

- The white paper, *Step-by-Step Guide to Kerberos 5 (krb5 1.0) Interoperability*, at: http://www.microsoft.com/windows2000/techinfo/planning/security/kerbsteps.asp.
- The white paper, *Windows Time Service*, under **Additional Reading** on the Web page on the Student Materials CD.
- Q216734, *How to Configure an Authoritative Time Server in Windows 2000.*
- Q147706, *How to Disable LM Authentication on Windows NT.*
- Q299656, *New Registry Key to Remove LM Hashes from AD & SAM.*

Considerations for Authenticating Web Users

IIS authentication protocols	Considerations
Anonymous	• Uses a single account • Does not require users to provide credentials
Basic	• Sends user names and passwords in plaintext • Supported by all browsers • Is secure if combined with SSL or TLS
Digest	• Uses a user name, password, and nonce to create the hash • Supported by all Web browsers • Introduces other vulnerabilities
Windows Integrated	• Is compatible with Internet Explorer only • Cannot be used with proxy servers or firewalls • Used for intranet Web sites
Certificate-based	• Requires a PKI • Does not require a user to enter a password

Key points

In a Microsoft network, Internet Information Services (IIS) version 5.0 authenticates Web-based users who access the network. IIS 5.0 uses the following authentication protocols:

- *Anonymous authentication*. Enables users to access a Web site without presenting credentials. All anonymous users are authenticated with the same account, which by default is IUSR_*Servername*, where *servername* is the name of the server running IIS.
- *Basic authentication*. Sends user name and password combinations across the network in plaintext that is encoded with base64 encoding. To use Basic authentication, users must have the right to log on locally to the server running IIS. All Web browser software supports Basic authentication, which can be used with proxy servers. To protect the authentication packets from interception, use Basic authentication only in combination with Secure Sockets Layer (SSL).
- *Digest access authentication*. Uses a user name and password and adds a random value called a *nonce* to create a hash to improve Basic authentication. Digest authentication requires that the server running IIS be a member of an Active Directory domain. However, user accounts that use Digest authentication must have their passwords stored in Active Directory by using reversible encryption, which introduces additional vulnerabilities. As a result, Digest authentication is rarely used.
- *Windows Integrated authentication*. Enables a computer running Microsoft Internet Explorer version 4.0 or later to automatically authenticate the user by using the cached credentials of the logged-on user without a prompt to the user. By default, servers running IIS 5.0 use the Kerberos authentication protocol, but will use NTLM if Kerberos authentication fails. Windows Integrated authentication works only with Internet Explorer. It does not work with proxy servers.

- *Certificate-based authentication.* Enables a user or computer to authenticate to a Web site on a server running IIS 5.0 by possessing a private key that is associated with an X.509 digital certificate. The certificate is mapped to a local user account or to a user account that is stored in Active Directory so that it can be used for authentication. Certificate-based authentication is the most secure authentication protocol for Web sites that are hosted on servers running IIS 5.0. However, you must deploy a public key infrastructure (PKI) to issue and manage certificates.

Note All authentication messages for File Transfer Protocol (FTP) service in IIS 5.0 are sent in plaintext.

Additional reading

For more information about IIS authentication methods, see:

- The white paper, *Designing Distributed Applications with Visual Studio .NET*, at: http://msdn.microsoft.com/library/en-us/vsent7/html/vxconIISAuthentication.asp.
- *IIS 5.0 Authentication Modes* from the *IIS 5.0 Resource Guide*, at: http://www.microsoft.com/windows2000/techinfo/reskit/en/IISbook/c09_iis_5.0_authentication_modes.htm.
- *IIS 4.0 and 5.0 Authentication Methods Chart*, at: http://www.microsoft.com/technet/prodtechnol/iis/maintain/featusability/authmeth.asp.
- Q264921, *INFO: How IIS Authenticates Browser Clients.*

Considerations for Authenticating RAS Users

Remote authentication protocols	Considerations
CHAP	• Requires that passwords are stored using reversible encryption • Is compatible with Macintosh and UNIX-based RAS clients • Disallows data encryption
MS-CHAP	• Used by Windows 95 clients • Supports only Microsoft clients
MS-CHAP version 2	• Performs mutual authentication • Installed by default as the RAS authentication protocol in Windows 2000 and later operating systems
EAP-TLS	• Requires PKI • Enables multifactor authentication

Key points

When designing authentication, consider how you are authenticating remote users who connect by dialing-up or through a virtual private network (VPN). You can use the following protocols:

- *CHAP*. The Challenge Handshake Authentication Protocol (CHAP) is a challenge-response authentication protocol that is documented in RFC 1994. It uses the Message Digest 5 (MD5) algorithm to hash the response to a challenge that the remote access server issues. Various vendors of dial-in servers and clients use CHAP.

  CHAP requires that user account passwords are stored using reversible encryption, which introduces additional vulnerabilities. If an attacker can intercept the entire CHAP authentication sequence, she can attack the password hash offline. Also, data cannot be encrypted when using the CHAP protocol. Therefore, CHAP is not a secure authentication protocol.

- *MS-CHAP*. Similar to CHAP, the Microsoft Challenge Handshake Authentication Protocol (MS-CHAP) is an encrypted authentication mechanism. MS-CHAP is also vulnerable to an attacker performing an offline attack on the user's password hash. Unlike CHAP, however, MS-CHAP does not require that passwords be stored using reversible encryption. Data is secured by Microsoft Point-to-Point Encryption (MPPE).

  Only implement MS-CHAP if you run older Microsoft operating systems that require it. Both CHAP and MS-CHAP are only as secure as the strength of users' passwords.

- *MS-CHAP version 2*. Offering additional security improvements to MS-CHAP, MS-CHAP version 2 (MS-CHAP v2) includes mutual authentication, separate session keys for transmitted and received data, and session key generation that is not entirely based on users' passwords.
- *EAP-TLS*. Extensible Authentication Protocol (EAP) - Transport Layer Security (TLS) provides authentication, data integrity, and data confidentiality services. It uses mutual authentication, negotiation of encryption algorithms, secure exchange of sessions keys, and message integrity. Use EAP-TLS if you implement multifactor authentication technologies, such as smart cards. EAP-TLS is the most secure remote authentication protocol.

Additional reading

For more information about remote access authentication protocols, see:

- The white paper, *Privacy Protected Network Access: Virtual Private Networking and Intranet Security*, under **Additional Reading** on the Web page on the Student Materials CD.
- The white paper, *RADIUS Protocol Security and Best Practices*, at: http://www.microsoft.com/technet/itsolutions/network/maintain/security/radiusec.asp.
- The white paper, *Cryptanalysis of Microsoft's PPTP Authentication Extensions (MS-CHAPv2)*, at: http://www.counterpane.com/pptpv2-paper.html.
- The white paper, *Virtual Private Networking with Windows 2000: Deploying Remote Access VPNs*, at: http://www.microsoft.com/technet/itsolutions/network/deploy/depovg/vpndeply.asp.
- Appendix D, "Authentication in CHAP, MS-CHAP, and MS-CHAP v2," in Course 2830, *Designing Security for Microsoft Networks*.

What Is Multifactor Authentication?

Factors	Examples
Passcode	• User name and password • PIN
Physical item	• Smart card • Hardware or software token
Personal characteristic of user	• Thumbprint • Voice

Use multifactor authentication when:

- **You want to confirm the identity of a user with more than a password**
- **Security is critical to your organization**

Key points

Multifactor authentication requires more than one type of credential to validate a user account. In general, there are three categories of credential types:

- Passcodes
- Physical items
- Personal characteristics

Using multiple factors to authenticate users greatly increases the difficulty for an attacker who wants to compromise a network. Multifactor authentication is especially useful to secure remote users, where physical verification of a user's identity is difficult; it is also useful with administrative accounts, where an extra level of security may be required.

In Windows 2000 and Windows XP, you can use Group Policy to require the use of smart cards when interactively logging on to the network, such as when using the Windows Logon screen or the Remote Desktop client. To prevent the account from being used for other types of logons, such as logons to network shares, reset the password to a random, complex password greater than 14 characters in length before you enable the Group Policy setting.

Additional reading

For more information about smart cards, see the white papers, *Smart Cards* and *Smart Card Logon*, under **Additional Reading** on the Web page on the Student Materials CD.

For more information about using personal characteristics for authentication, see the Biometric Consortium Web page, at: http://www.biometrics.org.

Considerations for Authenticating Applications and Network Devices

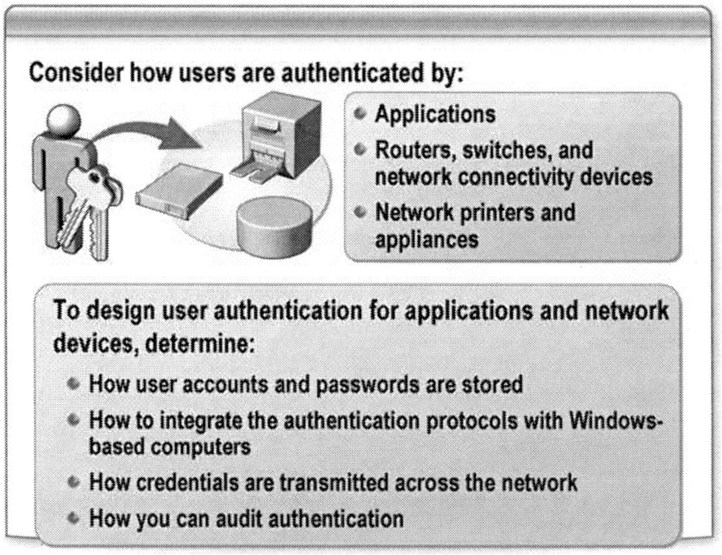

Key points

In addition to authentication protocols that the operating system uses, many applications and most network devices, printers, and appliances have their own authentication protocols.

As part of your security design, research the requirements of the applications and devices on your network. Also, work with the administrators who manage the applications and devices on your network to ensure that the authentication design is compatible with the applications and devices and with your overall security policy.

Practice: Risk and Response

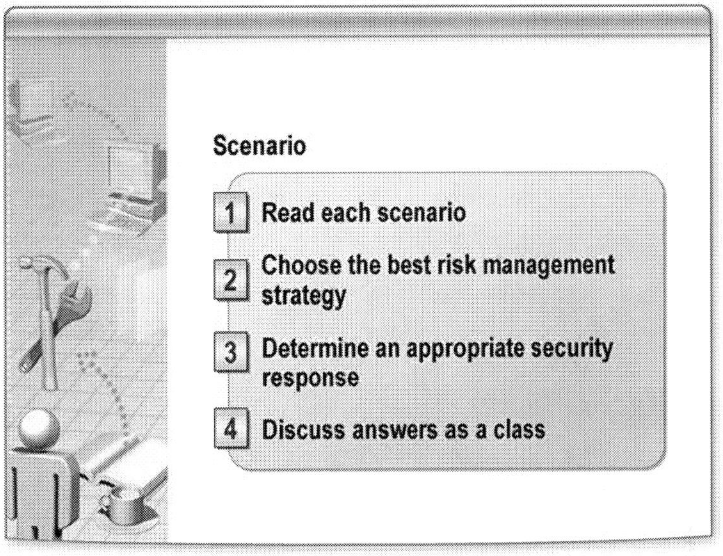

Introduction

For each scenario, choose whether to accept, mitigate, transfer, or avoid the risk presented, and then enter an appropriate security response.

Scenario	Risk strategy	Security response
Attacker intercepts LAN Manager password hashes that were sent with NTLM authentication messages.		
You must authenticate Web users securely. Web users use many types of Web browsers.		
Attacker creates a VPN connection to your network by guessing an administrator's password.		

Security Policy Checklist

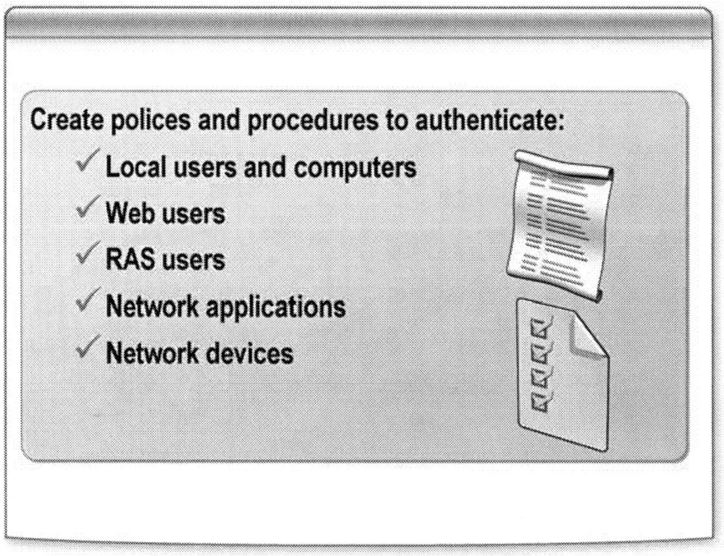

Checklist

Use the following checklist to guide your security design for authentication.

Phase	Task	Details
Planning	Model threats	STRIDE (Spoofing, Tampering, Repudiation, Information disclosure, Denial of service, and Elevation of privilege) and life cycle threat models
	Manage risks	Qualitative and quantitative risk analysis

Phase	Task	Details
Building	Create policies and procedures for authenticating:	Local users and computers Web users RAS users Network applications Network devices

Lab A: Designing Authentication Security

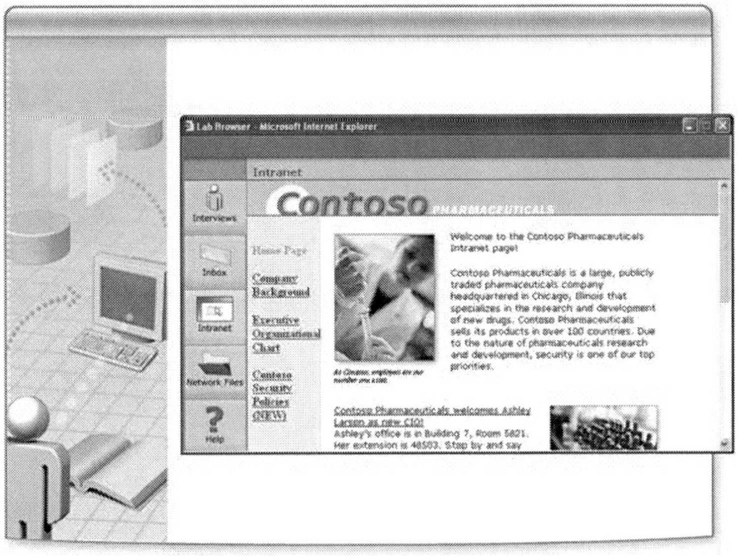

Objectives

After completing this lab, you will be able to apply security design concepts to authentication.

Scenario

You are a consultant hired by Contoso Pharmaceuticals to help the company design security for its network. Each lab uses an interactive application to convey scenario-based information. To begin a lab, on the desktop, click **Internet Explorer**; this opens a Web page that contains links to each lab. Click a link to begin a lab.

Estimated time to complete this lab: 30 minutes

Work with a lab partner to perform the lab.

► **To complete a lab**

1. Read Ashley Larson's e-mail in each lab to determine the goals for the lab.
2. Click **Reply**, and then type your answer to Ashley's questions.
3. Click **Send** to save your answers to a folder on your desktop.
4. Discuss your answers as a class.

Microsoft®
Training &
Certification

Module 9: Creating a Security Design for Data

Contents

Microsoft®

Overview

- **Determining Threats and Analyzing Risks to Data**
- **Designing Security for Data**

Introduction

In this module, you will learn how to determine threats and analyze risks to data in an organization. You will learn how to design access control for files and folders in order to protect data that is stored on network servers. You will also learn about considerations for encrypting and managing data.

Objectives

After completing this module, you will be able to:

- Determine threats and analyze risks to data.
- Design security for data.

Lesson: Determining Threats and Analyzing Risks to Data

- Overview of Access Control
- Why Securing Data Is Important
- Common Vulnerabilities to Data
- Practice: Analyzing Risks to Data

Introduction

Securing data means controlling access to it. You control access by using permissions. Attackers who can subvert or override permissions may be able to access data on your network.

Lesson objectives

After completing this lesson, you will be able to:

- Describe access control for data.
- Explain why securing data is important.
- List common vulnerabilities to data.

Overview of Access Control

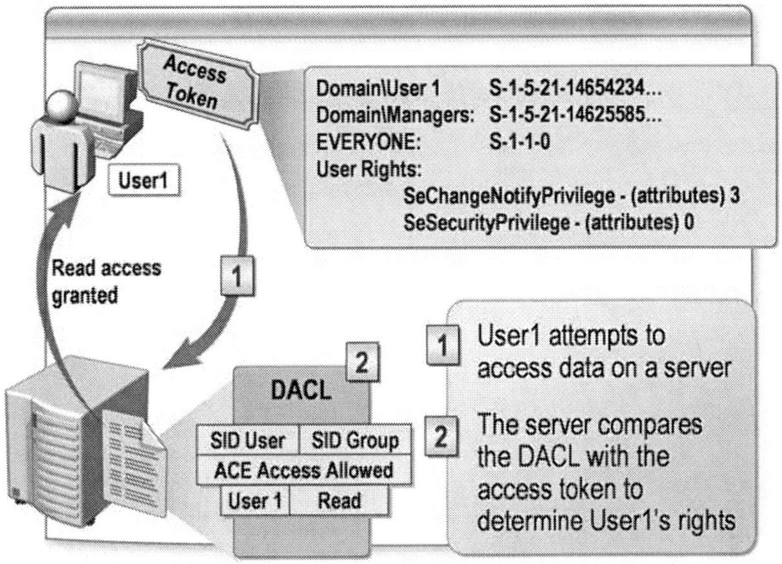

Key points

To control access to data, Microsoft® Windows® 2000 and Microsoft Windows XP use access tokens and discretionary access control lists (DACLs). Access tokens define the rights that a user account has. DACLs control the permissions to Active Directory® directory service objects and the folder and file objects in NTFS file system (NTFS).

When a user's credentials are validated during authentication, the user's computer receives and stores an access token. The access token contains the security identifier (SID) of the user account, the SID of each local and domain group that the user has membership in, and a list of the user rights for the user.

When a user attempts to access a resource, the SIDs in the access token are compared to the SIDs in the DACL. The user receives the corresponding permissions to each matching SID in the access token and DACL. The DACL of the resource contains an access control entry (ACE) for each permission that is assigned to the resource. The ACEs define the protections that apply to an object.

Additional reading

For more information about access control in Windows 2000 and Windows XP, see *Access Control Components*, at: http://msdn.microsoft.com/library/default.asp?url=/library/en-us/security/Security/access_control_components.asp.

Why Securing Data Is Important

Attacker	Threat	Example
External	Theft of laptop	An attacker steals a laptop from an employee's car, boots the laptop by using a floppy disk, and changes the Administrator password. The attacker uses the account to access files on the laptop.
Internal	Default permissions used and auditing not enabled	A network folder configured with default permissions contains a confidential file. An attacker copies the data and sells it to a competitor without being detected.

Key points

Data is vulnerable to threats from both external and internal attackers. For example:

External attacker scenario

An external attacker steals a laptop from an employee's car. Using a floppy disk to boot the computer, the attacker replaces the password of the Administrator account in the local Security Accounts Manager (SAM) database. The attacker then logs on to the laptop as Administrator and accesses the data.

Internal attacker scenario

An internal attacker discovers a server running Windows 2000 that stores confidential data in folders that are configured with default permissions. The attacker copies the data and sells it to a competitor. Because auditing was not configured, the IT staff cannot determine how the server was compromised or who stole the data.

Common Vulnerabilities to Data

Vulnerability	Example
Configuration of permissions	• Computers running Windows 2000 and Windows XP use default NTFS and share permissions • Permissions are assigned incorrectly • Administrators and users have improper rights
Physical security of data	• Computers are stolen • Hardware fails • A disaster destroys data
Corruption of data	• A virus corrupts or deletes data • Hardware fails and corrupts data • A user irreversibly encrypts a file • A user tampers with data

Key points

Data is vulnerable to three general threats:

- *Incorrect configuration of permissions.* A user is able to access data that should be restricted.
- *Physical security of data.* A user has local access and can defeat other security measures or physically destroy data.
- *Corruption of data.* For example, a virus or irreversible encryption can corrupt data.

When configuring physical and logical security of data, always assign the least amount of access and permissions that a user requires to complete her job duties.

Practice: Analyzing Risks to Data

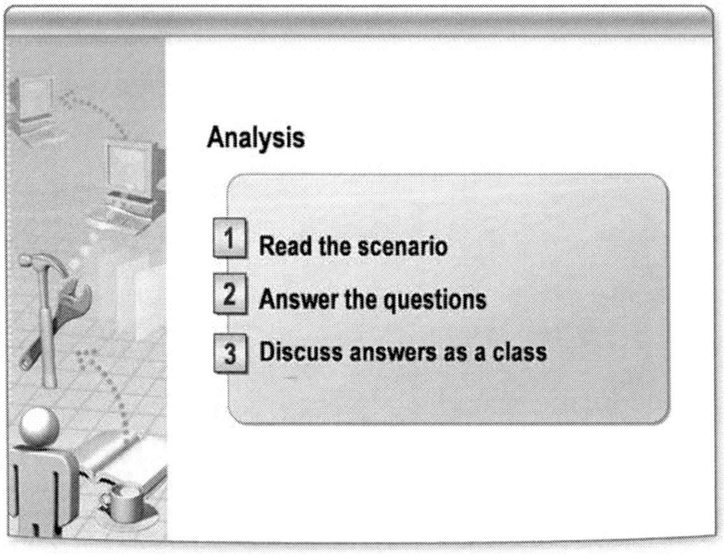

Introduction

After examining threats to data, Northwind Traders determined that if it stores all user data on a central data server and installs antivirus software on all client computers, the organization will reduce its Annual Loss Expectancy (ALE) for data by $150,000.

Question

What are some other threats to data that may prevent Northwind Traders from reducing the ALE by the anticipated amount?

Lesson: Designing Security for Data

- Steps for Designing an Access Control Model
- Considerations for Combining NTFS and Share Permissions
- Steps for Designing EFS Policies
- Guidelines for Managing Data Securely
- Practice: Risk and Response
- Security Policy Checklist

Introduction

You can secure access to data by ensuring that users have appropriate permission. An *access control model* is a methodology for assigning permissions to users and groups. You can also secure data by using NTFS with share permissions or by using encryption.

Lesson objectives

After completing this lesson, you will be able to:

- Design an access control model.
- Describe considerations when using NTFS in combination with share permissions.
- Design an Encrypting File System (EFS) policy.
- List guidelines for designing security for data.

Steps for Designing an Access Control Model

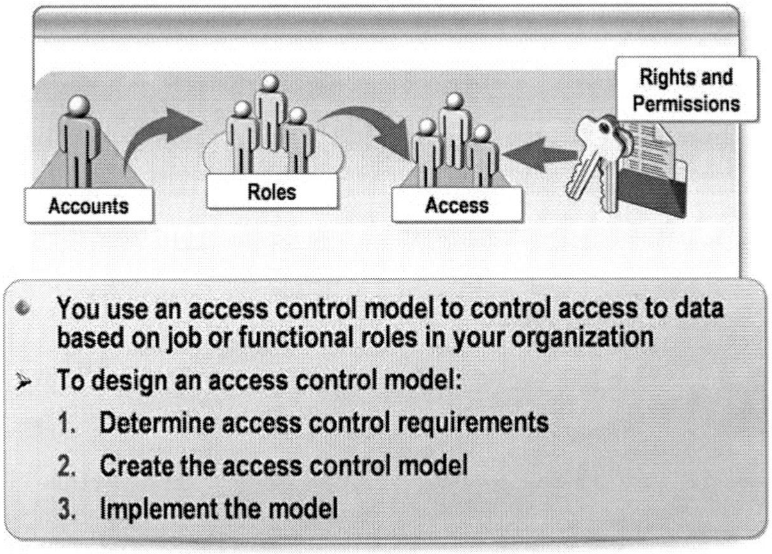

Key points

In Windows 2000 and Windows XP, you can apply access control to data and to the accounts that access data. You can use an access control model on accounts to isolate the security of resources from individual accounts. An access control model also greatly simplifies the application of security on resources.

AGDLP (account, global group, domain local group, permissions) is an access control model that you can use to implement security based on user roles in your organization. The AGDLP model places accounts in groups, places the groups in domain local groups, and then assigns permissions to the domain local groups.

To design an access control model based on the principle of AGDLP, follow these steps:

1. Determine access control requirements:
   a. Identify the jobs and functional roles in your organization.
   b. Determine the security levels for data on your network.
2. Create the access control model:
   a. Create global groups that correspond to jobs or roles.
   b. Create domain local groups and assign permissions to the groups.
3. Implement the model:
   a. Put accounts in the appropriate global groups.
   b. Put global groups in domain local groups, based on the security requirements of the global group.

Considerations for Combining NTFS and Share Permissions

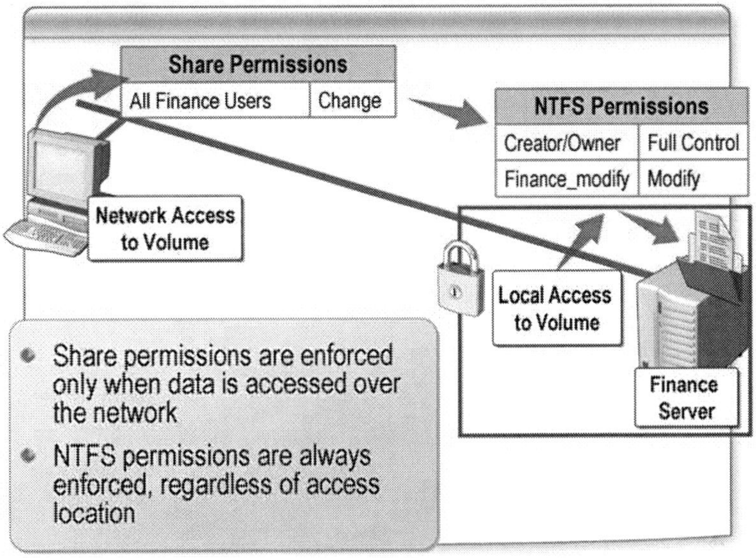

Key points

You can use NTFS and share permissions together to control the security of data. NTFS permissions are in effect when a user accesses data on an NTFS volume locally or remotely. Share permissions are in effect when the data is accessed remotely over a network.

All files and folders stored on an NTFS volume have an owner, who always has the permission to control the permissions to the resource. This ability can enable an owner to subvert a security policy enforced by an IT department. For example, a user in the Finance group creates a spreadsheet on a Finance server, which has membership restricted by a security policy to only Finance users. Because the owner of the spreadsheet has Full Control permissions on the spreadsheet, the owner could grant another user Full Control, even though that person might not belong to the Finance group.

By granting Change permissions to the group All Finance Users on the shared folder on the Finance server, the owner can still create files on the Finance server but is prevented from assigning Full Control permissions on files to other users unless the owner has local access to the volume.

Additional reading

For more information about NTFS and share permissions, see:

- The white paper, *Default Access Control Settings*, under **Additional Reading** on the Web page on the Student Materials CD.
- Q313398, *HOW TO: Control NTFS Permissions Inheritance in Windows.*
- Q318754, *HOW TO: Use Xcacls.exe to Modify NTFS Permissions.*
- Q301198, *HOW TO: Share Files and Folders Over a Network (Domain) in Windows 2000.*

Multimedia: How EFS Works

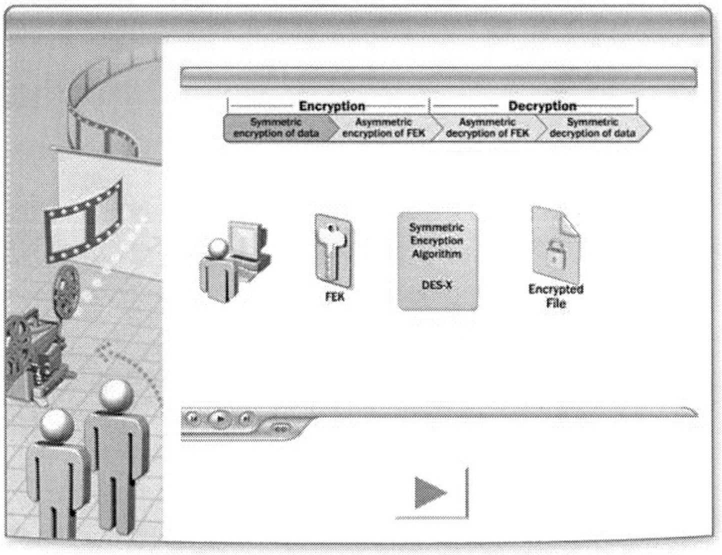

Key points

This animation shows how EFS uses both symmetric and asymmetric encryption to encrypt and decrypt data in Windows 2000 and Windows XP.

Additional reading

The animation is located in the **Media** folder on the Web page on the Student Materials CD. For more information about EFS, see the white paper, *Encrypting File System for Windows 2000*, under **Additional Reading** on the Web page on the Student Materials CD.

Steps for Designing EFS Policies

To design:	Determine:
1. Policies for encrypting files	• Data to encrypt using EFS • Who can use EFS • Data recovery agents (DRAs) • How to generate private keys for DRAs • Where to store private keys for DRAs • Additional security requirements for EFS
2. Procedures for recovering encrypted files	• Who can recover encrypted files • How to use a DRA to recover encrypted files
3. User education strategy	• How to use EFS • How EFS protects data • Data that EFS does not protect

Key points

EFS is a powerful tool for securing data. Used improperly, however, it can prevent legitimate users from accessing their data. To ensure the proper use of EFS in your organization, design:

1. *Policies for encrypting files.* If you do not have policies for properly using encryption, users may irreversibly encrypt files with no method for recovery. For example, an administrator encrypts all files on a server and then accidentally deletes his Administrator account.
2. *Procedures for recovering encrypted files.* Without a procedure, an administrator may expose the data recovery agent (DRA) to attackers, who could then use the compromised private key to decrypt all files on the network. For example, an administrator accidentally leaves a floppy disk on a user's desk that contains the administrator's private key.
3. *A user education strategy.* Train users or ensure that they take classes about how to use EFS. Without adequate training, users may be unaware of policies or may accidentally encrypt a file without knowing how to recover it. Or, lacking proper knowledge about EFS, users may have a false sense of security about its use. For example, a user may think that all files in an encrypted folder are also encrypted, and then may copy the file to a folder on a floppy disk that is not encrypted.

Additional reading

For more information about designing an EFS policy, see the white paper, *Encrypting File System in Windows XP and Windows .NET Server*, under **Additional Reading** on the Web page on the Student Materials CD.

Guidelines for Managing Data Securely

For each area:	Determine:
Data storage location	• How to store data on the network • What data to store locally
Backup strategy	• Who can back up and restore files • How frequently to back up files • How to secure backup media
Auditing	• How to audit data access • How to review data access audit logs
Management permissions	• Who manages data • Where to manage data
Hardware replacement	• How to use hardware redundancy technology • How often to replace hardware
Data retention	• How long to retain data on the network • How and where to archive data from the network

Key points

A proactive management strategy for data helps ensure that your data remains protected. Create policies to manage how your organization stores data and backs up data. Use auditing to ensure that access to data remains secure. Use management permissions to ensure the secure administration of data. Also determine an appropriate length of time that your organization retains data and how you use redundant hardware and hardware replacement schedules to protect against loss of data due to hardware failure.

Additional reading

For more information about managing data securely, see:

- The white paper, *Storage Management Operations Guide*, at: http://www.microsoft.com/technet/prodtechnol/windows2000serv/maintain/opsguide/stormgog.asp.
- The white paper, *Windows 2000 Server Disaster Recovery Guidelines*, under **Additional Reading** on the Web page on the Student Materials CD.
- The white paper, *Managing Windows 2000 Disks and Backup and Restore*, under **Additional Reading** on the Web page on the Student Materials CD.

Practice: Risk and Response

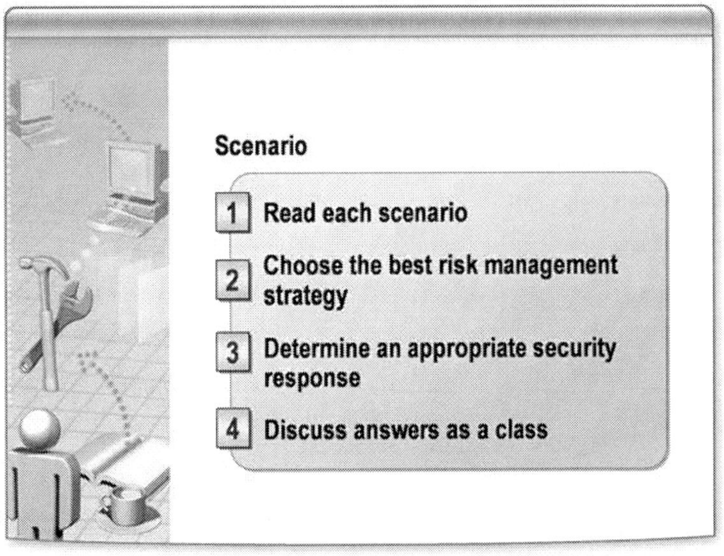

Introduction

For each scenario, choose whether to accept, mitigate, transfer, or avoid the risk that is presented, and then enter an appropriate security response.

Scenario	Risk strategy	Security response
Attacker steals a portable computer that contains critical data		
Many employees have physical access to data servers		
Disgruntled user encrypts all files on her computer before resigning from the organization		

Security Policy Checklist

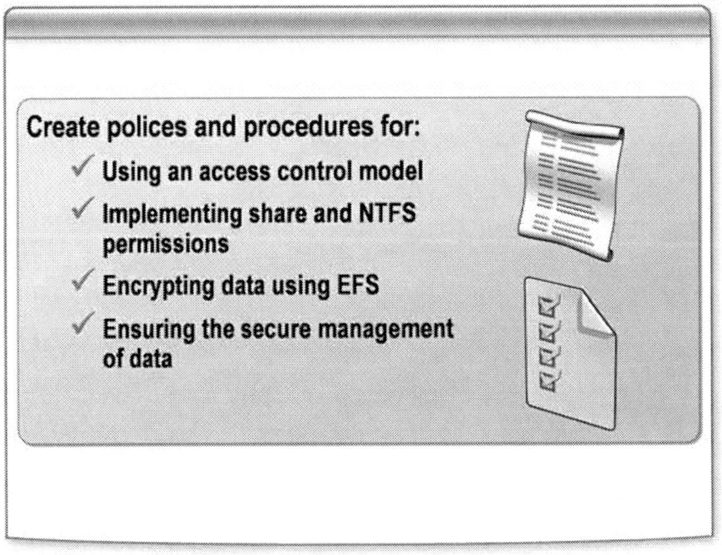

Checklist

Use the following checklist to guide your security design for data.

Phase	Task	Details
Planning	Model threats	STRIDE (Spoofing, Tampering, Repudiation, Information disclosure, Denial of service, and Elevation of privilege) and life cycle threat models
	Manage risks	Qualitative and quantitative risk analysis

Phase	Task	Details
Building	Create policies and procedures for:	Using an access control model Implementing share and NTFS permissions Encrypting data using EFS Ensuring the secure management of data

Lab A: Designing Security for Data

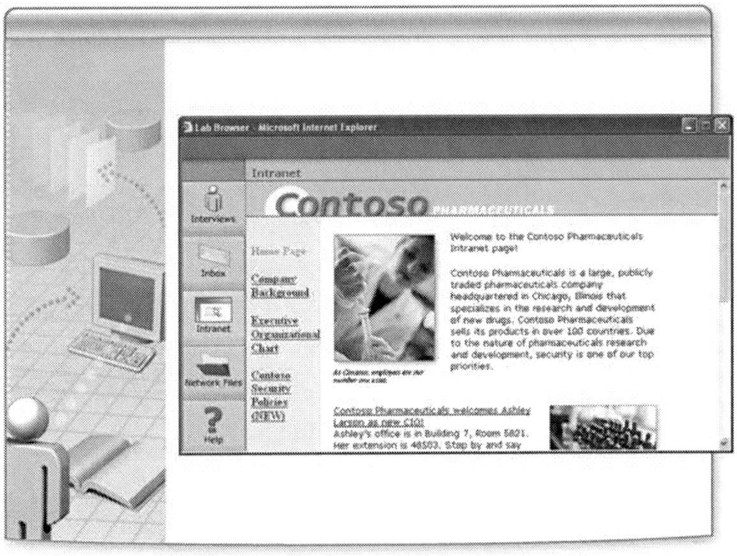

Objectives

After completing this lab, you will be able to apply security design concepts to data.

Scenario

You are a consultant hired by Contoso Pharmaceuticals to help the company design security for its network. Each lab uses an interactive application to convey scenario-based information. To begin a lab, on the desktop, click **Internet Explorer**; this opens a Web page that contains links to each lab. Click a link to begin a lab.

Estimated time to complete this lab: 30 minutes

Work with a lab partner to perform the lab.

► **To complete a lab**

1. Read Ashley Larson's e-mail in each lab to determine the goals for the lab.
2. Click **Reply**, and then type your answer to Ashley's questions.
3. Click **Send** to save your answers to a folder on your desktop.
4. Discuss your answers as a class.

Important In this lab, you can use a Microsoft Visio® file named CP File Permissions Template.vsd and add information to it. If you choose to use the template, rename the file and save it to the Lab Answers folder on your desktop for discussion.

Microsoft®
Training &
Certification

Module 10: Creating a Security Design for Data Transmission

Contents

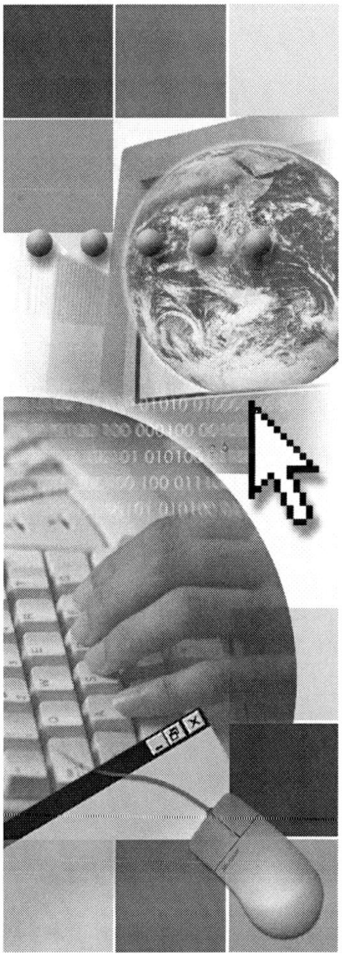

Microsoft®

Overview

- Determining Threats and Analyzing Risks to Data Transmission
- Designing Security for Data Transmission

Introduction

In this module, you will learn how to determine threats and analyze risks to data transmission in an organization. You will also learn how to design security for different types of data transmission, including traffic on local area networks (LANs), wide area networks (WANs), virtual private networks (VPNs), wireless networks, and the Internet.

Objectives

After completing this module, you will be able to:

- Determine threats and analyze risks to data transmission.
- Design security for data transmission.

Lesson: Determining Threats and Analyzing Risks to Data Transmission

- Overview of Data Transmission
- Why Securing Data Transmission Is Important
- Common Vulnerabilities to Data Transmission
- Practice: Analyzing Risks to Data Transmission

Introduction

You can protect data that is stored on your network by securing access to it, but when you transmit data across the network in your organization, the data becomes vulnerable to a variety of additional threats. Attackers can potentially intercept transmitted data, depending on how and where the data is transmitted.

Lesson objectives

After completing this lesson, you will be able to:

- Describe data transmission methods.
- Explain why securing data transmission is important.
- List common vulnerabilities that threaten transmitted data.

Overview of Data Transmission

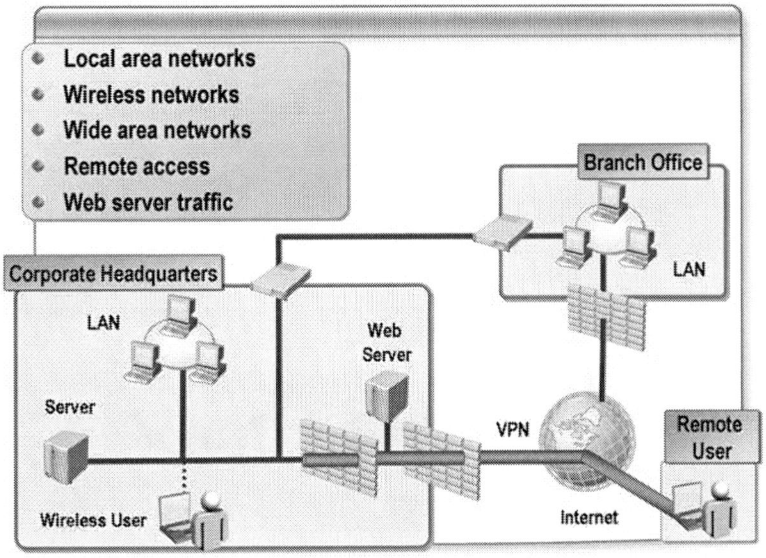

Key points

Data travels over many types of networks in an organization, with different levels of trust associated with them. For example, LANs are generally associated with a high degree of trust because they are located within an organization's physical facilities. Web server traffic is generally associated with a low level of trust because it crosses public links that are outside your organization's control.

When designing security for data transmission, determine the types of networks that your organization uses to transmit data. Common networks include LANs, wireless networks, WANs for branch offices and trusted partners, virtual private networks (VPNs) for remote users, and the Internet.

Why Securing Data Transmission Is Important

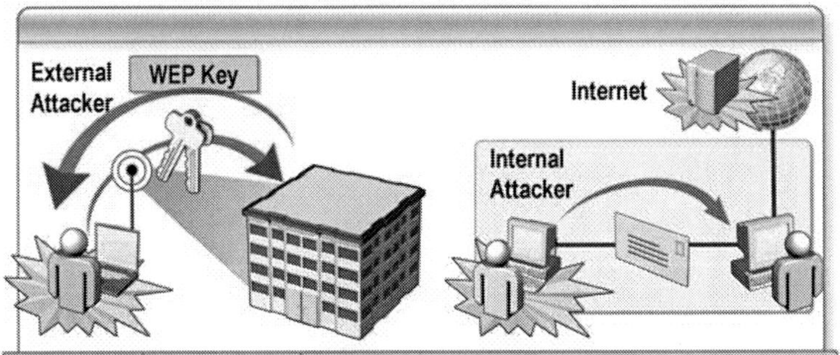

Attacker	Threat	Example
External	Network monitoring	Attacker intercepts wireless LAN packets that are secured with WEP, and then completes an offline attack on the WEP key. The attacker can now connect to the network locally.
Internal	E-mail forgery	Attacker forges an e-mail to the company president from another employee that contains hyperlinks to Web sites that contain offensive content.

External attacker scenario

An attacker sits in a car across the street from an organization and uses a high-powered antenna to intercept packets from the organization's wireless network. After intercepting packets, he performs an offline attack on the packets that were transmitted over the wireless network to obtain the Wired Equivalent Privacy (WEP) key. The attacker configures his portable computer with the WEP key for the organization's WAN and then connects to the organization's network.

Internal attacker scenario

An attacker forges e-mail from another employee and sends a message to the company president. The message contains links to Web sites that contain offensive content. The company terminates the employee who appeared to have sent the offensive e-mail message.

Common Vulnerabilities to Data Transmission

Vulnerability	Attacker:
Network monitoring	• Views authentication traffic • Reads e-mail packets • Views network management traffic • Reads wireless encryption packets
Identity spoofing	• Spoofs IP address to make packets appear to come from the internal network in order to bypass the access control list (ACL) on a router • Forges Internet Control Message Protocol (ICMP) packets to carry out an attack on a third party • Sends forged e-mail from a company official
Data modification	• Uses a man-in-the-middle attack to intercept network traffic • Modifies data in transit
Denial of service	• Floods a computer with Transmission Control Protocol (TCP) synchronization (SYN) messages • Uses multiple computers to automatically flood network

Key points

Threats and vulnerabilities to data transmission differ, depending on the mode of transmission and the goals of the attacker. Threats can range from passive monitoring to malicious disruption of traffic. For example, an attacker who wants to gain knowledge about data as it is transmitted can passively monitor the network from within an organization. This type of attack reveals data but does not interrupt data transmission.

However, an attacker who wants to stop the transmission of traffic entirely can attempt a denial of service (DoS) attack over the Internet that prevents legitimate traffic from flowing to and from a network.

Additional reading

For more information about threats to data transmission, see the white paper, *Security Threats*, at: http://www.microsoft.com/technet/security/bestprac/bpent/sec1/secthret.asp.

Practice: Analyzing Risks to Data Transmission

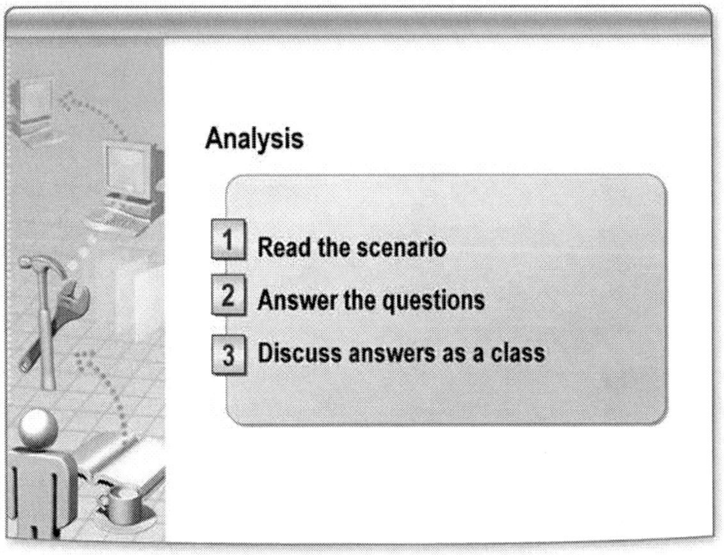

Introduction

Northwind Traders is implementing a Web site so that customers can view their order histories over the Internet. Management has asked you to help design a strategy for securing data transmission. To add security to Web transactions, one of the network administrators recommends using Secure Sockets Layer (SSL) on all sessions to the Web site. She also recommends purchasing and installing an SSL hardware accelerator card.

Management is reluctant to purchase the SSL certificate that is required for using SSL, which costs $2,500. You determine that the SSL hardware accelerator card costs approximately $1,500. After discussing the issue with the other network administrators, you determine that management does not understand the possible threats to the information that will be transmitted.

Question

How would you explain the threats to management to justify the cost of the SSL certificate and SSL hardware accelerator card?

Lesson: Designing Security for Data Transmission

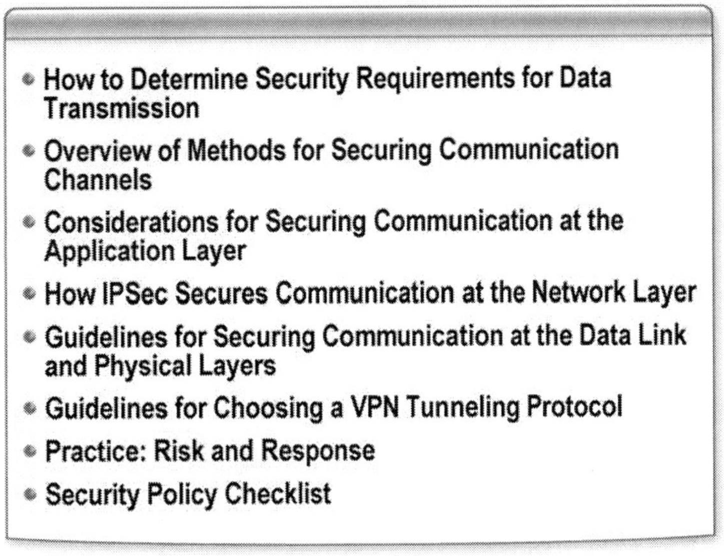

Introduction

Designing security for data transmission requires that you secure communication across the network at the different layers of the four-layer Department of Defense Internet model. Each layer is vulnerable to different threats and therefore requires different methods for securing transmitted data.

Lesson objectives

After completing this lesson, you will be able to:

- Determine security requirements for data transmission.
- List methods for securing communication channels.
- Describe considerations for securing communication at the application layer.
- Describe how Internet Protocol Security (IPSec) secures communication at the network layer.
- List guidelines for securing communication at the data link and physical layers.
- Choose a VPN tunneling protocol.

How to Determine Security Requirements for Data Transmission

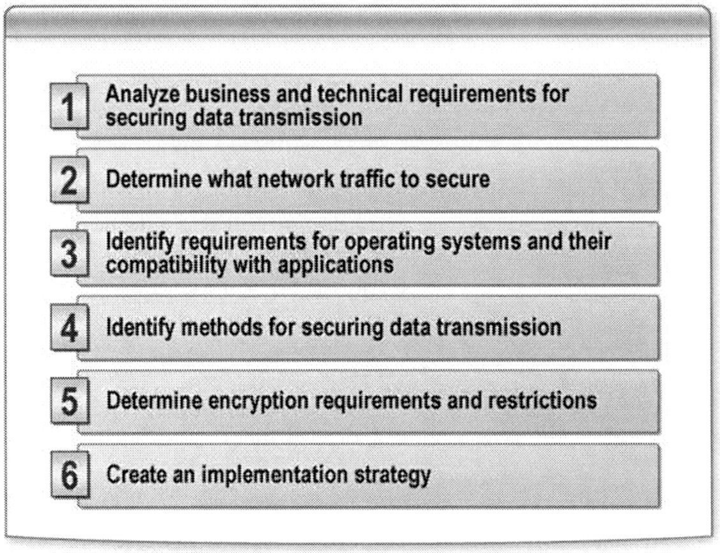

Key points

To determine security requirements for data transmission:

1. *Analyze business and technical requirements for securing data transmission*. Your organization may have specific security requirements for data. For example, you may require encryption of all customer data when it is transmitted over public networks.
2. *Determine what network traffic to secure*. Not all data transmissions require the same level of security. Determine what types of network traffic must be secured, the level of security that they require, and the networks that you use to transmit data.
3. *Identify requirements for operating systems and their compatibility with applications*. Your organization may use applications or operating systems that support different data transmission protocols. You will need to determine how to secure the data despite these differences.
4. *Identify methods for securing data transmission*. There are often several methods that you can use to secure data transmission. Identify the method that is cost effective and provides the level of security that your organization requires.
5. *Determine encryption requirements and restrictions*. Transmission protocols may use a variety of encryption methods. Determine what encryption algorithms to use and the level of encryption strength that is necessary to secure data transmissions. Government or industry regulations for using encryption algorithms may also affect your decision.
6. *Create an implementation strategy*. After you complete your design, ensure that you create an implementation strategy for the security methods, so that your organization deploys and implements them correctly.

Overview of Methods for Securing Communication Channels

Internet model layer	Methods for securing traffic include:
Application	• Secure Sockets Layer (SSL) or Transport Layer Security (TLS) • Server Messenger Block (SMB) signing • Secure Multiuse Internet Mail Extensions (S/MIME) • 802.1x
Network	• IPSec transport mode • IPSec tunnel mode
Data link	• Switches rather than hubs • Port authentication
Physical	• Strong physical security on wiring closets, data centers, ISPs, and co-location facilities • Restrictions on access to the LAN from public areas

Key points

A convenient way to understand data transmission security is to categorize where security can be applied at different layers of the Department of Defense Internet model.

You can use different methods of security to secure data transmission at the application, network, data link, and physical layers.

Note Consider using software that detects network adapters that are running in promiscuous mode.

Considerations for Securing Communication at the Application Layer

What each method provides:		Considerations:
SSL or TLS	Session encryption Session integrity Server authentication	• Is compatible with many applications • Is compatible with all operating systems • Requires the use of digital certificates • Degrades performance
SMB signing	Mutual authentication Data integrity	• Must be enabled on all computers • Is compatible with older operating systems • Can be deployed with GPO
S/MIME	Message encryption Message integrity Nonrepudiation	• Is used with e-mail applications • Requires digital certificates • Is often a complex deployment
802.1x	Mutual authentication Packet encryption Packet integrity	• Is used with wireless networks • Can be used with wired networks • Is used with network hardware • Requires a PKI

Key points

Security protocols at the application layer provide different services and levels of security.

The most common protocols include:

- *SSL or TLS*. These protocols use public key and symmetric key encryption for Transmission Control Protocol (TCP)-based communications. Both SSL and Transport Layer Security (TLS) provide session encryption and integrity and server authentication. SSL and TLS enable clients and servers to communicate in a way that prevents successful eavesdropping, tampering, or message forgery. Both SSL and TLS require the use of digital certificates. To improve the performance of these protocols, add hardware accelerator cards or additional CPUs to servers.
- *SMB signing*. Provides mutual authentication of Server Message Block (SMB) hosts for file and print services. Enabling signing also provides data integrity for SMB messages that are exchanged by SMB hosts, such as when a computer running Microsoft® Windows® 2000 Professional accesses a file share on a computer running Windows 2000 Server. SMB signing may significantly affect the performance of highly used servers, such as domain controllers. You must configure SMB signing on both clients and servers. You can use Group Policy objects to configure SMB signing.

- *S/MIME*. Secure Multipurpose Internet Mail Extensions (S/MIME) is a secure extension of MIME for exchanging digitally signed or encrypted e-mail messages. It protects e-mail messages from interception and forgery by proving message origin and data integrity and performing encryption. S/MIME requires the use of digital certificates.
- *802.1x*. Uses port-based authentication to provide authenticated network access for Ethernet networks, including wireless and wired networks. Port-based network access control uses the physical characteristics of a switched LAN infrastructure to authenticate devices that are attached to a LAN port. It also prevents access to the port if the authentication process fails. 802.1x requires a public key infrastructure (PKI) and a Remote Authentication Dial-In User Service (RADIUS) infrastructure.

Additional reading

For more information about data transmission protocols for the application layer, see:

- RFC 2246, *The TLS Protocol Version 1.0*, under **Additional Reading** on the Web page on the Student Materials CD.
- The white paper, *SSL Protocol Version 3.0*, at: http://wp.netscape.com/eng/ssl3/draft302.txt.
- The white paper, *Web Security*, at: http://www.microsoft.com/technet/security/prodtech/windows/iis/chaptr14.asp.
- The white paper, *Windows 2000 Server and Key Management Server Interoperability*, at: http://www.microsoft.com/technet/prodtechnol/exchange/exchange2000/maintain/optimize/win2kms.asp.
- The white paper, *Wireless 802.11 Security with Windows XP*, under **Additional Reading** on the Web page on the Student Materials CD.
- The white paper, *Enterprise Deployment of IEEE 802.11 Using Windows XP and Windows 2000 Internet Authentication Service*, under **Additional Reading** on the Web page on the Student Materials CD.
- The Web page, *802.1x Authentication*, at: http://msdn.microsoft.com/library/en-us/wceddk40/htm/cmcon8021xAuthentication.asp.

How IPSec Secures Communication at the Network Layer

Elements to configure:	Choices:
IPSec protocol	• Authentication Header (AH), Encapsulating Security Payload (ESP), or both
IPSec mode	• Transport mode or tunnel mode
Authentication protocol	• Kerberos, certificates, or preshared keys
Encryption settings	• For encryption: DES or 3DES for encryption • For integrity: SHA1 or MD5 for integrity • For key exchange: DH key exchange level 1 or 2
Filter list	• Source and destination IP addresses and ports
Filter actions	• Require security, request security, permit traffic, or block traffic

Key points

IPSec is a rule-based security protocol that protects data transmission at the network layer. When two IPSec-enabled computers communicate, they must agree on the IPSec configuration for the session. This agreement is called the *security association*.

IPSec uses the following encryption methods:

- *Data Encryption Standard (DES)*. Consists of a 56-bit symmetric cipher that is no longer considered secure.
- *Triple DES (3DES)*. Consists of a 128-bit symmetric cipher that is based on the DES algorithm.
- *Secure Hash Algorithm (SHA1)*. Creates a 160-bit hash. Required for compliance with Federal Information Processing Standards (FIPS).
- *Message Digest 5 (MD5)*. Creates a 128-bit hash.
- *Diffie-Helman (DH)*. Is an asymmetric key exchange protocol that is based on discrete logarithms.

For all computers that use IPSec, you must design IPSec policies that include the elements that are listed in the preceding slide. Additionally, consider how IPSec affects network performance, network monitoring, and intrusion detection software, as well as how you will deploy IPSec. Also, determine whether IPSec is compatible with any older or non-Microsoft operating systems that your organization uses.

Note By default, IPSec does not secure traffic from Kerberos version 5 authentication protocol in Windows 2000, Resource Reservation Protocol (RSVP), multicast traffic, broadcast traffic, or Internet Key Exchange (IKE). To secure Kerberos protocol traffic and RSVP, follow the instructions in Q254728, *IPSec Does Not Secure Kerberos Traffic Between DCs.*

Additional reading

For more information about IPSec, see:

- The white paper, *IP Security for Microsoft Windows 2000 Server*, under **Additional Reading** on the Web page on the Student Materials CD.
- The Web page, *IP Security Protocol (IPSec)*, at: http://www.ietf.org/html.charters/ipsec-charter.html.
- Q233256, *How to Enable IPSec Traffic Through a Firewall.*

Guidelines for Securing Communication at the Data Link and Physical Layers

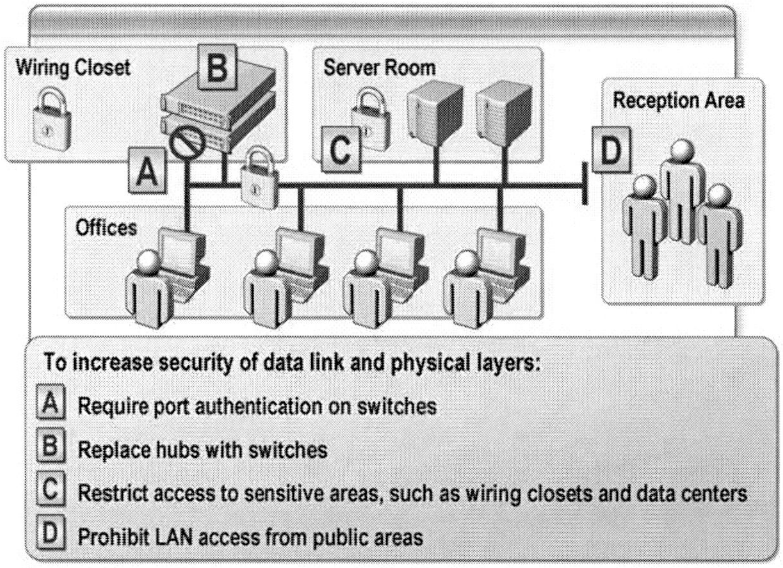

Key points

To prevent attackers from compromising data at the data link and physical layers:

1. *Require port authentication on switches*. You can use 802.1x to authenticate on a port-by-port basis all devices that connect to a switch. Use port authentication to prevent unauthorized devices from connecting to your organization's network.
2. *Replace hubs with switches*. You can make network packet sniffing much more difficult for attackers by replacing passive hubs with active switches.
3. *Restrict access to sensitive areas, such as wiring closets and data centers*. Only authorized personnel should have access to areas where network devices and communication links are physically located. Securing these areas can prevent an attacker from directly connecting to the network or sabotaging equipment.
4. *Prohibit LAN access from public areas*. These areas are generally associated with a low level of trust. Prohibit or greatly restrict access to LAN connections in public areas to prevent attackers from directly accessing your network.

Additional reading

For additional information about securing the physical and data link layers, see:

- The white paper, *Enterprise Deployment of IEEE 802.11 Using Windows XP and Windows 2000 Internet Authentication Service*, under **Additional Reading** on the Web page on the Student Materials CD.
- The Web page, *Sniffing FAQ*, at: http://www.robertgraham.com/pubs/sniffing-faq.html.

Guidelines for Choosing a VPN Tunneling Protocol

If you require:	You can use:	
	PPTP	L2TP/ IPSec
Compatibility with NAT	☑	
User authentication	☑	☑
Computer authentication		☑
Compatibility with other network devices and operating systems		☑
Support for workstations and servers running Windows NT 4.0	☑	☑

Key points

A VPN uses both public and private networks to create a network connection. Windows 2000 Server supports Point-to-Point Tunneling Protocol (PPTP) and Layer Two Tunneling Protocol (L2TP) for securing VPN connections.

- *PPTP*. A Layer 2 protocol that encapsulates Point-to-Point Protocol (PPP) frames in IP datagrams for transmission over IP-based networks, such as the Internet. PPTP uses the Microsoft Point-to-Point Encryption (MPPE) protocol to secure PPTP tunnels.
- *L2TP*. Encapsulates PPP frames that are sent over IP-based or connection-oriented networks, such as frame relay networks. When configured to use IP as its datagram transport, L2TP can be used as a tunneling protocol over the Internet. L2TP has no native encryption method. If you use L2TP in Windows 2000, you must use IPSec to secure the L2TP tunnel.

Considerations for using tunneling protocols include:

- *Compatibility with Network Address Translation (NAT)*. Until NAT-Traversal is fully supported, IPSec cannot be used over NAT, because NAT changes the IP header of packets. If the VPN tunnel passes over a NAT router, you must use PPTP.
- *User authentication*. Both PPTP and L2TP authenticate the user account that initiates the tunnel.
- *Computer authentication*. When using L2TP, IPSec certificates authenticate the Remote Access Service (RAS) client and the RAS server. PPTP does not authenticate computer accounts.
- *Compatibility with other operating systems*. L2TP and IPSec are supported by many operating systems and network devices. PPTP is primarily used by Windows-based computers.

- *Support for workstations running Microsoft Windows NT® version 4.0.* Windows NT 4.0 natively supports the PPTP protocol. With the addition of the L2TP/IPSec VPN client, released in July 2002, Windows NT 4.0 can also support the L2TP and IPSec protocols for VPN connections.

Additional reading

For more information about VPN tunneling protocols, see:

- The white paper, *Virtual Private Networking with Windows 2000: Deploying Remote Access VPNs*, under **Additional Reading** on the Web page on the Student Materials CD.
- The white paper, *Microsoft L2TP/IPSec VPN Client*, at: http://www.microsoft.com/windows2000/server/evaluation/news/bulletins/l2tpclient.asp.
- The Web page, *Virtual Private Networks*, at: http://www.microsoft.com/vpn.
- RFC 2637, *Point-to-Point Tunneling Protocol (PPTP)*, under **Additional Reading** on the Web page on the Student Materials CD.
- RFC 2661, *Layer Two Tunneling Protocol "L2TP"*, under **Additional Reading** on the Web page on the Student Materials CD.

Practice: Risk and Response

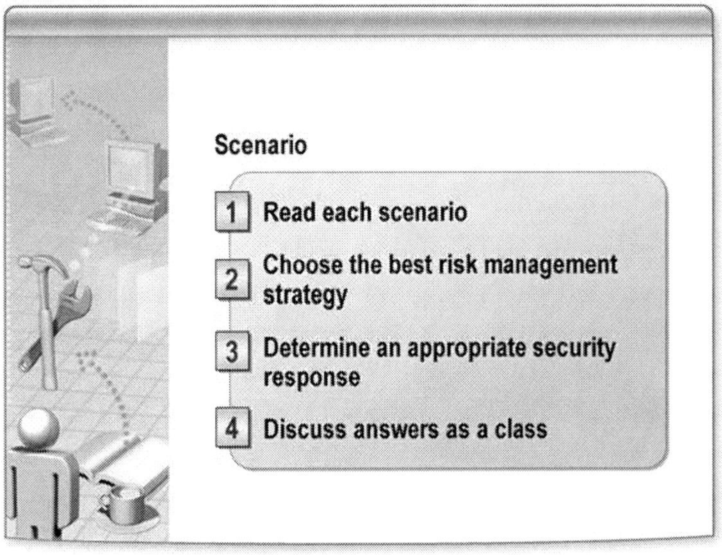

Introduction

For each scenario, choose whether to accept, mitigate, transfer, or avoid the risk that is presented, and then enter an appropriate security response. Then, answer the question.

Scenario	Risk strategy	Security response
Your organization places kiosk computers in the lobby so that visiting customers can check their e-mail. The kiosk is connected to the LAN.		
A network administrator discovers that packets on the network can be modified in transit.		

Question

In each scenario above, which is the greater threat: external attackers or internal attackers?

Security Policy Checklist

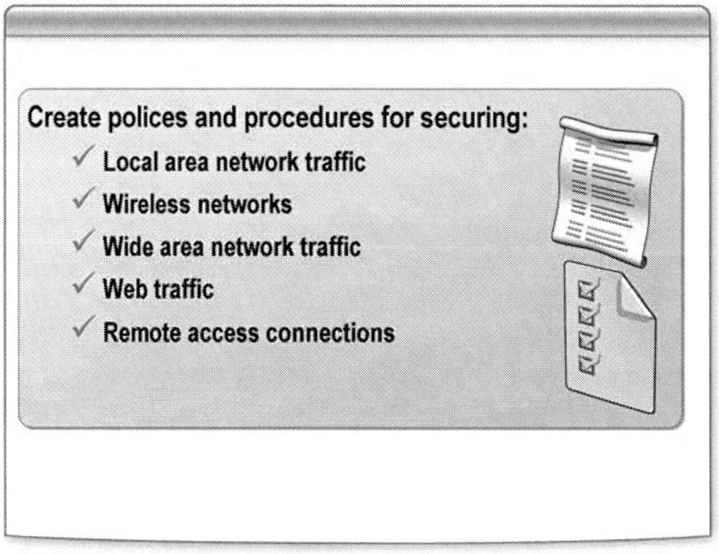

Checklist

Use the following checklist to guide your security design for data transmission.

Phase	Task	Details
Planning	Model threats	STRIDE (Spoofing, Tampering, Repudiation, Information disclosure, Denial of service, and Elevation of privilege) and life cycle threat models
	Manage risks	Qualitative and quantitative risk analysis

Phase	Task	Details
Building	Create policies and procedures for securing:	Local area network traffic
		Wireless networks
		Wide area network traffic
		Web traffic
		Remote access connections

Lab A: Designing Security for Data Transmission

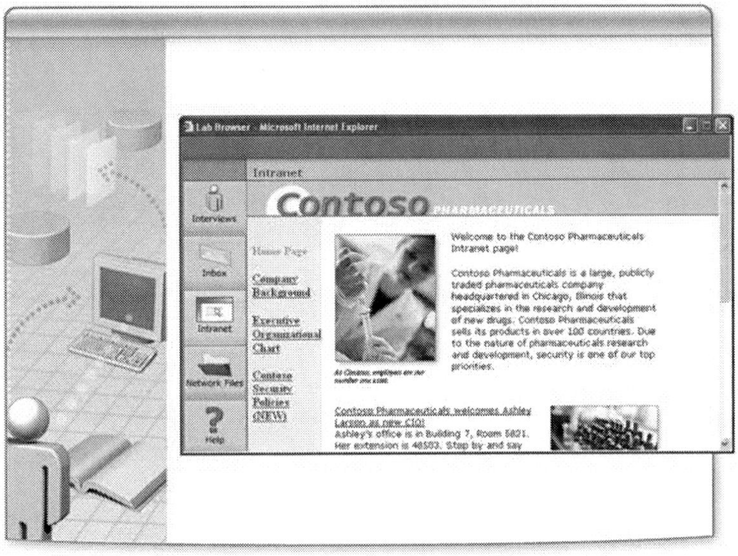

Objectives

After completing this lab, you will be able to apply security design concepts to data transmission.

Scenario

You are a consultant hired by Contoso Pharmaceuticals to help the company design security for its network. Each lab uses an interactive application to convey scenario-based information. To begin a lab, on the desktop, click **Internet Explorer**; this opens a Web page that contains links to each lab. Click a link to begin a lab.

Estimated time to complete this lab: 30 minutes

Work with a lab partner to perform the lab.

► **To complete a lab**

1. Read Ashley Larson's e-mail in each lab to determine the goals for the lab.
2. Click **Reply**, and then type your answer to Ashley's questions.
3. Click **Send** to save your answers to a folder on your desktop.
4. Discuss your answers as a class.

Course Evaluation

Your evaluation of this course will help Microsoft understand the quality of your learning experience.

At a convenient time before the end of the course, please complete a course evaluation, which is available at http://www.CourseSurvey.com.

Microsoft will keep your evaluation strictly confidential and will use your responses to improve your future learning experience.

Microsoft®
Training &
Certification

Module 11: Creating a Security Design for Network Perimeters

Contents

Microsoft®

Overview

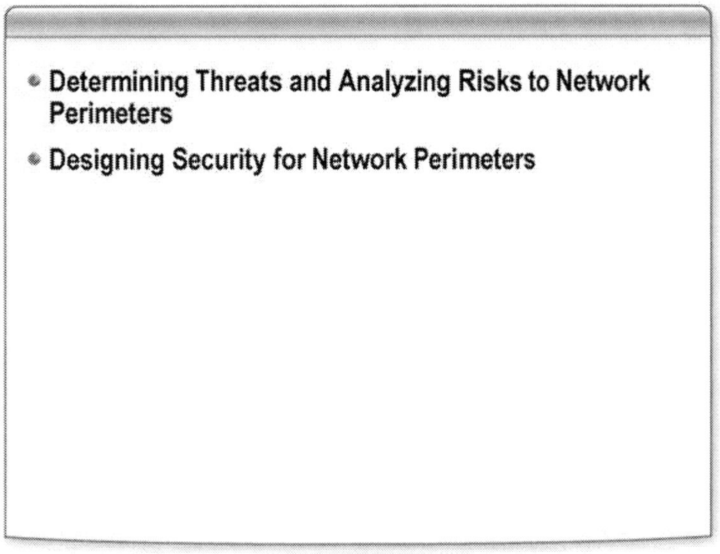

Introduction

In this module, you will learn how to determine threats and analyze risks to network perimeters. You will also learn how to design security for network perimeters, including screened subnets, and for computers that connect directly to the Internet.

Objectives

After completing this module, you will be able to:

- Determine threats and analyze risks to network perimeters.
- Design security for network perimeters.

Lesson: Determining Threats and Analyzing Risks to Network Perimeters

- What Is the Perimeter of a Network?
- Why Perimeter Security Is Important
- Common Vulnerabilities to Perimeter Security
- Practice: Analyzing Risks to Network Perimeters

Introduction

The perimeter, or boundary, of a network is where your organization ends and the area outside your organization begins. Perimeters are not always easy to identify. Attackers who penetrate weaknesses in your perimeter can potentially access information on your network.

Lesson objectives

After completing this lesson, you will be able to:

- Describe the perimeter of a network.
- Explain the importance of perimeter security.
- List common vulnerabilities to perimeter security.

What Is the Perimeter of a Network?

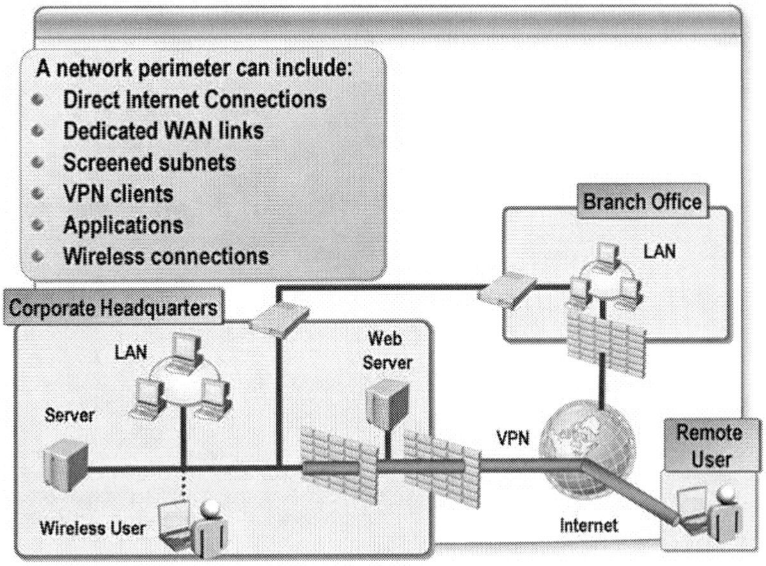

Key points

A perimeter is any point that connects to networks outside of an organization. In a typical network, perimeter points can include:

- *Direct Internet connections*. Any connection to the Internet from within an organization.
- *Dedicated WAN links*. Wide area network (WAN) links to branch offices, trusted partners, or other facilities outside of the organization.
- *Screened subnets*. Protected areas within a network that run services, such as business-to-business (B2B) services, that the organization exposes to public networks, such as the Internet.
- *VPN clients*. A virtual private network (VPN) tunnel to remote users who are accessing the internal network across a public network.
- *Applications*. Organizations may run applications that access the Internet or access services running in a screened subnet.
- *Wireless connections*. Access to wireless networks can often be gained from outside of an organization's physical facilities.

Why Perimeter Security Is Important

Attacker	Threat	Example
External	Information disclosure	An attacker runs a series of port scans on a network and creates a virtual network diagram and vulnerability list. The attacker uses this information to attack the network systematically.
Internal	Denial of service	An employee opens an e-mail message from an external Web-based e-mail account that contains a new worm virus. The virus infects the internal network from inside the perimeter.

Key points

Assets are vulnerable to threats from both external and internal attackers. For example:

External attacker scenario

An external attacker runs a series of port scans on a network. The attacker uses the information to create a network diagram of the perimeter, including computers in the screened subnet, operating systems of network devices and computers, services running in the screened subnet, and the level of security that is implemented on the network. The attacker researches known vulnerabilities of these network devices, computers, and services, and then attacks the network systematically.

Internal attacker scenario

An employee receives an e-mail from a friend through an external Web-based e-mail account. When the employee opens a file that is enclosed in the e-mail, a new worm virus automatically spreads to all computers on the internal network. The traffic from the spreading virus slows legitimate traffic, resulting in a denial of service (DoS) for network users.

Common Vulnerabilities to Perimeter Security

Vulnerability	Example
Exposure of network information	• TCP and UDP port scans • Internet Control Message Protocol (ICMP) packet scans of network perimeters • Capturing of service banners • Analysis of packets
Lack of control over infrastructure	• Unauthorized Web servers • Forgotten connections to the Internet • Unmanaged VPN clients • Uncontrolled use of applications
Exposure of computers to attack	• Denial-of-service attacks • Exposure of account information • E-mail worms • Unauthorized access to data • Destruction of data

Key points

Of all the areas of your network, the network perimeter has the greatest exposure to public networks and therefore is one of the areas most threatened by attack. Before Internet connectivity became common, an organization's network often maintained only one connection to a public network.

Today, Internet access, remote access, and branch office connectivity have become vital to the operation of an organization. As organizations increase their requirements for connectivity, the difficulty of managing network connections increases, and so does the risk that information and computers may be exposed to attack.

Additional reading

For more information about common attacks to network perimeters, see:

- The Web page, *Hacking Methods*, on the Internet Security Systems Web site, at: http://www.iss.net/security_center/advice/Underground/Hacking/Methods/Technical/default.htm.
- The white paper, *Managing the Threat of Denial-of-Service Attacks*, on the CERT Coordination Center Web site, at: http://www.cert.org/archive/pdf/Managing_DoS.pdf.

Practice: Analyzing Risks to Network Perimeters

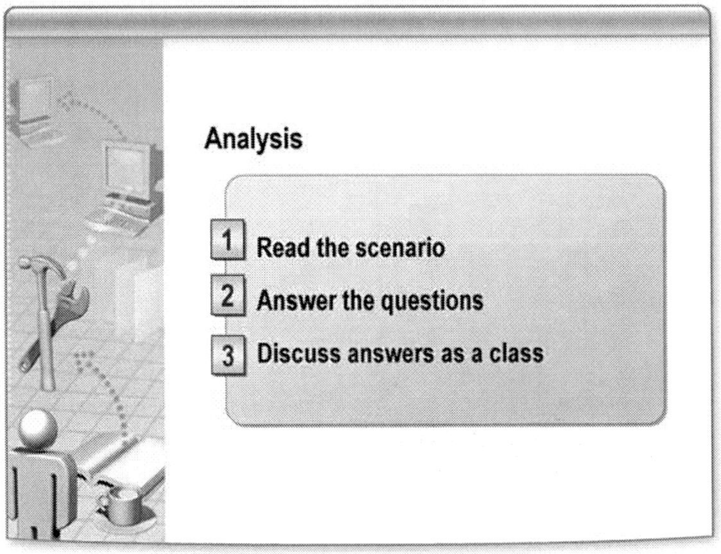

Introduction

Northwind Traders has 10,000 users who work in one facility. All users have computers running Microsoft® Windows® 2000 that belong to an Active Directory® directory service domain. Northwind Traders recently deployed a Web server so that employees can retrieve their e-mail messages.

The IT manager has asked you to explain how a Land attack and a SYN flood attack (or SYN-ACK attack) can prevent users from retrieving their e-mail. Use the Internet to locate information about how Land and SYN-ACK attacks affect perimeter security.

Questions

1. What is a Land attack, and how can it prevent users from receiving their e-mail messages?

2. What is a SYN-ACK or SYN flood attack, and how can it prevent users from receiving their e-mail messages?

Lesson: Designing Security for Network Perimeters

- Common Network Perimeter Designs
- Steps for Designing Secure Screened Subnets
- How Perimeter Devices Protect a Network
- Guidelines for Protecting Computers on a Perimeter
- Practice: Risk and Response
- Security Policy Checklist

Introduction

A perimeter of a network is by nature a place of low trust. You must ensure that your network perimeter is secure and that it provides the services that you, your customers, and your partners require. Identify the perimeter, decide what services you will provide in the perimeter, and determine how you will securely manage and monitor these services. You can also use firewalls and hardware devices to secure your network perimeter from attack.

Lesson objectives

After completing this lesson, you will be able to:

- Describe common network perimeter designs.
- Explain the steps for designing a secure screened subnet.
- Explain how perimeter devices protect a network.
- List guidelines for protecting computers on a perimeter.

Common Network Perimeter Designs

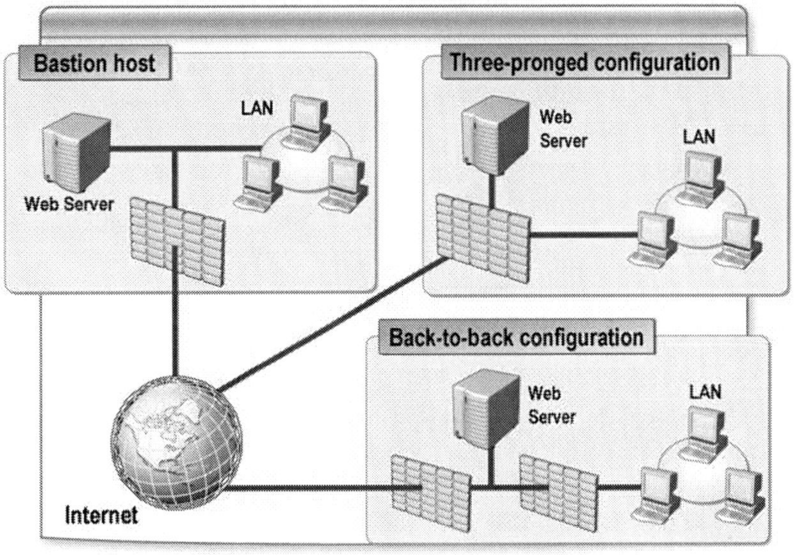

Key points

The design of a secure network perimeter includes protection for the internal network or local area network (LAN). On the perimeter, you can use a firewall or a *screened subnet*, which is an area of limited trust on networks, such as a Web server that is exposed to the Internet. A screened subnet is sometimes called a DMZ, demilitarized zone, or a perimeter network, because it is often a small network located on the edge of the main network. You can use routers and firewalls to screen traffic that goes in and out of a screened subnet.

Types of network perimeters include:

- *Bastion host.* Acts as the main connection for computers on the internal network that are accessing the Internet. As a firewall, the bastion host is designed to defend against attacks that are aimed at the internal network. Smaller networks typically use bastion hosts to protect the internal network from intruders.

  A bastion host uses two network adapters, one connected to the internal network and one connected to the Internet. This configuration physically isolates the internal network from potential intruders on the Internet. However, the bastion host is only a single line of defense between an internal network and the Internet.

- *Three-pronged configuration.* Gives users on the Internet limited access to network resources, while preventing unwanted traffic to computers that are located on the LAN. A three-pronged configuration uses a firewall with three network adapters—one connected to the LAN, one connected to a screened subnet that is separate from the LAN, and one connected to the Internet. A three-pronged configuration isolates the internal network from the Internet and also permits limited access from the Internet and the internal network to the screened subnet.

- *Back to back configuration*. Places the screened subnet between two firewalls. The two firewalls are connected to the screened subnet; one firewall is connected to the Internet, and the other firewall is connected to the internal network. In this configuration, there is no single point of access from the Internet to the LAN. To reach the internal network, an attacker would need to get past both firewalls.

Additional reading

For more information about designing screened subnets, see:

- The *Design a Firewall System* practice on the CERT Coordination Center Web site, at: http://www.cert.org/security-improvement/#practices.
- The white paper, *ISA Server Installation and Deployment Guide*, under **Additional Reading** on the Web Page on the Student Materials CD.

Steps for Designing Secure Screened Subnets

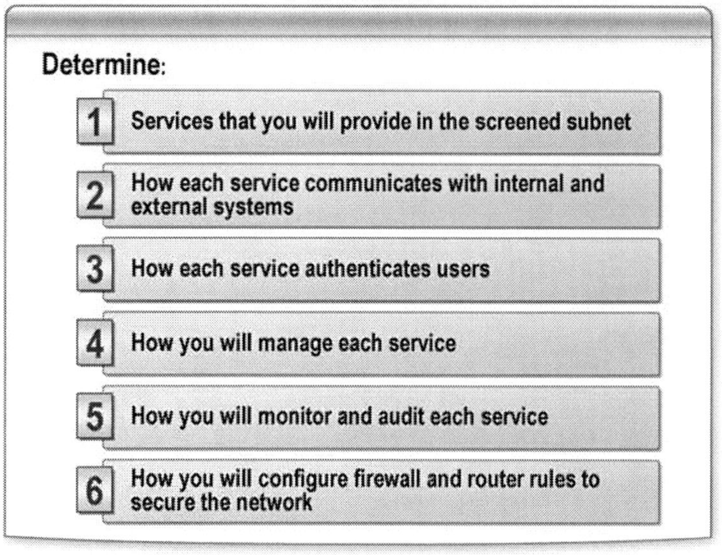

Key points

When designing secure screened subnets, determine:

1. *Services that you will provide in the screened subnet.* The computer that runs each service in the screened subnet, such as Simple Mail Transfer Protocol (SMTP) and Web servers, must be secured against threats to the service.
2. *How each service communicates with internal and external systems.* Determine which protocols and ports each service requires for inbound and outbound communication. The firewall administrator uses this information to configure ingress and egress filtering.
3. *How each service authenticates users.* Determine how you will authenticate users and the security that the authentication protocol provides. Ensure that users can be authenticated securely. It is very difficult to detect attackers who have gained valid credentials due to a poorly designed authentication strategy.
4. *How you will manage each service.* Determine how you will manage services that run on the internal network and from the Internet. Be sure to include processes for applying security patches to the computers that run each service.
5. *How you will monitor and audit each service.* Determine how you will audit each service, how often you will audit each service, and who will be responsible for monitoring the audit logs for suspicious events.
6. *How you will configure firewall and router rules to secure the network.* Use the information from steps 1 to 5 to determine how to configure the firewalls and routers. Work with your firewall administrator to implement and test the configurations.

Additional reading

For more information about determining the protocols and ports that services use, see:

- The list, *Port Numbers*, at the Internet Assigned Numbers Authority (IANA) Web site, at: http://www.iana.org/assignments/port-numbers.
- The list, *Protocol Numbers*, at the IANA Web site, at: http://www.iana.org/assignments/protocol-numbers.
- Q281336, *How to Determine Which Program Uses or Blocks Specific TCP Ports.*
- Q289241, *A List of the Windows 2000 Domain Controller Default Ports.*

How Perimeter Devices Protect a Network

Device	Secures network by using:
Router	• Packet filtering • Routing rules
Firewall	• Packet filtering • Stateful packet inspection • Application gateway • Server publishing • User-based authentication • Intrusion detection

Routers and firewalls do not:

- **Filter traffic that does not pass through them**
- **Defend against attacks after a network has been penetrated**
- **Stop traffic that appears legitimate**
- **Make intelligent decisions based on packet contents**
- **Inspect encrypted traffic**

Key points

You can secure screened subnets by using the following security mechanisms on routers and firewalls:

- *Packet filtering.* Permits or blocks IP-based packets according to packet filtering rules that include criteria such as source and destination IP addresses and ports.
- *Routing rules.* Determine how to route network traffic after it arrives at the router. You can configure router rules to permit or deny traffic to certain networks.
- *Stateful packet inspection.* Prevents TCP and User Datagram Protocol (UDP) traffic from traversing ports after initial communication has been established.
- *Application gateway.* Uses detailed knowledge of how an application communicates with other applications to communicate securely with outside networks.
- *Server publishing.* Makes services available to the Internet from a screened subnet or internal network without direct connectivity to the Internet.
- *User-based authentication.* Enables network administrators to determine which users can access different types of Internet resources. Administrators can also track each user's use of Internet resources.
- *Intrusion detection.* Passive or active monitoring that detects possible security compromises and reports them to administrators.

Additional reading

For more information about firewalls, see:

- The white paper, *Security with Internet Security and Acceleration Server 2000*, under **Additional Reading** on the Web page on the Student Materials CD.
- The white paper, *Deploying Firewalls*, at: http://www.sei.cmu.edu/pub/documents/sims/pdf/sim008.pdf.

Guidelines for Protecting Computers on a Perimeter

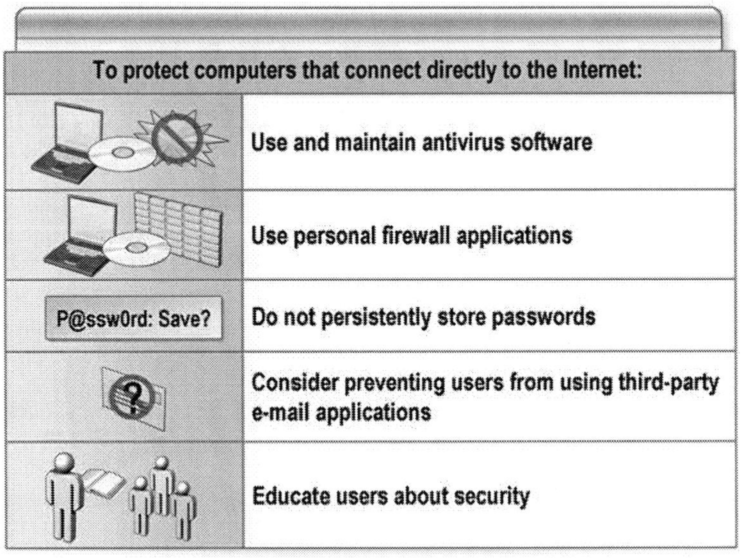

Key points

For computers or traveling users that connect directly to the Internet or other networks that are not trusted, follow these guidelines:

- *Use and maintain antivirus software.* Third-party antivirus software can prevent attacks from such threats as viruses, Trojan horse applications, and worms.
- *Use personal firewall applications.* Internet Connection Firewall (ICF) and third-party personal firewalls are smaller versions of enterprise firewalls that provide protection from attackers on the Internet.
- *Do not persistently store passwords.* Users that store passwords, such as Remote Access Service (RAS) or logon passwords, on their computers expose their user accounts and the network to attack.
- *Consider preventing users from using third-party e-mail applications.* Any e-mail applications that access the Web can spread viruses because they circumvent the mail servers that use the organization's firewall.
- *Educate users about security.* Increasing user awareness through information campaigns and training can help change behavior and prevent users from creating network vulnerabilities.

Additional reading

For more information, see:

- The Web page, *5-Minute Security Advisor - Using the Internet Connection Firewall*, at: http://www.microsoft.com/technet/columns/security/5min/5min-204.asp.
- The Web page, *Virus Alerts*, at: http://www.microsoft.com/technet/security/virus/alerts/default.asp.
- The white paper, *Securing Mobile Computers with Windows XP Professional*, under **Additional Reading** on the Web page on the Student Materials CD.

Practice: Risk and Response

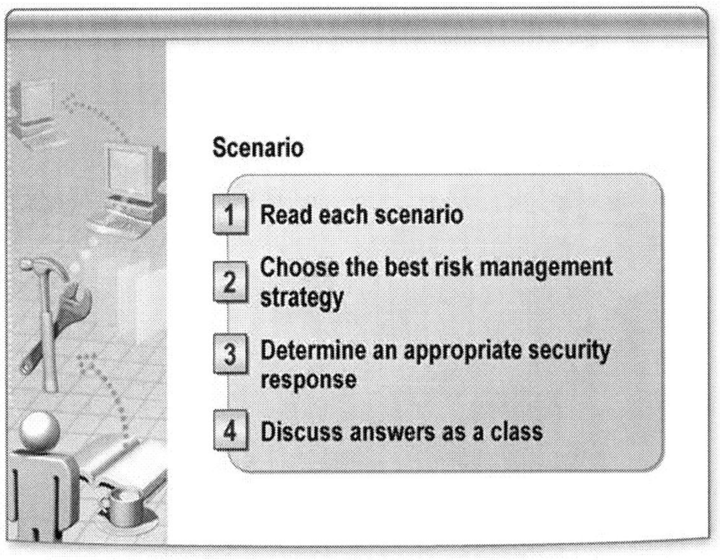

Introduction

For each scenario, choose whether to accept, mitigate, transfer, or avoid the risk presented, and then enter an appropriate security response.

Scenario	Risk strategy	Security response
A home user with a cable modem connects to the corporate network by using VPN		
Your organization uses a bastion host firewall to protect a small branch office		

Security Policy Checklist

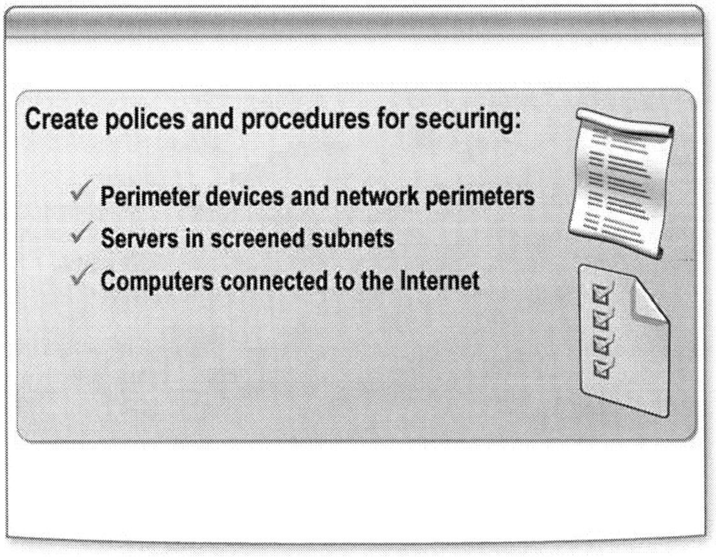

Checklist

Use the following checklist to guide your security design for network perimeters.

Phase	Task	Details
Planning	Model threats	STRIDE (Spoofing, Tampering, Repudiation, Information disclosure, Denial of service, and Elevation of privilege) and life cycle threat models
	Manage risks	Qualitative and quantitative risk analysis

Phase	Task	Details
Building	Create policies and procedures for securing:	Perimeter devices and network perimeters Servers in screened subnets Computers connected to the Internet

Lab A: Designing Security for Network Perimeters

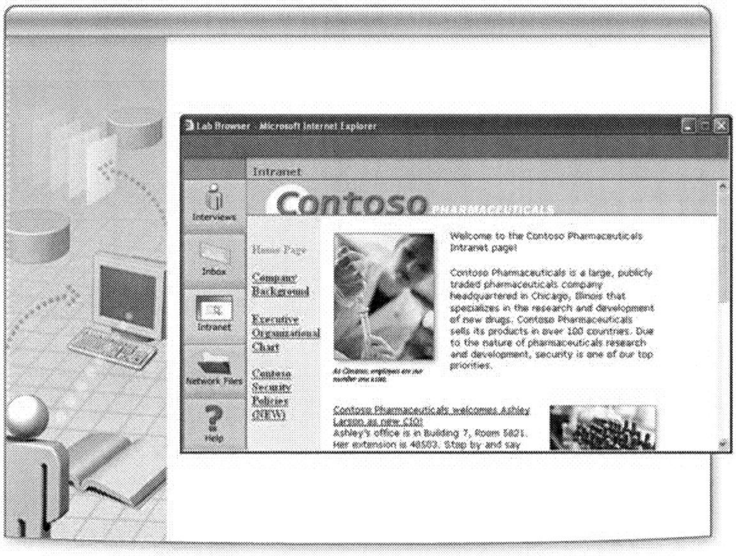

Objectives

After completing this lab, you will be able to apply security design concepts to network perimeters.

Scenario

You are a consultant hired by Contoso Pharmaceuticals to help the company design security for its network. Each lab uses an interactive application to convey scenario-based information. To begin a lab, on the desktop, click **Internet Explorer**; this opens a Web page that contains links to each lab. Click a link to begin a lab.

Estimated time to complete this lab: 30 minutes

Work with a lab partner to perform the lab.

► **To complete a lab**

1. Read Ashley Larson's e-mail in each lab to determine the goals for the lab.
2. Click **Reply**, and then type your answer to Ashley's questions.
3. Click **Send** to save your answers to a folder on your desktop.
4. Discuss your answers as a class.

Microsoft®
Training &
Certification

Module 12: Designing Responses to Security Incidents

Contents

Microsoft®

Overview

- Introduction to Auditing and Incident Response
- Designing an Audit Policy
- Designing an Incident Response Procedure

Introduction

Network security for an organization is an exercise in prevention. A good security design that is properly implemented will prevent a majority of the most common attacks. However, it is very likely that an attacker will eventually penetrate the defenses that you design.

When an attack happens, the key to limiting damage is early detection and a rapid and orderly response. Auditing is an important tool to help you detect network abnormalities that may indicate attacks. An incident response procedure is a series of steps that you design in advance to guide your organization during a security incident.

Objectives

After completing this module, you will be able to:

- Explain the importance of auditing and incident response.
- Design an auditing policy.
- Design an incident response procedure.

Lesson: Introduction to Auditing and Incident Response

- **The Auditing Process**
- **Why Auditing Is Important**
- **What Is an Incident Response Procedure?**
- **Why an Incident Response Procedure Is Important**

Introduction

Auditing and incident response provide you with the means to detect and maintain a record of network events. They also give you a procedure to respond to events that you determine are attacks.

Lesson objectives

After completing this lesson, you will be able to:

- Describe the auditing process.
- Explain why auditing is important.
- Describe an incident response procedure.
- Explain why an incident response procedure is important.

The Auditing Process

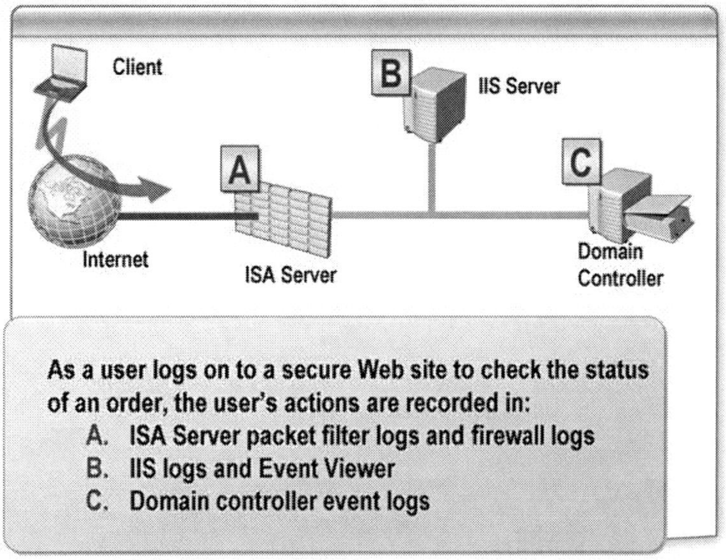

Key points

Auditing records specific events on a network. By auditing events on computers and applications, you can compare the audit logs on each computer to understand the actions of a user or an attacker.

For example, consider a computer running Microsoft® Windows® 2000 Server and also Microsoft Internet Security and Acceleration (ISA) Server that is functioning as a firewall. ISA Server protects a Web site on a computer running Windows 2000 Server and Internet Information Services (IIS). When a customer on the Internet accesses the Web server, he is authenticated by Basic authentication over Secure Sockets Layer (SSL) to an Active Directory® directory services domain controller.

In this example, when you enable auditing on the computers and applications, you can determine a user's actions by examining the following:

1. *Packet filter log file.* By analyzing the packet filter log file, you determine that a computer with the IP address 131.107.1.31 created a SSL session with the Web server, which is published on the ISA Server firewall, for approximately 4 minutes, from 13:27 Pacific Daylight Time (PDT) to 13:31 PDT.
2. *Security event log file from the IIS server and the IIS log file.* By analyzing the Security event log file on the Web server, you determine that a user attempted to log on by using the account Ben and failed twice before succeeding at 13:29:07 PDT.

   By analyzing the IIS log file, you determine that the computer with the IP address 131.107.1.31 used a computer running Windows 2000 and Microsoft Internet Explorer version 5.01 to attempt to enroll a certificate from the *Certsrv* Web site.
3. *Security event log file from the domain controller.* By analyzing the Security event log file on the domain controller, you determine that the user who logged on by using the account Ben failed to log on twice due to using a bad password before ultimately succeeding.

Note To ensure that you can accurately compare audit logs from different computers and resources, synchronize the times of all audited computers and resources on your network.

Additional reading

To analyze the log files that are used in this example, see the files in the Log files folder, under **Additional Reading** on the Web page on the Student Materials CD.

Why Auditing Is Important

Attacker	Threat	Example
External	Brute force attack	After many failed attempts, an attacker gains access to the network, creates a legitimate user account, and uses it to access information on the network.
Internal	Misuse of administrator rights	A help desk administrator uses administrative rights to change his supervisor's password to read her e-mail and access personnel records.

External attacker scenario

An attacker locates a Simple Mail Transfer Protocol (SMTP) server in the screened subnet of a company. The attacker generates random passwords and runs a script that attempts to use the passwords to log on to the SMTP server. After two weeks and several thousand attempts, the attacker discovers the correct password for the account named Administrator. The attacker then uses this account to create accounts to access information on the network. Because auditing is not enabled, there is no record of the failed logon attempts or of the creation of additional user accounts.

Internal attacker scenario

A help desk administrator uses administrative rights to temporarily change the password of his supervisor's account, and then uses the new password to log on to the network. The help desk administrator reads his supervisor's e-mail and accesses her personnel records to determine the salaries of his coworkers. The administrator changes the password to its original setting. Because auditing is not enabled, there is no record of the security incident.

What Is an Incident Response Procedure?

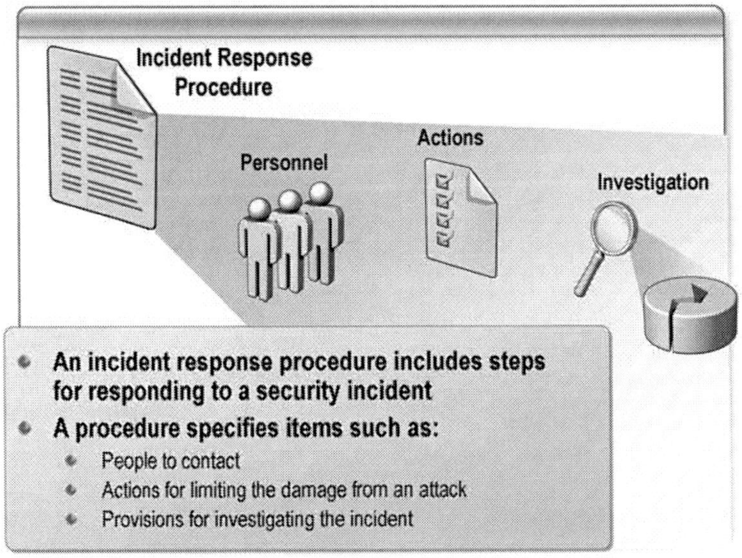

Key points

Incident response describes how your organization reacts to an attack or other types of security incidents on your network. Too often, in an effort to respond quickly, organizations respond to security incidents in an ad-hoc manner. Mistakes due to chaotic responses can cause loss of prestige, assets, and revenue. Poor incident response also makes it difficult to learn about the origins of the incident or how to prevent similar incidents from occurring in the future.

By creating and using an incident response procedure, individuals in your organization can respond efficiently during and after a security incident.

An incident response procedure can help your organization:

- Prevent the mishandling of potential evidence.
- Contain the spread of the security incident.
- Limit the damages that may result from the security incident.
- Control the release of information about the security incident.
- Quickly recover from the effects of a security incident.

Why an Incident Response Procedure Is Important

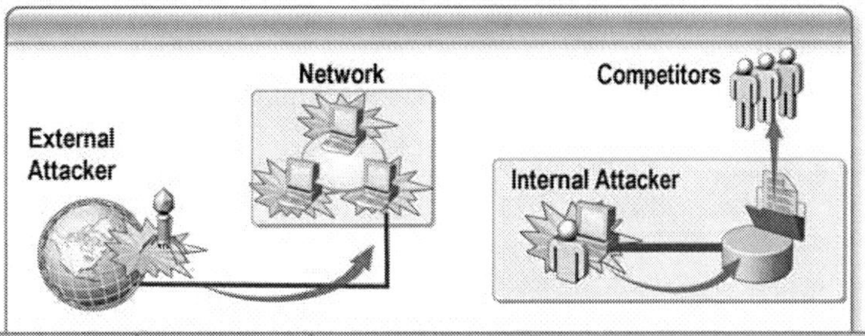

Attacker	Threat	Example
External	Uncoordinated response	A virus over the Internet exploits a known vulnerability on the network. Despite previous attacks, the organization does not identify and respond to the virus until all computers on the network are infected.
Internal	Failure to maintain the chain of evidence	A company suspects that an employee is selling confidential information to a competitor. During the investigation, a routine network update changes files on the suspect's computer.

External attacker scenario

A virus that an external attacker created penetrates the internal network from the Internet by exploiting a known vulnerability. Despite previous virus attacks, the organization struggles to identify the attack. Some network administrators recognize the virus and remove it from computers, only to discover that those computers are infected again from the network. By the time the organization identifies the virus and communicates the information to all administrators, all computers on the network are infected.

Internal attacker scenario

A company notices that a competitor appears to receive advanced knowledge about its marketing plans. The company suspects that one of its employees is selling confidential information to the competitor. Management attempts to detect and isolate the *chain of evidence*, or the records that will indicate that the suspect actually committed a crime. During the investigation, a routine update to the network changes several files on the suspect's computer and renders the evidence on the computer inadmissible in court.

Lesson: Designing an Audit Policy

- Steps for Planning an Audit Policy
- Guidelines for Creating a Framework for Auditing
- Common Auditing Tools and Sources
- Guidelines for Designing an Audit Review Process
- Practice: Risk and Response
- Security Policy Checklist

Introduction

You use an audit policy to audit specifically for security threats. To design an audit policy, use a framework to help you determine what to audit, how to audit, and when and how to review the data that you collect.

Lesson objectives

After completing this lesson, you will be able to:

- List steps for planning an audit policy.
- Explain guidelines for creating an auditing framework.
- Describe common auditing tools.
- Explain guidelines for reviewing audit data.

Steps for Planning an Audit Policy

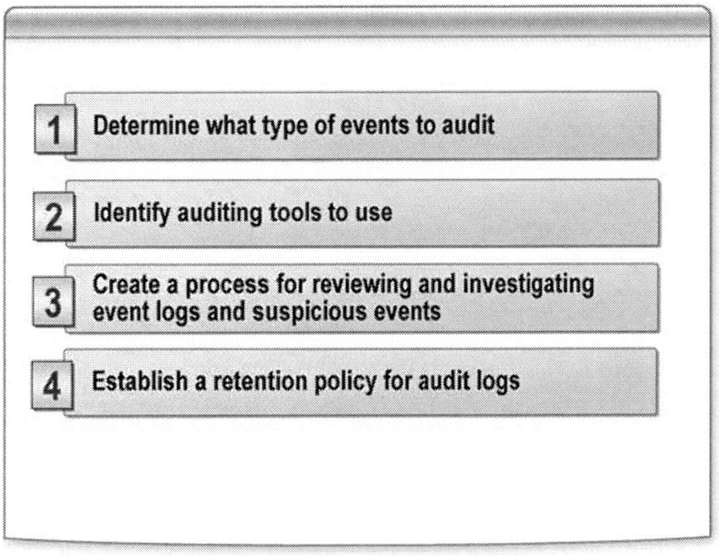

Key points

By planning an audit policy for security, you can ensure that the events that you audit help your organization meet business and technical goals, that you audit all required events on all relevant computers and resources, and that you monitor the log files in a timely and organized manner.

Complete the following steps:

1. *Determine what type of events to audit.* Work with business and technical decision makers to determine what types of events to audit. Excessive auditing often degrades system performance, which makes it more difficult to locate suspicious events.
2. *Identify auditing tools to use.* Work with your IT staff to identify the appropriate auditing tools to record events that you decide to audit.
3. *Create a process for reviewing and investigating event logs and suspicious events.* Work with technical decision makers to assign responsibility for reviewing audit log files. Also, create a process with the IT staff for reviewing and investigating suspicious events.
4. *Establish a retention policy for audit logs.* Define how long your organization will retain audit logs and how the logs will be stored.

Guidelines for Creating a Framework for Auditing

Create audit statements that define:

- **The general type of security event that you want to track**
- **The audit event details that will best record a security event**
- **The computers or resources to be audited**

Audit statement component	Example
Type of event	To track user logon attempts to the network...
Event details	...log successful and failed logon attempts, time of day, the type of logon, and origin of the attempt...
Audit point	...for all users and domain controllers

Key points

Audit only events and resources that you need to track later. Globally auditing all events will cause event logs to grow to an unmanageable size.

An *audit statement* helps you define what events to monitor, the level of detail to audit, and the computers or resources to audit. By creating audit statements, you ensure that you only audit events that are relevant to business goals or technical requirements. Audit statements also help to ensure that you audit events on all necessary computers and network devices to capture the intended action.

Common Auditing Tools and Sources

Resource:	Tools and sources:
Operating systems	• Event Viewer • EventComb • Microsoft Operations Manager • Custom scripts
Web sites	• IIS logs • URLScan
Network perimeters	• Router logs • Firewall logs • Packet filtering logs • Proxy logs
Applications	• Application-specific logs • Intrusion-detection software • Antivirus software • Microsoft Operations Manager

Key points

You can choose from a variety of auditing tools and sources to record and examine events on your network. Auditing tools record and report events in different ways. To help identify how each tool records and reports common events, consider using a test environment to record different types of events.

Additional reading

For more information about auditing tools, see:

- The Web site, *Microsoft Operations Manager*, at: http://www.microsoft.com/mom.
- Q302372, *HOW TO: Configure Logging in ISA Server*.
- Q313437, *HOW TO: Enable Logging in IIS 5.0*.
- Chapter 6, "Auditing and Intrusion Detection," in *Security Operations Guide for Windows 2000 Server*, under **Additional Reading** on the Web page on the Student Materials CD.

Guidelines for Designing an Audit Review Process

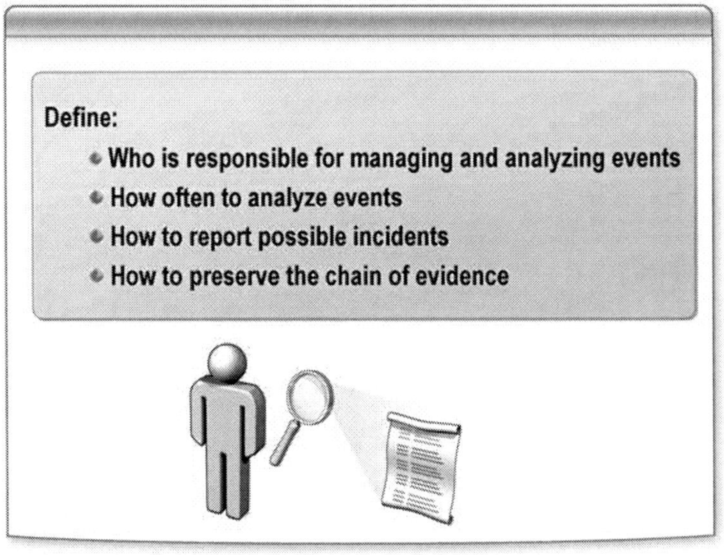

Key points

You can examine audit logs to determine whether a security incident is underway, to investigate a security incident, and to provide evidence of a security violation.

When designing an audit review process, define:

- *Who is responsible for managing and analyzing events.* You must ensure that individuals are held responsible for managing and analyzing events for abnormalities. Ensure that the employees who analyze events can determine whether the recorded events are normal. For example, you may want managers to review the logon times of their employees for abnormal behavior. Additionally, you can use custom scripts to automate searching for certain events that your organization considers suspicious.
- *How often to analyze events.* Ensure that employees who are responsible for analyzing events review the audit logs regularly. The maximum interval between reviews should be frequent enough to detect suspicious behavior before the security of the network is compromised.
- *How to report possible incidents to management.* Define how the employees who are responsible for analyzing security events will escalate suspicious events or possible security incidents, and to whom they should report events. This planning will help your organization initiate its incident response procedure when necessary.
- *How to preserve the chain of evidence.* Define how your organization maintains and preserves audit log files to ensure that they are usable in a security investigation and, if necessary, admissible in court as legal evidence.

Practice: Risk and Response

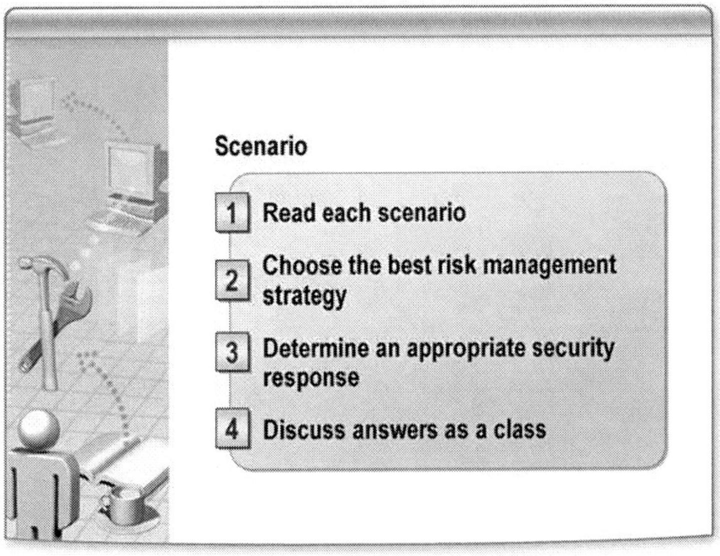

Introduction

For each scenario, choose whether to accept, mitigate, transfer, or avoid the risk that is presented, and then enter an appropriate security response.

Scenario	Risk strategy	Security response
Auditing is not enabled. If an attacker compromises the network, it would be difficult for the organization to prove that the security incident occurred.		
Although auditing is enabled, no one is responsible for reviewing the audit logs.		
Auditing is enabled, and events are stored in a central database on a server. The firewall administrator is concerned that an attacker could obtain critical information on the network from the events stored in the database.		

Security Policy Checklist

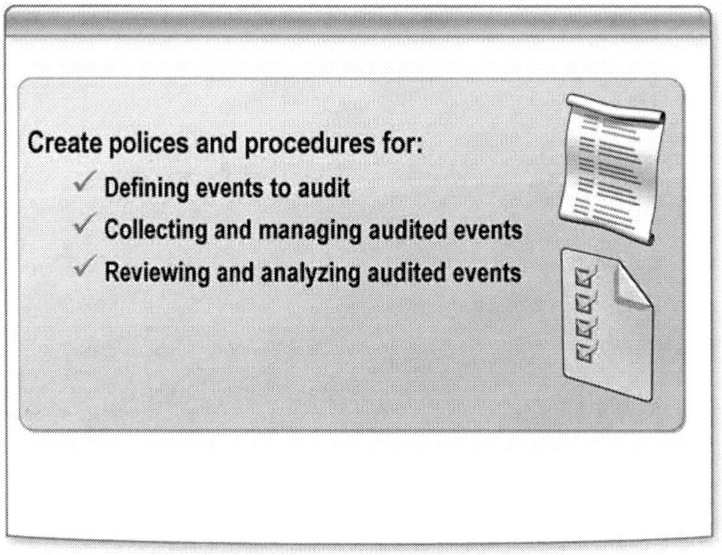

Checklist

Use the following checklist to guide your security design for an audit policy.

Phase	Task	Details
Planning	Model threats	STRIDE (Spoofing, Tampering, Repudiation, Information disclosure, Denial of service, and Elevation of privilege) and life cycle threat models
	Manage risks	Qualitative and quantitative risk analysis

Phase	Task	Details
Building	Create policies and procedures for securing:	Defining events to audit Collecting and managing audited events Reviewing and analyzing audited events

Lesson: Designing an Incident Response Procedure

- Steps for Planning an Incident Response Procedure
- Guidelines for Creating an Incident Response Team
- What to Include in a Communication Plan
- Common Indicators of Security Incidents
- Guidelines for Analyzing a Security Incident
- Methods for Limiting Damage from an Attack
- Guidelines for Documenting Security Incidents
- Practice: Risk and Response
- Security Policy Checklist

Introduction

The goals of an incident response procedure are to ensure safety and to limit the damage from an attack. Designing an incident response procedure and assembling a team to implement the procedures will help your organization respond to security incidents in an organized and efficient manner.

Lesson objectives

After completing this lesson, you will be able to:

- Explain the steps for planning an incident response procedure.
- Describe guidelines for assembling a team to respond to incidents.
- List items to include in a communication plan.
- Identify common indicators of security incidents.
- Describe guidelines for analyzing an incident.
- Limit damage from an attack.
- Discuss guidelines for documenting incidents.

Steps for Planning an Incident Response Procedure

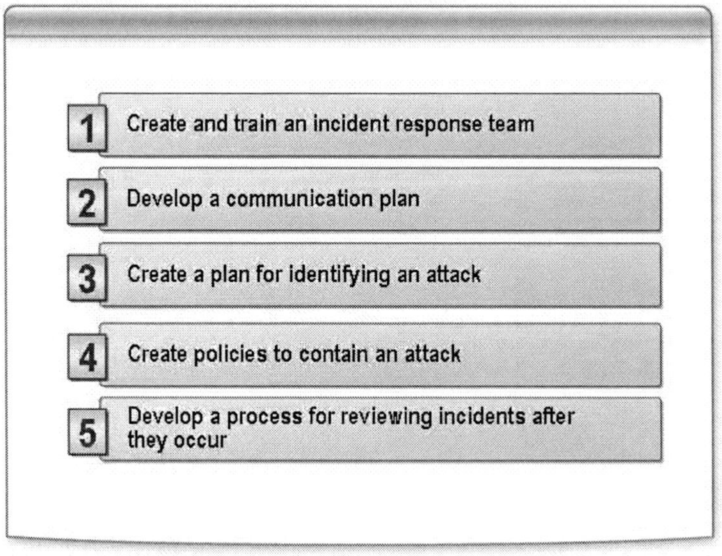

Key points

An incident response procedure is a systematic approach to responding to security incidents, and one that you prepare before an incident occurs. The first and most important goal of an incident response procedure is to protect human life and safety. Secondary to that, an incident response policy protects confidential information, other information, hardware, and software. It also minimizes disruption to computers and resources that a security incident can cause.

Use the steps in the preceding slide to organize your design. Also include plans in your procedure for the following:

- Informal investigation of security incidents
- Criminal investigation of security incidents
- Controlling the spread of information about the security incident
- Recovering from the security incident

Additional reading

For more information about planning an incident response procedure, see:

- RFC 2350, *Expectations for Computer Security Incident Response*, under **Additional Reading** on the Web page on the Student Materials CD.
- Chapter 7, "Responding to Incidents" in *Security Operations Guide for Windows 2000 Server*, under **Additional Reading** on the Web page on the Student Materials CD.

Guidelines for Creating an Incident Response Team

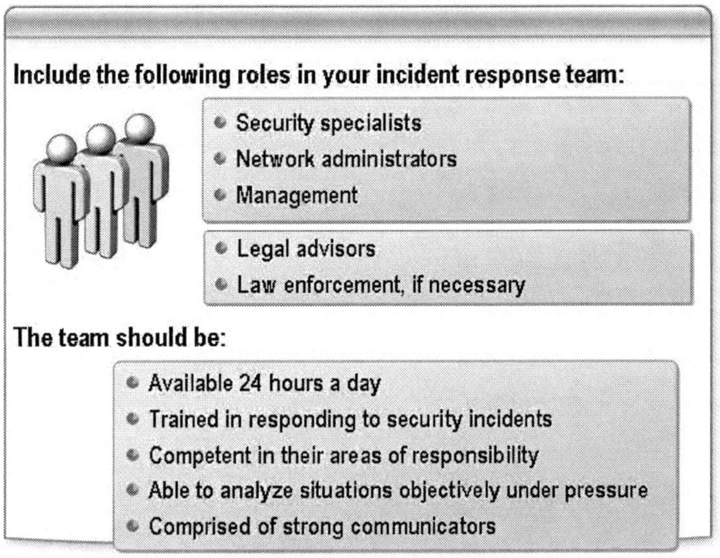

Key points

An incident response team should be as small as possible to ensure a rapid and efficient response to incidents; but it should be large enough to possess a diverse set of skills. Ensure that the following roles are represented in your team:

Role	Responsibility
Security specialist	Assesses and investigates security incidents and advises management about how to respond
Network administrator	Provides information about the network and computer configurations and help to assess the damage
Management	Makes critical decisions on a case-by-case basis about security incidents, such as how to respond to an incident and how to communicate the incident to the public
Legal advisor	Advises management about criminal prosecution and external communications
Law enforcement, if necessary	Performs criminal investigation and prosecution of attackers

In addition, ensure that your team is:

- *Available 24 hours a day*. Security incidents can occur at any time of the day or year. Ensure that your team is available to provide rapid response to incidents.
- *Trained in responding to security incidents*. Individuals who have experience or training in responding to incidents will help your team respond in a rational and orderly manner.
- *Competent in their areas of responsibility*. To avoid conflicts among team members during a crisis, clearly define roles and responsibilities and ensure that team members possess skills and expertise in their areas of specialty.
- *Able to analyze situations objectively under pressure*. Responding to security incidents often involves making difficult decisions under significant pressure and time constraints. Team members must be able to analyze a situation quickly and objectively.
- *Strong communicators*. It may be necessary for team members to communicate with internal and external groups, including managers, upset customers, media, and law enforcement.

Note It is recommended that all team members sign confidentiality agreements to mitigate against premature disclosure, either internally or externally, of confidential information that is discovered during an investigation.

Additional reading

For more information about creating a security incident response team, see *Creating a Computer Security Incident Response Team: A Process for Getting Started*, at: http://www.cert.org/csirts/Creating-A-CSIRT.html.

What to Include in a Communication Plan

Include in your communication plan:

- **Triggers that define when to contact each member of the incident response team**
- **Contact information for all team members**
- **Substitute team members and contact information**
- **Procedures for communicating securely among team members**
- **Incident details that each team member will receive**
- **How team members communicate details of the incident outside the team**

Key points

Inconsistent or poorly timed communication can make it difficult to resolve a security incident. Include in your communication plan:

- *Triggers that define when to contact each member of the incident response team.* You may decide to involve certain team members at different points during a response. For example, notify your chief information officer (CIO) if you detect an unknown virus on the network, but do not notify her if the virus is known.
- *Contact information for all team members.* Create and distribute a list that includes all relevant contact information for your team. Make sure that you keep the contact information up to date and in a location where all team members can find it.
- *Substitute team members and contact information.* Ensure that you maintain substitute representatives and their contact information in the event that you cannot contact a team member.
- *Procedures for communicating securely among team members.* To maintain confidentiality about an incident while it is occurring, create procedures to ensure secure communication among the team. Security measures can range from instructing team members not to leave handwritten notes about the incident in public areas, to requiring team members to communicate by using secure or encrypted channels, such as encrypted e-mail or phone lines.
- *Incident details that each team member receives.* Managing information about the incident will help you respond proactively rather than reactively. Consider what each team member needs to know about the incident.

- *How team members communicate details of the incident to nonteam members*. For many reasons, such as shareholder confidence, your organization may choose to keep the security incident confidential. To prevent information from being leaked to nonteam members or to the public, create clear guidelines about how to communicate details about the security incident and who should communicate the information. For employees who are not on the incident response team, such as corporate public relations representatives, determine what they need to know about the incident.

Common Indicators of Security Incidents

Area	Examples
Network irregularities	• Network performance decreases • Accounts are used at irregular times
System irregularities	• Audited events increase significantly • System performance decreases • Computers crash or reboot mysteriously
Direct reporting of events	• Users report security incidents • A new virus is published • Intrusion detection software detects an incident
Physical indicators	• Hardware is missing • Visible signs exist of physical compromise
Business indicators	• Confidential information is published on the Internet or in print • Competitor appears to possess trade secrets

Key points

Although many abnormal events on a network are harmless, some may indicate security incidents. Investigate all abnormal events to determine their causes and to confirm whether the events present a security risk.

Additional reading

For more information about investigating security incidents, see *Detecting Signs of Intrusion*, at: http://www.cert.org/security-improvement/modules/m09.html.

Guidelines for Analyzing a Security Incident

To identify:	Determine:
Symptoms	• How is the event occurring? • What are the symptoms of the attack?
Origin	• Where is the attack originating? • Is the point of origin connected to the attacker?
Entry point	• How is the attack entering the network? • Is the attacker exploiting a known vulnerability?
Intent	• What does the attacker appear to be trying to accomplish? • Is there a pattern to the attack?
Severity	• What is at risk? • How serious is the risk?
Exposure	• What systems have been compromised? • How are the systems compromised?

Key points

After you determine that an event is a security incident, use the guidelines that are listed in the preceding slide to determine the scope of the incident. Notify the members of the incident response team as dictated by the triggers in your communication plan.

Ensure that your plan includes procedures for preserving the chain of evidence when you identify and isolate the attack. It is strongly recommended that you create a checklist for network administrators to use to analyze a security incident. You can use the questions on the preceding slide as guidelines when creating your list.

Additional reading

For more information about analyzing security incidents, see "Job Aid 4: Incident Response Quick Reference Card," in *Security Operations Guide for Windows 2000 Server*, under **Additional Reading** on the Web page on the Student Materials CD.

Methods for Limiting Damage from an Attack

Resource	Examples
Networks	• Disconnect affected networks from the corporate network • Disconnect corporate network from the Internet • Block TCP/IP ports
Computers	• Remove infected computers from the network • Remove computers with sensitive information from the network • Deploy security hotfixes and service packs to unpatched computers
Applications	• Change passwords on compromised and sensitive accounts • Update antivirus scanning engines and signature files • Update intrusion detection systems and inspect log files
Physical security	• Replace locks and key codes • Increase physical security

Key points

After ensuring the safety of employees and other people, the incident response team must determine how to contain and limit the damage from the attack. This is often one of the most difficult decisions to make, because the team may possess limited information about the attack and yet be under enormous pressure from key stakeholders to act decisively.

Ensure that the method that you choose to limit damage is proportionate to the potential impact of the security incident. For example, detection of a series of port scans on your ISA Server firewall does not justify disconnecting your organization's connection to the Internet.

Additional reading

For more information about limiting damage from an attack, see:

- "Job Aid 3: Attacks and Countermeasures," in *Security Operations Guide for Windows 2000 Server*, under **Additional Reading** on the Web page on the Student Materials CD.
- The white paper, *Microsoft Security Toolkit: Compromised Systems*, at: http://www.microsoft.com/technet/security/tools/tools/detect.asp.

Guidelines for Documenting Security Incidents

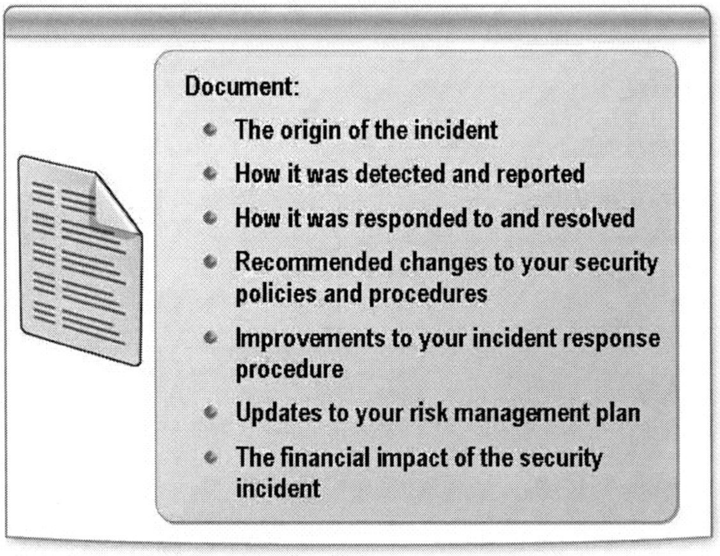

Key points

After the team resolves a security incident, schedule a meeting to discuss how the team reacted. Documenting the incident and reviewing the team's actions may help the team respond more effectively to the next security incident.

Use the guidelines in the preceding slide as a framework for gathering feedback during the meeting. It may be embarrassing to revisit actions that, in hindsight, are considered mistakes, but careful review and assessment will enable you to update your procedures and improve the team's response to future incidents.

Practice: Risk and Response

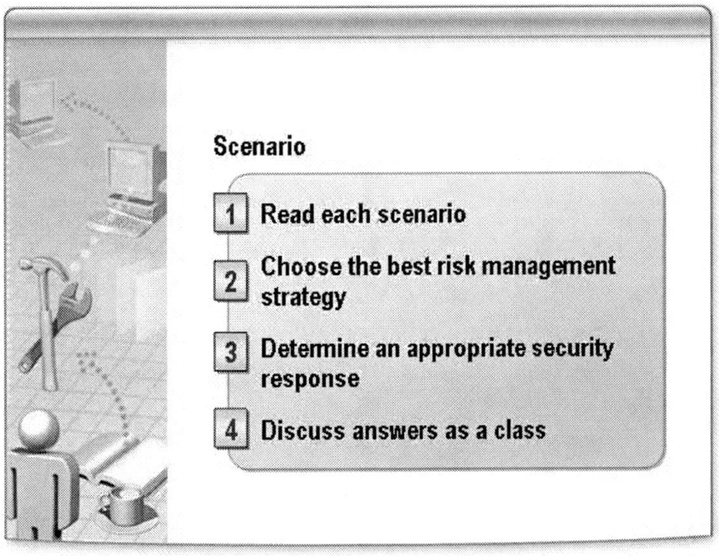

Introduction

For each scenario, choose whether to accept, mitigate, transfer, or avoid the risk that is presented, and then enter an appropriate security response.

Scenario	Risk strategy	Security response
Security incidents are reported prematurely and to inappropriate people		
Security incidents are leaked to the media before the team has met to discuss the incidents		
Despite a properly defined incident response plan, management fears that if an attacker gains access to the company's customer database, it could result in damages of more than $10 million		

Security Policy Checklist

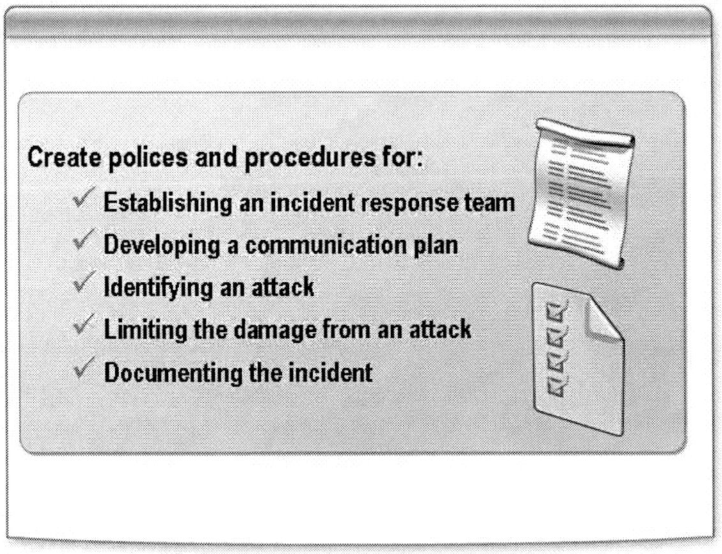

Checklist

Use the following checklist to guide your security design for an incident response procedure.

Phase	Task	Details
Planning	Model threats	STRIDE (Spoofing, Tampering, Repudiation, Information disclosure, Denial of service, and Elevation of privilege) and life cycle threat models
	Manage risks	Qualitative and quantitative risk analysis

Phase	Task	Details
Building	Create policies and procedures for:	Establishing an incident response team
		Developing a communication plan
		Identifying an attack
		Limiting the damage from an attack
		Documenting the incident

Lab A: Designing an Incident Response Procedure

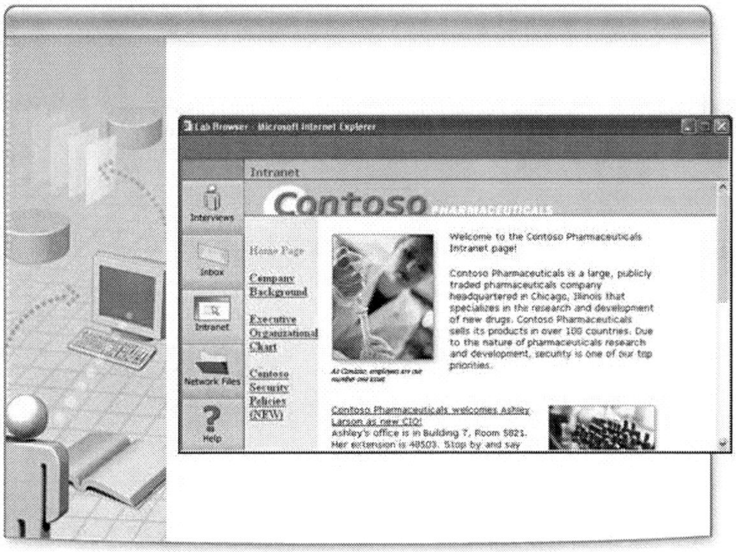

Objectives

After completing this lab, you will be able to apply security design concepts to incident response procedures.

Scenario

You are a consultant hired by Contoso Pharmaceuticals to help the company design security for its network. Each lab uses an interactive application to convey scenario-based information. To begin a lab, on the desktop, click **Internet Explorer**; this opens a Web page that contains links to each lab. Click a link to begin a lab.

Estimated time to complete this lab: 30 minutes

Work with a lab partner to perform the lab.

► **To complete a lab**

1. Read Ashley Larson's e-mail in each lab to determine the goals for the lab.
2. Click **Reply**, and then type your answer to Ashley's questions.
3. Click **Send** to save your answers to a folder on your desktop.
4. Discuss your answers as a class.

Course Evaluation

Your evaluation of this course will help Microsoft understand the quality of your learning experience.

To complete a course evaluation, go to http://www.CourseSurvey.com.

Microsoft will keep your evaluation strictly confidential and will use your responses to improve your future learning experience.

Microsoft®
Training &
Certification

Appendix A: Designing an Acceptable Use Policy

Contents

Microsoft®

Overview

- Analyzing Risks That Users Introduce
- Designing Security for Computer Use

Introduction

This appendix presents information about determining threats and analyzing risks that users can introduce to a network. You will learn how to define what is considered to be an acceptable use of computers, accounts, Internet access, applications, and the network.

Objectives

After completing this appendix, you will be able to:

- Analyze risks that users introduce.
- Design security for computer use.

Lesson: Analyzing Risks That Users Introduce

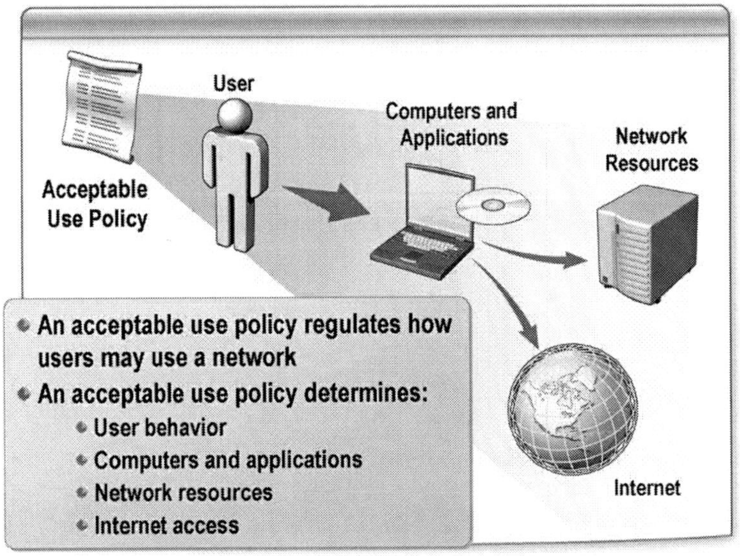

Introduction

Every organization must decide what is acceptable behavior for users and computers. Lax acceptable use policies may leave the organization vulnerable to attack. However, policies that are overly restrictive may inhibit business practices and may be subverted or ignored by employees.

Lesson objectives

After completing this lesson, you will be able to:

- Describe an acceptable use policy.
- Explain why an acceptable use policy is important.
- List common vulnerabilities that users introduce through behavior.

What Is an Acceptable Use Policy?

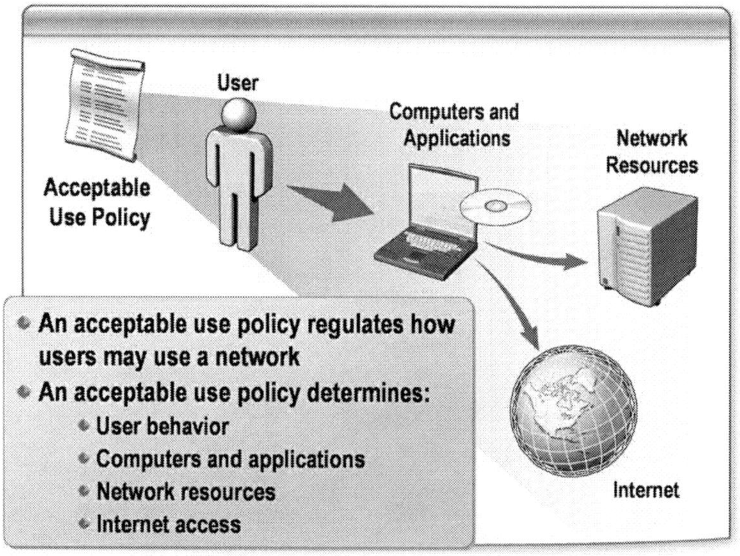

Key points

Acceptable use policies are administrative policies designed to regulate how users use computers and network resources.

Acceptable use policies are often created for situations where technical policy implementations:

- *Are not possible*. For example, your organization may create an acceptable use policy that prohibits users from discussing legal affairs of the company in public areas in order to prevent information from being overheard by eavesdroppers.
- *Are not cost effective*. For example, you organization may have a policy that restricts Web browsing to only approved sites, but the software application required to restrict Web browsing may be too expensive to purchase and implement.
- *Violate a user's right to privacy*. For example, your organization may want to create a security policy that audits user passwords to ensure that they are not easily guessable, but doing so would violate privacy laws.

Why an Acceptable Use Policy Is Important

Attacker	Threat	Example
External	User indiscretion	An employee leaves her portable computer at home unattended and unlocked. Her child deletes critical files from the corporate network.
Internal	Unsupported application	An employee installs an unauthorized application with known vulnerabilities on a computer that is connected to the corporate network. An attacker exploits the vulnerability to attack the network.

External attacker scenario

A user leaves her company-issued portable computer unattended at home while connected to the corporate network by using a virtual private network (VPN) tunnel. Her child approaches the keyboard and deletes critical files from the corporate network, resulting in data loss.

Internal attacker scenario

An employee installs an application on his computer that is not permitted by company policy. The application has known vulnerabilities, which an attacker exploits to gain control of the computer. The attacker uses the computer to attack the network.

Common Vulnerabilities That Users Introduce

Area	Vulnerabilities
Confidential information	• Public discussion of confidential data • Weak passwords
Computers and applications	• Theft or loss of computer • Unsupported or unapproved applications
Network	• Personal use of network • Misuse of remote access accounts
Internet access	• Personal use of the Internet • Exposure of the network to malicious, offensive, or illegal content

Key points

Many networks must endure malicious or disgruntled users who will attempt to intentionally subvert network security. However, most of the security threats that users introduce to networks are a result of:

- *A lack of training*. For example, a user may not know the difference between passwords that are easy for attackers to guess and those that are difficult to guess.
- *Failure to provide due care*. For example, a user may leave his portable computer in his automobile while parking in a public parking lot.
- *Misuse of network resources*. For example, a computer is exposed to a virus when a user downloads an unsigned Microsoft® ActiveX® component from a malicious Web site that promises access to pirated software.

Lesson: Designing Security for Computer Use

- Steps for Designing an Acceptable Use Policy
- Guidelines for Acceptable Use for Users
- Guidelines for Acceptable Use of Computers and Applications
- How to Define Acceptable Use of a Network
- How to Define Acceptable Use of Internet Access
- Security Policy Checklist

Introduction

An acceptable use policy encompasses computers as well as applications, network resources, and access to the Internet. The limits that you place on user behavior must be appropriate, realistic, and enforceable. You must also ensure that your users are aware of the rules that you create.

Lesson objectives

After completing this lesson, you will be able to:

- List the steps for designing an acceptable use policy.
- Explain guidelines for acceptable use of users, computers, applications, networks, and the Internet.

Steps for Designing an Acceptable Use Policy

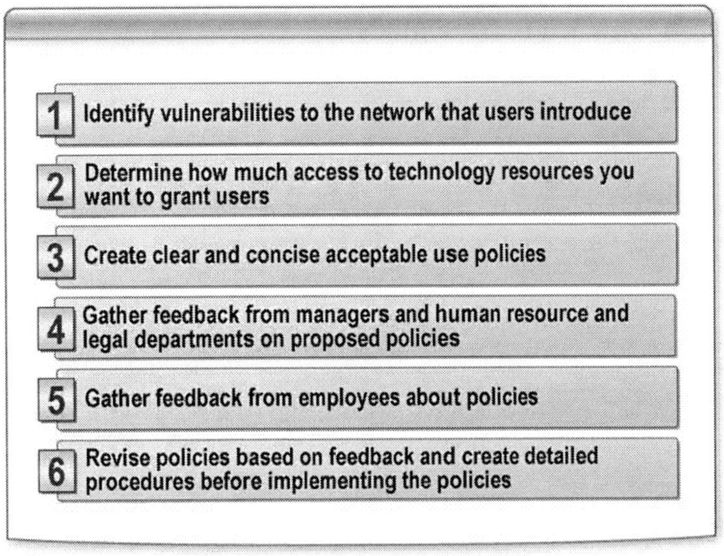

Key points

To design an acceptable use policy, follow these steps:

1. *Identify vulnerabilities to the network that users introduce.* Predict threats and vulnerabilities that users might introduce to network resources.

2. *Determine how much access to technology resources you want to grant users.* To ensure that users have the least privilege to network resources that is necessary for them to complete their job duties, determine the minimum level of access to resources that job roles require.

3. *Create clear and concise acceptable use policies.* Based on the information gained from completing the first two steps, create clear and concise acceptable use policies that are plainly written and easy for users to follow.

4. *Gather feedback from managers and human resource and legal departments on proposed policies.* To ensure that the acceptable use policies are appropriate, enforceable, and do not violate employee rights, ensure that management, human resource, and legal departments review and approve acceptable use policies.

5. *Gather feedback from employees about policies.* To ensure that acceptable use policies do not disrupt business processes, and to obtain backing from employees, gather feedback on proposed policies.

6. *Revise policies based on feedback and create detailed procedures before implementing the policies.* After incorporating the feedback from all stakeholders, work with human resources to create and implement acceptable use policies.

Guidelines for Acceptable Use for Users

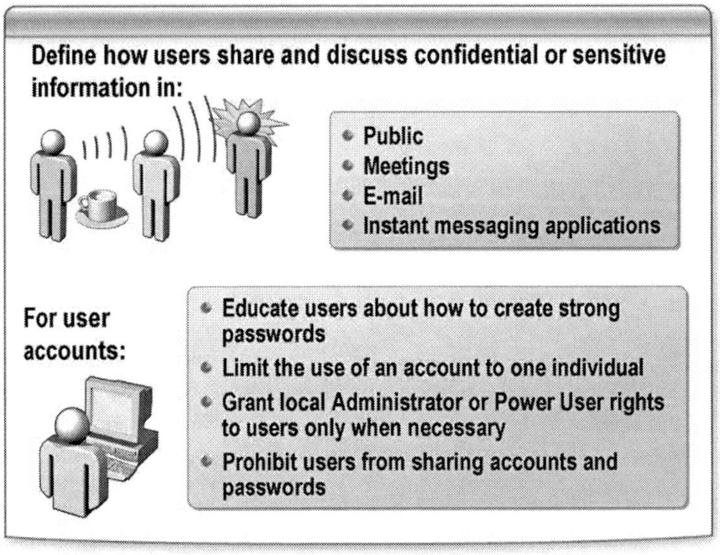

Key points

Two important acceptable use policies for users pertain to how users:

- *Manage information.* To protect confidential information from exposure, create guidelines for managing these categories of information. You may need to further categorize information to create these guidelines. For example, you may want to create separate guidelines for legal information and human resources information, even though both have been categorized as confidential.
- *Use accounts.* To prevent accounts from being easily compromised by attackers, create acceptable use policies that determine how to use accounts and how to create and managed passwords. Because you must trust that users handle their user accounts with due care, create training and guidance for users on how to comply with the acceptable use policies.

Guidelines for Acceptable Use of Computers and Applications

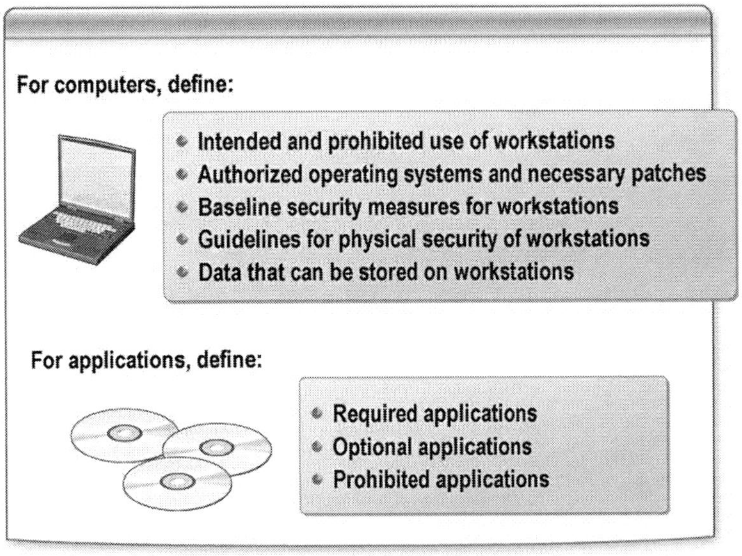

Key points

To prevent computers from unnecessary exposure to attackers, create acceptable use policies based on the guidelines in the preceding slide.

Note You can use Software Restriction policies in Microsoft Windows® XP to restrict which applications are permitted to run.

How to Define Acceptable Use of a Network

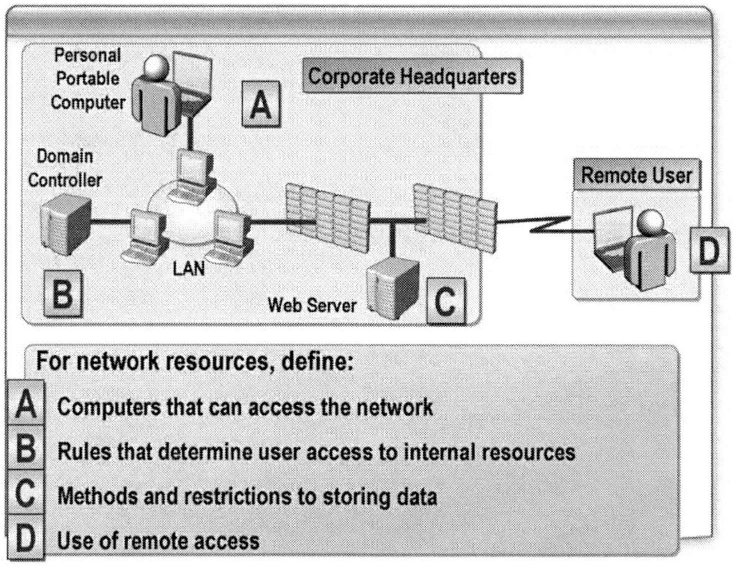

Key points

To ensure that users do not expose resources on the network to attackers, include guidelines in your acceptable use policy for:

1. *Computers that can access the network.* A user may connect her home computer to the network to steal company software.
2. *Rules that determine user access to internal resources.* A user may abuse access to internal resources, such as color laser printers.
3. *Methods and restrictions to storing data.* A user may use a network share to store illegally obtained music files and then share them to users on the Internet by using peer-to-peer file sharing protocols.
4. *Use of remote access.* A user may use a remote access connection to the organization to view illicit content on the Internet.

How to Define Acceptable Use of Internet Access

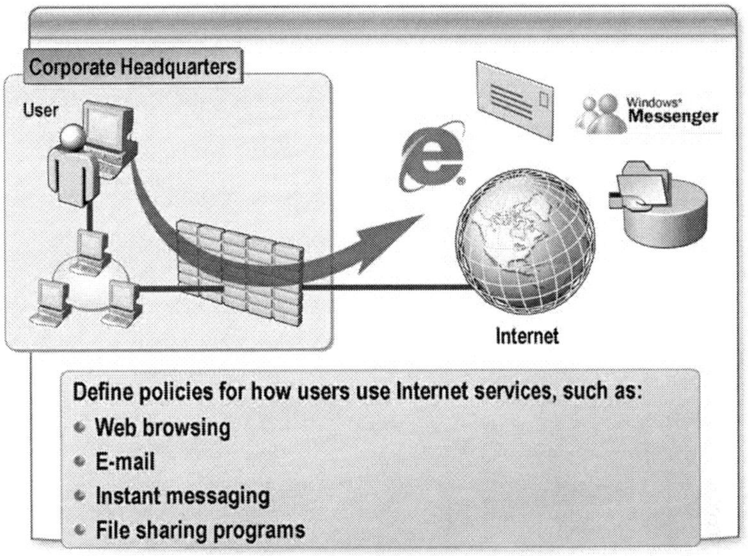

Key points

Because the Internet is an untrusted network, applications that connect to the Internet can provide direct access for attackers to your internal network.

To enforce acceptable use policies regarding Internet use, you can often combine the policies with implementations of technical policies, such as firewall rules and software that screens Web content.

Security Policy Checklist

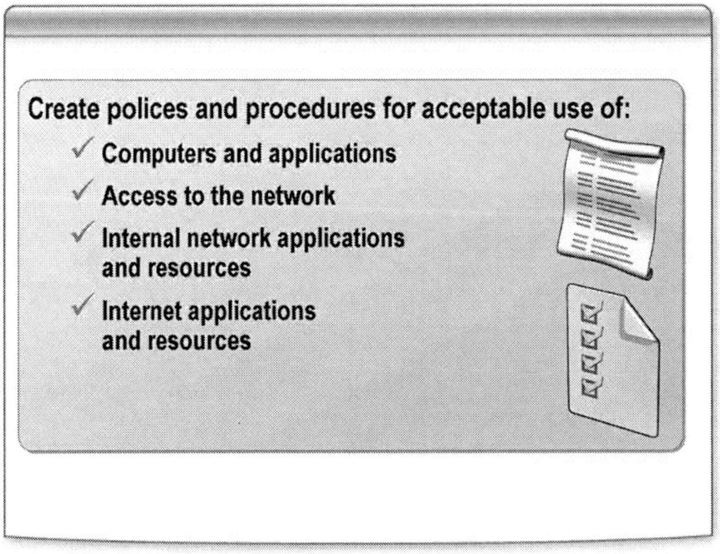

Checklist

Use the following checklist to guide your security design for acceptable use.

Phase	Task	Details
Planning	Model threats	STRIDE (spoofing, tampering, repudiation, information disclosure, denial of service and elevation of privilege) and life cycle threat models
	Manage risks	Qualitative and quantitative risk analysis

Phase	Task	Details
Building	Create policies and procedures for acceptable use of:	Computers and applications Access to the network Internal network applications and resources Internet applications and resources

Microsoft®
Training &
Certification

Appendix B: Designing Policies for Managing Networks

Contents

Microsoft®

Overview

- Analyzing Risks to Managing Networks
- Designing Security for Managing Networks

Introduction

In this appendix, you will learn how to determine threats and analyze risks to network management. You will also learn how to design security for network management, including specifying who can manage a network, what tools are permitted, and what procedures administrators must follow.

Objectives

After completing this appendix, you will be able to:

- Determine threats and analyze risks to network management.
- Design security for network management.

Lesson: Analyzing Risks to Managing Networks

- What Is a Network Management Policy?
- Why Network Administration Policies Are Important
- Common Threats to Network Administration

Introduction

You use a network management policy to specify how to manage your network in a secure manner. Improper management can introduce vulnerabilities as easily as can improper user behavior. Because administrators have greater permissions and access than users, the potential risks due to mismanagement are great.

Lesson objectives

After completing this lesson, you will be able to:

- Describe a network management policy.
- Explain why a network management policy is important.
- List common vulnerabilities to network management.

What Is a Network Management Policy?

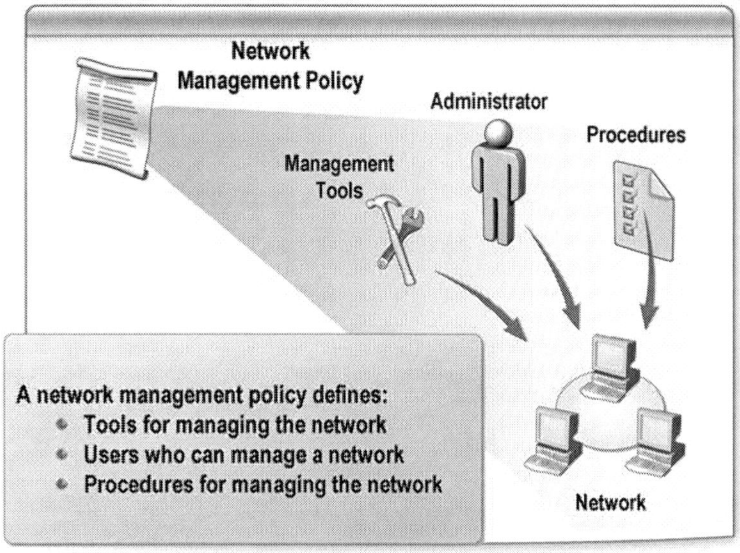

Key points

An organization must always trust its network administrators to use their rights and permissions legitimately on the network. Because of this trust, organizations require policies that regulate who can receive rights and permissions to manage network resources. You must also create policies to ensure that network resources are managed in a secure manner and that there are procedures for protecting network administrators against attackers.

Why Network Management Policies Are Important

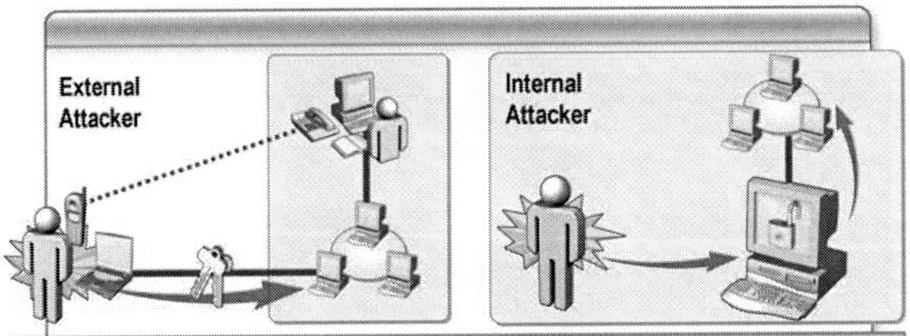

Attacker	Threat	Example
External	Social engineering	An attacker calls a company's help desk, posing as a newly hired network administrator who needs to reset the password of a company official. The attacker uses the official's account to steal company secrets.
Internal	Unlocked workstation	An administrator logs on to a computer by using his administrator account, then leaves the computer unlocked before going to a meeting. An attacker uses the administrator's computer to attack the network.

External attacker scenario

An attacker calls the help desk of a company posing as a newly hired network administrator. The attacker convinces the help desk administrator to reset the password of a company official. Because no procedure exists for verifying identity, the help desk administrator performs the reset of the password. The attacker uses the compromised account to attack the network.

Internal attacker scenario

An administrator logs on to a computer by using his administrator account, then leaves the computer unattended and unlocked while attending a meeting. An internal attacker sees the unlocked computer and uses it to attack the network under the security context of the administrator.

Common Threats to Network Management

Area	Threats
Network management model	• Poor decisions about security • Accounts that have excessive administrative rights • Incomplete background checks of a prospective administrator
Access to information	• Social engineering attacks that manipulate administrators • Sensitive information found by sifting through garbage
Diligence	• Failure to lock unattended workstations and servers • Critical resources in unsecured physical locations • Failure to perform security tasks in a timely manner
Tools	• Use of unapproved tools to manage a network • Failure to secure communication channels that are used to manage a network

Key points

Network administration itself may be a threat to the security of information if the overall design of the network management model is weak, if the organization fails to perform due diligence in protecting administrator account credentials, or if network administration tools are used in such a way that they leak information to attackers. Network administrators in particular are susceptible to social engineering attacks because of the elevated rights and permissions that they hold.

Lesson: Designing Security for Network Administrators

- Steps for Designing Secure Management of Networks
- Common Network Management Models
- Guidelines for Delegating Administrative Control
- Guidelines for Acceptable Use of Network Management Tools
- Guidelines for Network Management Security
- Guidelines for Protecting Against Social Engineering
- Security Policy Checklist

Introduction

A management model describes how an organization administers and manages its network. Different models have advantages and disadvantages regarding security. In your organization, you must ensure that those who manage your network follow the security guidelines that you establish.

Lesson objectives

After completing this lesson, you will be able to:

- Explain the steps for designing secure management of networks.
- Describe common network management models.
- Explain guidelines for delegating administrative control and acceptable use of network management tools.
- List guidelines for network administration security.
- Protect against social engineering.

Steps for Designing Secure Management of Networks

1. Identify and optimize the network management model used by the organization
2. Determine who can manage the network and what parts they manage
3. Predict threats to managing the network
4. Create a list of approved network management tools and techniques
5. Design and create polices and procedures for managing the network

---

Key points

To design secure management of the network, follow these steps:

1. *Identify and optimize the network management model used by the organization.* The network management model that your network uses is the foundation of how you make decisions regarding security.

2. *Determine who can manage the network and what parts they manage.* Ensure that administrators have only the rights and permissions that they require for the job role or function.

3. *Predict threats to managing the network.* By predicting threats to network management, you can design security countermeasures and processes to protect your organization.

4. *Create a list of approved network management tools and techniques.* Use only approved tools and techniques to prevent against attackers exploiting vulnerabilities.

5. *Design and create polices and procedures for managing the network.* Design policies and procedures to standardize the management of the network.

Common Network Management Models

Model	Characteristics
Centralized	• A small group makes all network management decisions • Network administration is performed from a central location • Strong security is provided at the expense of flexibility
Decentralized	• Autonomous groups make many network management decisions • Network administration is performed at multiple locations • It may be required by medium- and large-sized networks that have geographical, geopolitical, or language complexities
Outsourced	• Trusted third parties perform network management • Outsourcing can provide expertise that your organization may lack
Hybrid	• Centralized, decentralized, or outsourced network management models are combined • It is the most common network management model

Key points

The network management model of an organization is the foundation of how decisions about security are made. Each organization must determine which network management model best satisfies its business requirements. Most network management models are hybrids of centralized, decentralized, or outsourced models.

Guidelines for Delegating Administrative Control

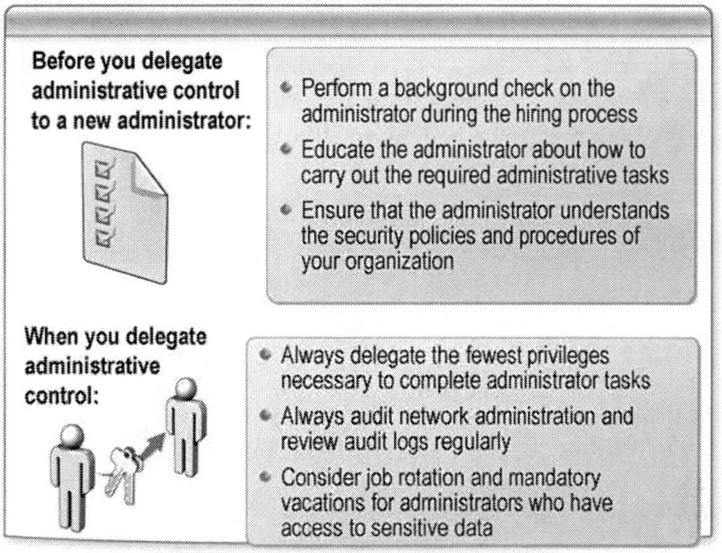

Key points

Because your organization must place its trust in its network administrators, grant administrator rights and permissions only to trustworthy and responsible employees. This is especially important for employees to whom you grant broad rights and permissions, such as domain administrator rights.

Before delegating administrative control:

- *Perform a background check on the administrator during the hiring process.* Requiring prospective employees to undergo a background check during the hiring process provides some assurance that the prospective employee is trustworthy.
- *Educate the administrator about how to carry out the required administrative tasks.* To protect the network from being managed in a non-secure manner, ensure that the administrator understands how to complete her job duties securely.
- *Ensure that the administrator understands the security policies and procedures of your organization.* To help protect a network administrator from social engineering attacks (and, thereby, becoming a threat to the security of the network himself), ensure that all network administrators receive training and understand security policies and procedures.

When delegating administrative control:

- *Always delegate the fewest privileges necessary to complete administrator tasks.* Granting administrators more rights or permissions than required to complete their job duties is a security risk.
- *Always audit network administration and review audit logs regularly.* By auditing the completion of network management tasks and reviewing the audit logs, you can help ensure that administrators are using their authority for legitimate proposes.
- *Consider implementing job rotation and mandatory vacations for administrators who have access to sensitive data.* Job rotations and mandatory vacations for network administrators enable an organization to independently verify that their administrators are using their authority legitimately.

Additional reading

For more information on delegating administrative rights and permissions, see the white paper, *Design Considerations for Delegation of Administration in Active Directory*, at: http://www.microsoft.com/technet/prodtechnol/ad/windows2000/plan/addeladm.asp.

Guidelines for Acceptable Use of Network Management Tools

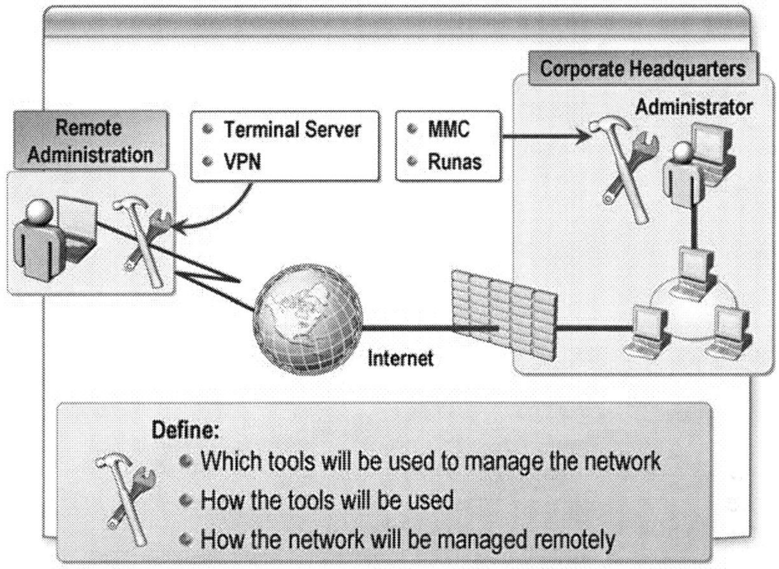

Key points

Inappropriate use of network management tools can reveal administrator credentials and information to attackers. Many network management tools are available, such as Terminal Services, virtual private network (VPN) tunnels, and the Microsoft Management Console (MMC).

You must also consider how administrator credentials are used on your network. For example, you may create a security policy that only allows administrators to use their administrator account from specified computers, or to only use their administrative credentials by using the *runas* service.

Guidelines for Network Management Security

Function	Guidelines for policies and procedures
Use of Administrator accounts	• Place limits on administrator authority • Prohibit use of administrator account for daily use • Prohibit use of administrator rights to monitor employees
Use of administration tools	• Specify how to use remote administration tools securely • Prohibit using attacker tools on the network without approval
Performance of daily tasks	• Follow policies and procedures when completing frequently occurring tasks • Create and update log files for change management

Key points

Network management security is a combination of people, processes, and technology. Design and create security policies and procedures for each of these areas, and ensure that network administrators comply with them.

Guidelines for Protecting Against Social Engineering

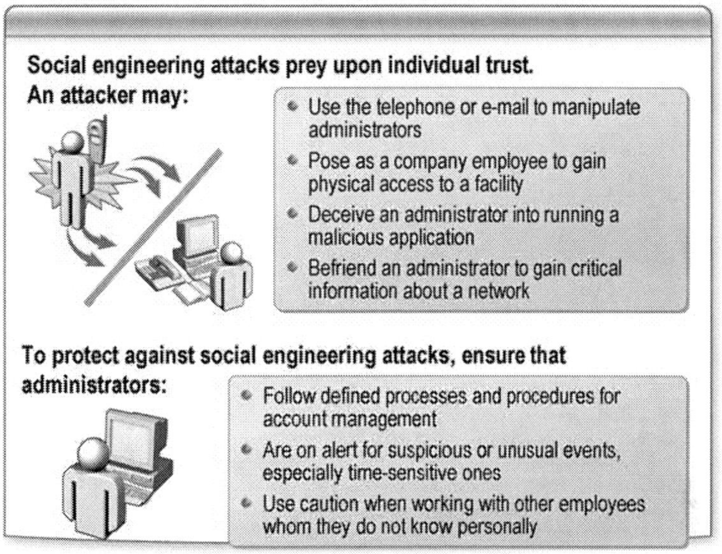

Key points

Social engineering attacks prey upon the trust of people. Attackers often use social engineering attacks to target network administrators because the administrators have high levels of access to resources on the network.

Social engineering attacks can be difficult to defend against. Educate your network administrators about common indicators of social engineering attacks, such as requests to carry out administrative tasks that break security policy, using friendships to get the administrator to do something that breaks security policy, or unusual requests that must be fulfilled immediately.

Security Policy Checklist

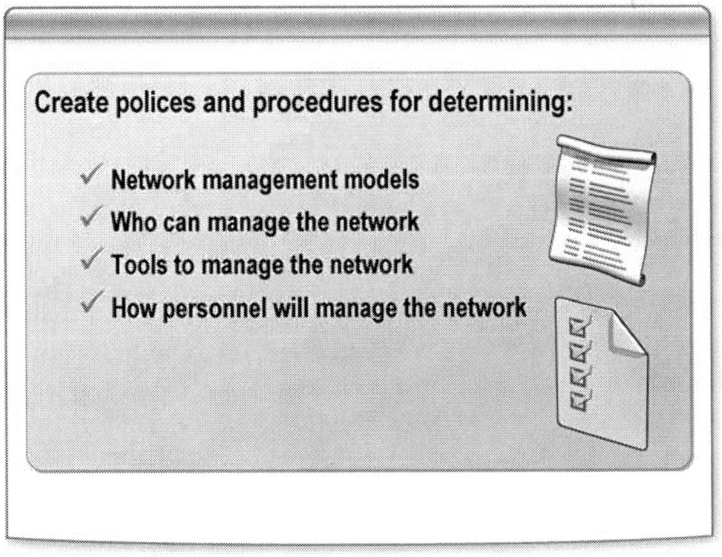

Checklist

Use the following checklist to guide your security design for network management.

Phase	Task	Details
Planning	Model threats	STRIDE (spoofing, tampering, repudiation, information disclosure, denial of service and elevation of privilege) and life cycle threat models
	Manage risks	Qualitative and quantitative risk analysis

Phase	Task	Details
Building	Create policies and procedures for determining:	Network management models Who can manage the network Tools to manage the network How personnel will manage the network

Microsoft®
Training &
Certification

Appendix C: Designing an Operations Framework to Manage Security

Contents

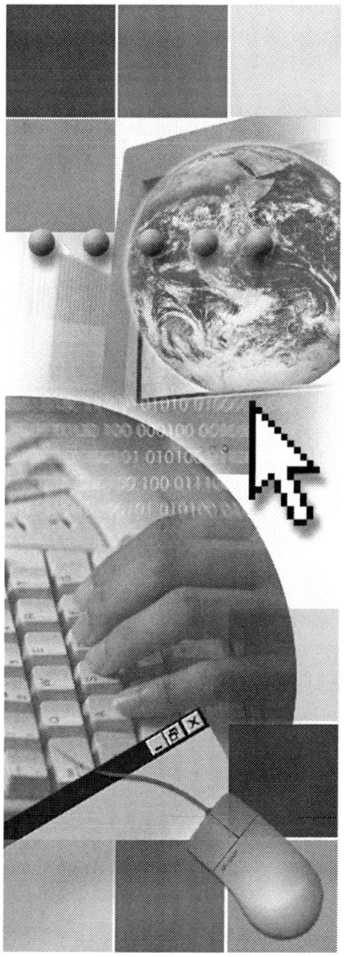

Microsoft®

Overview

- Analyzing Risks to Ongoing Network Operations
- Designing a Framework for Ongoing Network Operations

Introduction

In this appendix, you will learn how to help ensure the management of ongoing security operations. To maintain the security of network operations, you must ensure proper management of the security design and design a change management framework to meet changing security needs and conditions.

Objectives

After completing this appendix, you will be able to:

- Analyze risks to ongoing network operations.
- Design a framework for ensuring secure network operations.

Lesson: Analyzing Risks to Ongoing Network Operations

- Management of Ongoing Network Operations
- Why Security of Network Operations Is Important
- Common Vulnerabilities to Network Operations

Introduction

Ongoing network operations are the everyday administration and management of your network. The actions performed to maintain the network may conflict with security policy or introduce vulnerabilities that your design did not anticipate.

Lesson objectives

After completing this lesson, you will be able to:

- Explain the concept of ongoing management of network operations.
- Explain why securing network operations is important.
- List common vulnerabilities to network operations.

Management of Ongoing Network Operations

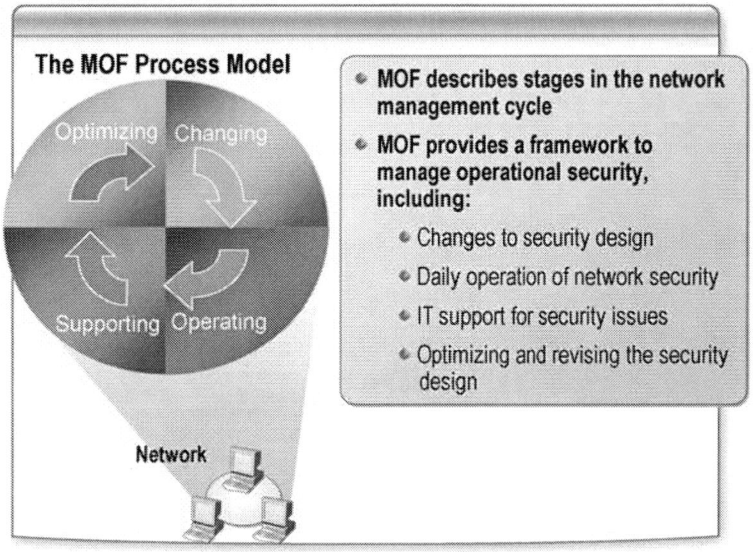

Key points

The Microsoft Operations Framework (MOF) is a comprehensive suite of operational guidance materials that encompass people, processes, and technologies. MOF provides a framework for effectively managing production systems within information technology (IT) environments, including network security.

Additional reading

For more information on MOF, see the white paper, *Process Model for Operations*, under **Additional Reading** on the Web page on the Student Materials CD.

Why Security of Network Operations Is Important

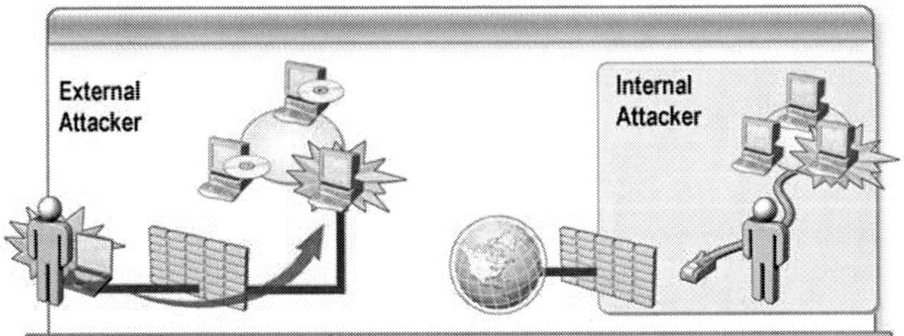

Attacker	Threat	Example
External	No change and configuration management	A software company releases a new security hotfix to patch a recently discovered vulnerability. An attacker exploits the vulnerability on the network before administrators apply the patch to all computers.
Internal	Security procedures not followed	An administrator notices a potential security compromise but is unsure how to report it. The administrator decides to remove the corporate network from the Internet.

External attacker scenario

A software company releases a new security update that secures a recently discovered vulnerability. Because the organization lacks policies for managing the deployment of updates, an attacker is able to exploit the vulnerability on the network before administrators apply the patch to all computers.

Internal attacker scenario

An administrator notices a potential security compromise but is unsure how to report it. The administrator decides to remove the corporate network from the Internet, causing the company to lose productivity and revenue from their e-commerce Web site.

Common Vulnerabilities to Network Operations

Vulnerability	Example
Inadequate plan for change management	• New security patches are applied irregularly or not at all • Administrators and users lack proper training on securing new applications
Poor operations plan	• Users do not follow security policies and procedures • Administrators do not regularly test backup media
Weak support structure	• Security incident goes unreported • IT support services are not reliable
Failure to revise policy	• New security risks are not added to risk management plan • Policies and procedures become outdated

Key points

The ongoing operation of a network can introduce vulnerabilities into the security of a network, even if you have a security design in place.

Planning for ongoing network operations during the design of network security can help prevent vulnerabilities from subverting your security policy.

Lesson: Designing a Framework for Ongoing Network Operations

- Steps for Planning a Security Operations Framework
- Guidelines for Change Management
- Guidelines for Daily Security Operations
- Guidelines for Supporting Security Policies and Procedures
- Guidelines for Using Service Level Agreements
- Guidelines for Optimizing Security Policies and Procedures
- Security Policy Checklist

Introduction

By planning for ongoing operations in your security design, you can help ensure that changes to the network as a result of daily operations do not adversely affect network security. Ongoing operations also involve support of the policies and procedures that you design, and ensure that service level agreements (SLAs) exist to maintain network operations.

Lesson objectives

After completing this lesson, you will be able to:

- Describe steps for planning a framework for secure operations.
- Describe guidelines for:
  - Change management.
  - Daily security operations.
  - Supporting security policies.
  - Using SLAs.
  - Optimizing security policies.

Steps for Planning a Security Operations Framework

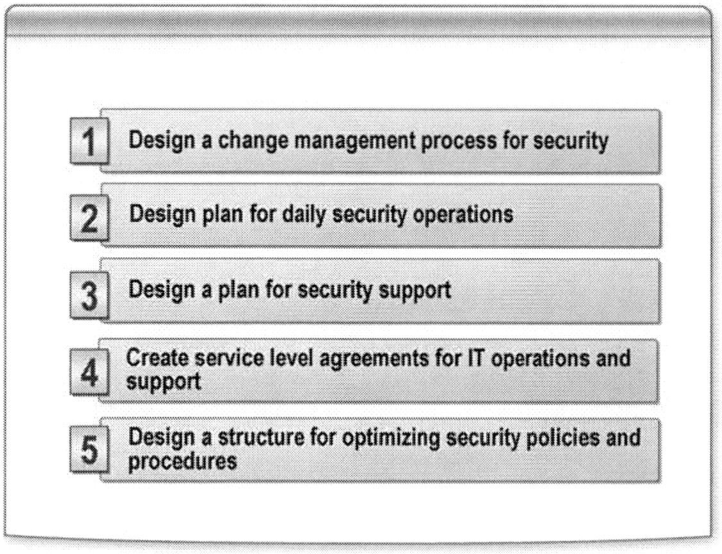

Key points

To design a security operations framework:

1. *Design a change management process for security.* Managing change on your network ensures that the security of your network is maintained when you make changes to the network.
2. *Design plan for daily security operations.* By designing a plan for daily security operations, you can ensure that all routine tasks related to security are completed.
3. *Design a plan for security support.* A security support plan ensures that users can escalate security related issues in an orderly and responsive manner.
4. *Create service level agreements for IT operations and support.* SLAs for IT operations and support ensure that all parties know what to expect from each other.
5. *Design a structure for optimizing security policies and procedures.* Like change management, optimization refers to changes that your security policy may require; however, it is based less on physical changes to your network and more on improving the overall design.

Guidelines for Change Management

A change management process reduces:

- Time to deployment
- Cost of updating hardware and software
- Disruption of business continuity

Phase	Example
Identify	When new security hotfixes are released...
Review	...the hotfixes will be tested on all applicable platforms...
Approve	...and approved by the CIO within 24 hours...
Implement	...and will be deployed according to the approved procedure for deploying security hotfixes.

Key points

Change management describes how you manage changes to your network so that you ensure consistency and manageability. The objective of the change process is to introduce new technologies, systems, applications, hardware, tools, and processes, as well as changes in roles and responsibilities, into the IT environment quickly and with minimal disruption to service.

Change management includes changes to all aspects of your network that are relevant to the running, support, and maintenance of systems in the managed environment. Change management includes hardware, communications equipment, system software, applications software, processes, procedures, roles, responsibilities, and documentation.

A change management plan has four phases:

- *Identify*. Defines condition that initiates the change management plan.
- *Review*. Defines the process for evaluating change.
- *Approve*. Defines how the decision is made to act on the change.
- *Implement*. Defines how the change will be implemented.

Guidelines for Daily Security Operations

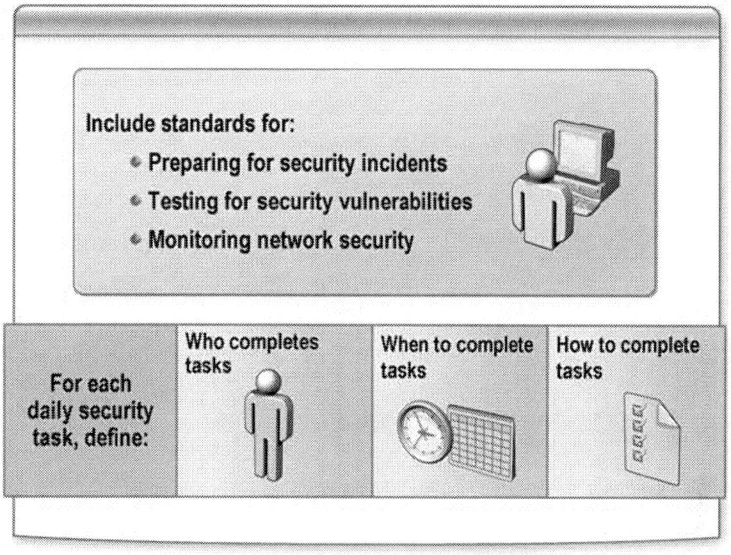

Key points

Managing security on a network can be an overwhelming task for many IT staffs. To ensure completion of daily operations tasks, define who will complete each task, when each task must be completed, and how the task will be completed.

Assignments of tasks will vary. Some tasks, such as monitoring network security, might be accomplished by many people on a daily basis. Other tasks, such as incident response preparation, may be the responsibility of a single person and take several weeks to complete.

Additional reading

For more information on managing daily IT operations, see "Chapter 8: Network Administration" of the *Operations Guide for the Internet Data Center Microsoft System Architecture Guide*, at: http://www.microsoft.com/technet/itsolutions/idc/oag/oagc08.asp.

Guidelines for Supporting Security Policies and Procedures

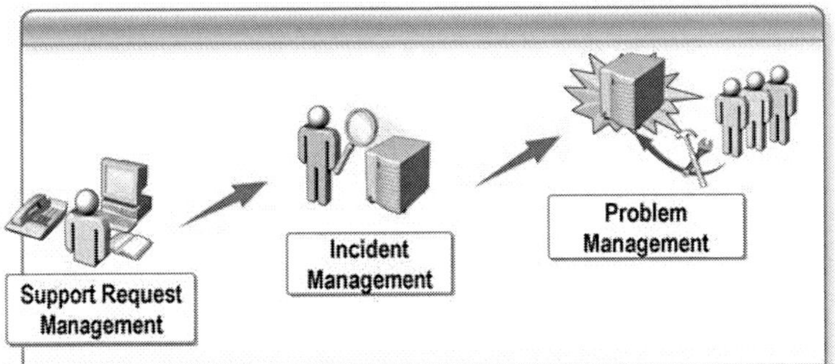

Phase	Responsibilities
Support request management	• Receives support requests from users • Escalates support issues
Incident management	• Resolves routine support requests • Escalates complex support requests and security incidents
Problem management	• Identifies and resolves underlying causes of problems • Incorporates results in organizational learning

Key points

To ensure that security issues are escalated and resolved properly and in a timely manner, create processes for supporting network security.

There are three main phases to supporting network security:

- *Support request management.* Acts as the first point of contact for users regarding security issues. Support requests are typically handled by first level support administrators, such as help desk administrators, who can gather the information that is required to escalate the support issue.
- *Incident management.* Resolves most security issues, including routine requests such as account management and authorization requests. At this stage, security administrators or network administrators typically resolve support requests.
- *Problem management.* Resolves all issues not resolved in earlier phases, including complex issues and security incidents. Support requests at this phase are typically handled by security specialists and network engineers who work closely with IT management.

Guidelines for Using Service Level Agreements

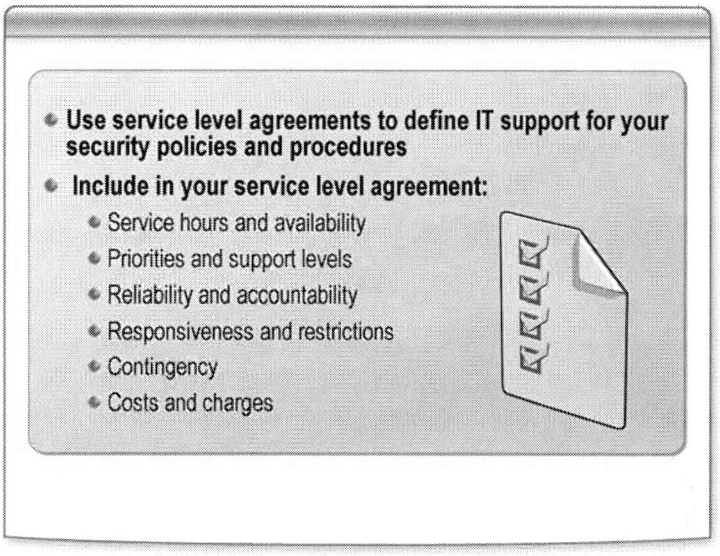

Key points

SLAs define support levels for policies and procedures. Organizations typically use SLAs to provide a minimum expectation of service between departments in order to ensure business continuity. You can also use SLAs to justify the use of resources such as hardware, software, and personnel. Many organizations use SLAs to award salary bonuses to departments based on the department's performance as measured against its SLA.

Additional reading

For more information on creating SLAs, see "Chapter 15: Service Level Management" in the *Operations Guide of the Internet Data Center Microsoft System Architecture Guide*, at: http://www.microsoft.com/technet/itsolutions/idc/oag/oagc15.asp.

Guidelines for Optimizing Security Policies and Procedures

Include measures in your security operations design for:

- Preventing interruptions to network services over time
- Recovering from security incidents as networks change
- Improving security polices and procedures over time

Activities include:

- Identifying new threats and vulnerabilities
- Updating risk management plans
- Improving daily procedures and processes
- Incorporating organizational learning from each incident response
- Testing disaster recovery plans on a regular basis
- Training new IT staff in security policies and procedures

Key points

The goal of optimizing your organization's security policies and procedures is to lower cost and improve performance, capacity, and availability in the delivery of IT services. By incorporating optimization measures in your security operations design, you can help ensure that your organization's security policies and procedures will benefit from lessons learned during ongoing support. Ideally, your organization will be able to better prevent interruptions to network services, recover from security incidents more quickly, and develop more effective security policies and procedures.

Failure to optimize your organization's security policies and procedures may result in the security policies and procedures quickly becoming obsolete and ineffective.

Security Policy Checklist

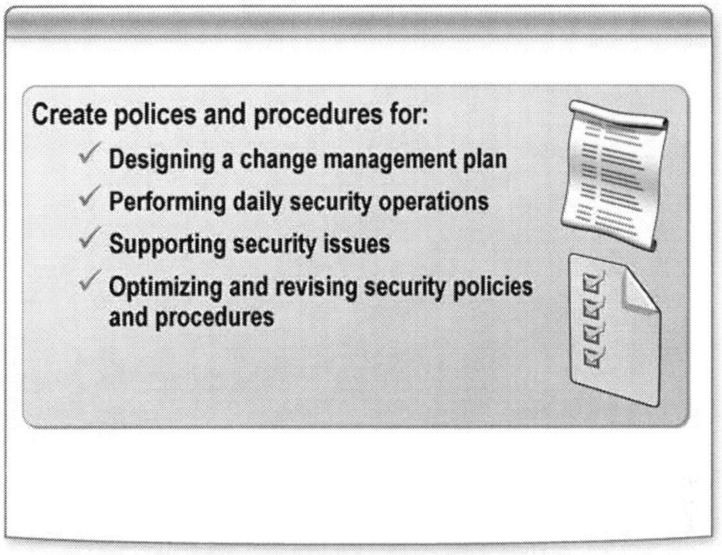

Checklist

Use the following checklist to guide your security design for ongoing network operations.

Phase	Task	Details
Planning	Model threats	STRIDE (spoofing, tampering, repudiation, information disclosure, denial of service and elevation of privilege) and life cycle threat models
	Manage risks	Qualitative and quantitative risk analysis

Phase	Task	Details
Building	Create policies and procedures for:	Designing a change management plan
		Performing daily security operations
		Supporting security issues
		Optimizing and revising security policies and procedures

Microsoft®
Training &
Certification

Appendix D: Authentication in CHAP, MS-CHAP, and MS-CHAP v2

Microsoft®

CHAP

Challenge Handshake Authentication Protocol (CHAP) authentication is an exchange of three messages:

1. The remote access server sends a CHAP Challenge message containing a session ID and an arbitrary challenge string.
2. The remote access client returns a CHAP Response message containing the user name in plain text and a hash of the challenge string, session ID, and the client's password using the MD5 one-way hashing algorithm.
3. The remote access server duplicates the hash and compares it to the hash in the CHAP Response. If the hashes are the same, the remote access server sends back a CHAP Success message. If the hashes are different, a CHAP Failure message is sent.

MS-CHAP

MS-CHAP authentication is an exchange of three messages:

1. The remote access server sends an MS-CHAP Challenge message containing a session ID and an arbitrary challenge string.
2. The remote access client returns an MS-CHAP Response message containing the user name in plain text and a hash of the challenge string, session ID, and the MD4 hash of the client's password using the MD4 one-way hashing algorithm.
3. The remote access server duplicates the hash and compares it to the hash in the MS-CHAP Response. If the hashes are the same, the remote access server sends back an MS-CHAP Success message. If the hashes are different, an MS-CHAP Failure message is sent.

MS-CHAP v2

MS-CHAP v2 authentication is an exchange of four steps:

1. The remote access server sends an MS-CHAP v2 Challenge message to the remote access client that consists of a session identifier and an arbitrary challenge string.
2. The remote access client sends an MS-CHAP v2 Response message that contains:
   - The user name.
   - An arbitrary peer challenge string.
   - A Secure Hash Algorithm (SHA) hash of the received challenge string, the peer challenge string, the session identifier, and the MD4-hashed version of the user's password.
3. The remote access server checks the MS-CHAP v2 Response message from the client and sends back an MS-CHAP v2 Response message that contains:
   - An indication of the success or failure of the connection attempt.
   - An authenticated response based on the sent challenge string, the peer challenge string, the client's encrypted response, and the user's password.
4. The remote access client verifies the authentication response and, if it is correct, uses the connection. If the authentication response is not correct, the remote access client terminates the connection.

MSM2830ACP/C90-03171

0 99751 06684 7

B1201051914